PERSON CENTERED ASTROLOGY

by
DANE RUDHYAR

Publisher/CSA Press
Lakemont, Georgia/30552

Copyright © 1976
by CSA Press
Lakemont, Ga. 30552

Standard Book Number 0-87707-192-6

Library of Congress Catalog No. 76-50756

Printed for the publisher in the United States of
America by CSA Printing & Bindery, Inc.

*To Marcia Moore
in warm and grateful friendship*

RECENT BOOKS
By
Dane Rudhyar

Occult Preparations for a New Age (Quest Books, Theosopical Publishing House, Wheaton, Illinois, 1974)

The Sun is Also a Star (E.P. Dutton and Co., New York, 1975)

From Humanistic to Transpersonal Astrology (Seed Center, Palo Alto, 1975)

White Thunder, poems (A paperback reprint of a long unavailable book by Seed Center, Palo Alto, 1976)

Seedman, a special issue of *Human Dimensions* magazine devoted entirely to the life and works of Dane Rudhyar, including color reproductions of paintings.

We Can Begin Again—Together (Distributed by Seed Center, Palo Alto)

Zodiacal Signatures (words by Dane Rudhyar; drawings made by Forrest 'Judge' Johnson from early Rudhyar sketches. Stellar Energy Exchange, Guerneville, CA, 1976)

These books, and all the older ones, can be obtained by writing to Leyla Rael, 3635 Lupine Avenue, Palo Alto, California 94303.

NEW BOOKS

to be released during the Winter, 1977

Astrology and the Modern Psyche (C. R. C. S. Publications, Davis, California)

Culture, Crisis and Creativity (Quest Books, Theosophical Publishing House, Wheaton, Illinois)

CONTENTS

ASTROLOGY FOR NEW MINDS

1. Astrology for New Minds — 13
2. Astrology in the Archaic Ages — 19
3. What is Astrology For? — 24
4. The Event-Oriented Environmental Approach — 30
5. The Person-Centered, Harmonic Approach — 39
6. Will and the Self-Maintaining Power of Form — 56

THE ASTROLOGY OF SELF-ACTUALIZATION AND THE NEW MORALITY

7. Event-Orientated and Person-Centered Astrology — 71
8. Astrology as a Discipline of Mind — 82
9. Astrology as Karma Yoga — 100
10. The New Morality — 110

FORM IN ASTROLOGICAL SPACE AND TIME

11. What is Form? — 121
12. The Basic Structure of Cyclic Processes — 132
13. The Aspects Formed During the Hemicycle of Spontaneous and Instinctual Action — 142
14. The Geometrical Principle of Formation of Aspects — 155

FIRST STEPS IN THE STUDY OF BIRTH-CHARTS

15. The "Signature" of the Whole Person — 175
16. Planetary Patterns — 186
17. The Moment of Interpretation — 226

THE PLANETARY AND LUNAR NODES

18. Orbital Astrology and the Nodes — 239
19. The Latitude Cycle — 253
20. The Moon's Nodes in a Birth-Chart — 266
21. The Moon's Nodes Cycle — 284
22. The Planets and the Nodes — 294

INTERPRETING A BIRTH-CHART AS A WHOLE

23. Preliminary Considerations — 303
24. President Franklin D. Roosevelt's Birth-Chart — 323
25. A Young Man's Chart — 352

EPILOGUE — 377

FOREWORD

What is astrology *for*?

It occurs only to a very few people to ask this question. If they are studying, practicing or merely reading about astrology, most persons take for granted that astrology is a way of predicting future events with at least a fair degree of accuracy and of determining what are good or bad times for performing various kinds of acts — starting an enterprise, getting married, investing money, buying clothes, etc. Individuals who are concerned with psychological problems and are eager to know more objectively the weaknesses and strengths of their character come to astrology for somewhat different reasons. They want to understand themselves better. They also want to discover what makes other people behave or feel the way they do, so to be able to use this knowledge in dealings with them.

From these two points of view astrology can be considered, broadly speaking, a "science." A science is a method of gaining a knowledge of what is around us, and of predicting what is going to happen when various factors in our environment act upon each other — for instance, when certain chemicals combine to produce accurately foreseeable reactions. Such a knowledge, if it has proven reliable in a large number of carefully identified and measured instances, can be called "scientific," whatever the method to gain the knowledge has been.

"Reliability" in knowledge can best be attained when one deals with external facts and material substances. It can have only a statistical character when a knowledge of, either infinitely small particles of matter (or units of energy), or of human beings is sought. Still, such a statistical kind of knowledge can be quite reliable, if properly used; witness the atom bomb or much that pertains to the social-political field of mass propaganda. It is said that "knowledge is power"; and this is quite evident. However, the usually unasked question is: Why is power valuable — or what is the value of what this power will be used *for*?

This book is the outcome of an initiative which I took during the evening of February 26, 1969, when I decided to start the International Committee for Humanistic Astrology. The reason I made this move was that I strongly felt the need to state as clearly and widely as possible that astrology could be given an altogether different meaning. I sensed that today many individuals, especially in the younger generations, while fascinated by astrology, actually were asking for something that the "scientific," analytical approach could not give them. They were seeking a *way of life* in which their relationship as individuals to the universe would be given a constructive meaning. They wanted not so much to know the "how," as to realize in a new, cosmic way, the "why" of their existence. They wanted to be *made whole,* and to discover how best to achieve this.

There obviously is a fundamental difference between the type of experimental psychology taught in most universities and the depth-psychology of Carl Jung. College psychology analysis separates and studies intricate processes occurring in the physical body (especially the nervous systems and the brain). It tries to learn how these processes operate and are related to conscious and unconscious reactions. It does this by using ingenious instruments and setting up complex and largely artificial experiments with animals and human subjects. It thus obtains a mass of raw data which the experimental psychologist tries to piece together. On the other hand, the type of psychology connected with the names of Jung and Ira Progoff, and Dr. Assagioli's Psychosynthesis, is essentially a *purposive* type of psychology — a "healing way." It is meant to *reveal* powerful archetypes and to

Foreword

evoke a "function of reconciliation," an "image of salvation." It aims at allowing the unconscious powers within the person to release their "message" to the consciousness, through dreams or other closely related psychological materials. The basis of this type of psychology or psychosynthesis is to acquaint us with a subliminal *language,* a language of images rich with symbolical meaning.

For more than 40 years I have tried to show that astrology likewise is in its deepest aspect a symbolical language. It does not have to claim that planets exert direct "influences" upon man through mysterious rays; in fact many of the techniques it uses cannot be logically justified on that basis. Assuredly man is "influenced" by the ever-changing "fields of forces" which the Earth, the solar system and the galaxy constitute; but to say this is very different from what astrological textbooks and magazines incessantly repeat. To analyze carefully day after day and year after year how the position of the various celestial bodies are related to the birth-chart and to deduce from this what most probably is to happen may be an intriguing game; but this does not touch the essential purpose of astrology. This purpose is not so much to tell us what we will meet on our road, as it is to suggest *how to meet it* — and the basic reason for the meeting. Which quality in us, which type of strength is needed to go through *any specific phase of our total unfoldment as an individual person.* This has little to do with whether the events, or the persons met during this particular phase, are to be catalogued as "good" or "bad." What is important is not the event — any event — but whether or not we are able to meet it with best results in terms of our growth.

The several essays which constitute this volume were published as a series of booklets during the years 1969, 1970 and 1971. Thousands of each booklet were sold and they elicited remarkably warm responses. It seems imperative therefore to reprint the entire series as a single book. My thanks go to Mr. and Mrs. Ed O'Neal whose warm interest made these publications possible, and to my dear wife, Tana, who labored diligently, not only with the typing of the manuscripts, but with the routine work involved in our most informal Committee.

Because of the ever mounting demands on my time and decreasing physical vitality, I am no longer able to carry on contacts with the people who wish to join I.C.H.A. However, a group of friends and students in Berkeley have volunteered to carry on the work.* I am sure they will do so with a younger and fresher spirit, and they plan to establish a closer rapport with all the friends of Humanistic Astrology.

In closing may I add that I have only a warm regard for astrologers who are striving to establish astrology on a more secure and dependable foundation through the use of "scientific" techniques, and especially for those who are trying to "re-think" astrology in terms of more philosophical and harmonic concepts. My only aim, in this "humanistic" approach has been to stand against the present de-personalizing trends which augur so badly for our Western civilization, and to place the individual person at the place where it belongs in astrology, i.e., at the center of its concern. I am concerned with persons, not with a system or a profession — persons who live and struggle toward the actualization of their fullest potential of being, NOW.

Dane Rudhyar
November 21, 1971

---

*Publisher's Note: In 1975, I. C. H. A. was discontinued, having accomplished the main purpose of its formation.

ASTROLOGY FOR NEW MINDS

1

Astrology for New Minds

To define astrology is as difficult a task as to define, let us say, philosophy, psychology, or even medicine. Not only are there many schools or systems of philosophy, psychology and medicine, but a definition which would fit the respective purposes of these various systems and be acceptable to all is well-nigh impossible. At first thought it would seem that medicine obviously refers to the type of activity aimed at curing illnesses; for some, however, medicine is the *art* of restoring and maintaining health in human *individual persons;* while for others it is primarily, if not exclusively, the *science* of suppressing *disease.* "Official" medicine in America follows mainly the second line of approach; but even here, and far more so in Europe (and totally so in ancient China), the first mentioned attitude and goal is considered by numerous physicians (homeopaths, naturopaths, osteopaths and the great variety of "healers") as characterizing the one basic function of medicine.

There is as well an abundance of varieties of modern and ancient psychologies or philosophies. Old India classified them into six great systems, all of which were considered valid, in as much as each was seen as befitting a particular type of mind, consciousness, or stage of human development. It is almost impossible today to define what psychology means, for to some it refers to the study of the nervous system, the brain and the effects of drugs upon the body, while to others it is "a Way of healing" aiming at helping individuals to fulfill their innermost potentialities along the fourfold path of sensation, feeling, thought and intuition, and to realize the "Self" as core of the integrated and integral "person." Psychologists who stress the use of statistics and tests are called "clinical" or, in a broader sense, "behaviorists"; others work along the lines of Freudian psychoanalysis, Jungian depth-psychology, individual psychology, etc. The recent development of what has been called a "Third Force" in psychology — linking the names of Moreno, Goldstein, Maslow, Rogers, Allport, Assagioli, Frankl, etc. — has stressed a "humanistic" approach to psychology which emphasizes a process of self-actualization and self-fulfillment through "peak experiences," expansion of consciousness, and more encompassing and open approaches to inter-personal relationships. A new movement has just been initiated by Anthony Sutich and his co-workers under the name of "transpersonal psychology" which further emphasizes the value of transcendent factors, of meditation and of spontaneous imagery rising from the depths of the psyche; and Asiatic disciplines (Hindu Yoga, Japanese Zen, Dervish techniques) are being incorporated into various systems of personal and superpersonal development. Psychology might be said to refer to the "soul" or the "psyche"; but who would be able to find definitions for these confusing terms acceptable to psychologists of all schools?

A similar situation exists in the field of what is generally termed astrology. The word "astrology" is still associated in the minds of a great many people with the study of the stars; but actually most astrologers today pay no attention at all to stars. They deal with the Sun, the Moon, the planets — and other factors of a less tangible nature, such as the intersection of planetary orbits and the Arabian Parts. But what the astrologer studies is not even material planets with mass, for in his calculations he is concerned in most cases only with the periodical motions of abstracts points, the centers of the planets. He deals with the interactions between these periodical motions, i.e., with the relationships between the cycles of the planets as they move at different speeds within the solar system and are observed from the Earth. Today the main way in which the astrologer measures these cyclic motions and their interaction (i.e. "aspects") is by plotting the planets' positions at a given moment upon a frame of reference called the zodiac; but there are also less commonly used frames of reference. Even with respect to the zodiac a basic ambiguity exists, for the term "zodiac" can be defined in two ways. There is the zodiac of "signs" and the zodiac of "constellations" — and to add to the confusion, signs and constellations bear the same names.

The zodiac of *signs* is the path traced during an entire year by the Sun in its *apparent* motion in relation to the distant stars — which are called "fixed," though they actually move very slowly, each in a somewhat different direction. We know today that this "tropical" zodiac is actually the orbit of the Earth as it revolves around the Sun; and astronomers call it "the ecliptic." The twelve signs of the zodiac are simply twelve equal 30-degree divisions of the ecliptic. This zodiac relates to the phenomenon of the seasons, and deals with the cyclically changing relationship of the Earth to the Sun — the Sun being the source of most of the energies which circulate within the electro-magnetic field which the solar system constitutes; but there are also energies flowing constantly from our vast Galaxy, within which our Sun is only one of billions of stars, and each planet may also have energies of a sort within its own globe.

The zodiac of *constellations* refers to groupings of stars located along and on either side of the plane of the ecliptic. As the Sun appears to move, month after month, in relation to the "fixed" stars, it passes over these twelve zodiacal constellations — Aries, Taurus, Gemini, etc.; that is to say, a line drawn from the Earth to the Sun would, if prolonged immensely, touch, month after month, one constellation after another.

Though in the popular mind, and even among astronomers who usually look at astrology with a prejudiced eye, Aries, Taurus, Gemini, etc., are believed to refer to actual groups of stars, *most* astrologers in fact mean by these terms the first, second, third, etc., *signs* of the zodiac. And today, because of the motion of the earth-globe called the "precession of the equinoxes" — a motion defining a long cycle of nearly 26,000 years — the constellations and the signs, though bearing the same names, do not coincide. A quite vocal though relatively small group of astrologers claims that the zodiac of the constellations (also called the *sidereal* zodiac) is the only one that has any validity — a claim based on the study of astrological records mostly pre-dating the Greek period of history. The great majority of astrologers, and all popular magazines and newspapers base their charts and interpretation on the zodiac of signs (the tropical zodiac).

The conflict between the proponents of the two zodiacs is only one of the many divergences of opinions found in the numerous astrological schools of the present day. But, as in the cases of medicine and psychology, back of the many divergent opinions and interpretations, techniques and systems, one can distinguish some fundamental differences of approach to the very meaning of human existence.

I spoke above of what has been called the Third Force in psychology, Humanistic Psychology, differentiating itself from, on the one hand, a medically oriented Freudian psychology and, on the other, the type of experimental laboratory psychology mainly taught in colleges which used the today fashionable techniques of "science." A rather similar division can be made in the field of present-day astrology. There is the traditional or "classical" type of predictive astrology which is mainly interested in predicting events, whether at the popular fortune-telling level or in a somewhat more sophisticated manner. There is also of recent date an astrology which tries to adopt the scientific methods of research, statistical analysis and the like, and which seeks to be recognized and taught in colleges as a reputable science. Then there are those astrologers who are by nature philosophically as well as psychologically inclined and for whom the one basic aim of astrology is to help individual persons to discover and gradually to actualize and fulfill, in the best possible way, the potentialities inherent in their total being.

I have recently called this last type of astrological approach "Humanistic astrology" for in some way it parallels the humanistic or Third Force psychology. It is the purpose of this booklet to define broadly the basic nature, purpose and implications of Humanistic astrology in contrast to the more traditional astrology whose essential aim is to predict future events.

2

Astrology in the Archaic Ages

The tradition-oriented astrologer finds himself in a somewhat awkward position, even if he or she is not aware of it, because an astrology having its roots in ancient Chaldea, Egypt or India was undoubtedly the product of the type of thinking and of feeling-response to life which produced the philosophies and religions of archaic cultures. Yet it is applied to circumstances and individuals living in an era dominated by scientific thinking, and by the use of empirical and rationalistic techniques — a thinking which has not yet fully emancipated itself from a mechanistic, strictly causal approach to phenomena.

During the "vitalistic" ages preceding the sixth century B.C. in the Mediterranean world, and in tribal cultures dominated by agriculture and livestock-raising, and by local conditions within a narrowly restricted geographical environment, man's approach to the universe was deeply religious; and religion was essentially ritualistic and based on the vivid feeling that everything was alive. The stars and the planets were the radiant bodies of gods. The One Life of the Universe operated everywhere through the polarities represented by the two "Lights" (Sun and Moon), and found itself differentiated as it passed through the concentric celestial spheres ruled by the planets. These planets were Administrators or Regents in their own realms; they affected all living things and all men, just as the administrators of the big empires of Egypt, Mesopotamia, Persia affected the people of their provinces. The same was true in ancient China where the Emperor — at first the one and only "Celestial" — was considered the intermediary between the celestial order of the Sky and the chaotic interplay of men, beasts, storms and cataclysms prevailing on the earth-surface. Around the Emperor stood four astrologers representing the four seasons of the year whose task it was to interpret the dictates of the Sky and the stars.

Such an archaic approach to the universe was very beautiful and had great meaning — and we can learn a great deal from it. But it is alien to the classical, rationalistic and Christian mentality. Nevertheless, most of the basic symbols of astrology which Europe and America inherited from the ancient world through Alexandrian and Greco-Roman writers can be traced to what the archaic minds of the vitalistic ages conceived to be the facts of the universe. Perhaps some Chaldean and Egyptian Wise Men and priests saw things differently; but, if so, they hid their knowledge under myths which were passed on to succeeding generations for many centuries.

The astrologer of the present-day who relies on all that has been traditionally recorded, particularly by Ptolemy and his European successors usually accepts their statements literally — often made in the form of brief aphorisms — very much as an engineer, builder or aviator accepts the complex formulas he finds in his books of instructions which tell him what to do under such and such circumstances. These formulas are reliable. He knows that if he took the trouble to re-study the laws of physics he once learned in college he would be able to see exactly *why* they work. But the situation is basically different for the modern astrologer who has memorized the old aphorisms and the many meanings of planets, aspects, houses, rulerships, etc., he still finds in textbooks repeating the old tradition.

The situation is different because he is dealing with the end-product of an archaic religious attitude to life which has become alien to him, and the experiential basis of which, try as he may, he cannot *feel*, even if he can somewhat comprehend intellectually the general meaning of anciently recorded statements and apply them. What he finds in applying them is very often disappointing; it may have a very confusing, if not destructive, psychological effect. Why? Because the mentality and the feeling-responses of modern men and women are no longer those of archaic Chaldea or Egypt; and even our geographical and cosmic environment may differ from that of men living nearly 3,000 years ago in certain regions of the Earth.

To this, the tradition-bound astrologer would probably reply that if the old aphorisms and rules do not seem to be reliable it is because they are wrongly or ineffectually applied and referred to the wrong zodiac. To him the old rules were devised by generations of ancient astrologers who used empirical methods of observation, and who were indeed "scientists" in their own field, astrology.

As I see it, such a type of reply indicates that one *projects* upon the men of a long past culture our present-day mentality and its rationalistic-empirical approach. Nothing that I know of the type of thinking and records whose origin can be traced to before the sixth century B.C. permits me to believe that the astrology which we have inherited from the old Mediterranean and Near-Eastern cultures originated in such a manner. Another type of mental faculty, perhaps a "psychic" faculty of attunement to the great rhythms of the universe or some kind of "Revelation" was most likely involved — in accord with the then prevailing vitalistic and ritualistic mentality of the period. In terms of such a mentality this ancient astrology could be considered completely valid and effectual. It expressed the character and the basic principles of the universe as these ancient people experienced it. We do not experience and respond to it in the same way.

One might retort: "Did not the laws of gravity and, in general, of mechanics work out then in the same way as they do now? Why should not planetary aspects and planetary influences act today just as they operated then?"

We can assume they did, though it is not at all

certain that the so-called universal constants are actually unchangeable if one considers very long periods of time or very vast distances in space. The belief in such constants is one of the undemonstrable postulates of modern science. As I wrote in my just published book "BIRTH PATTERNS FOR A NEW HUMANITY: A Study of Astrological Cycles Structuring the Present World-Crisis,": is the rate of growth of a human body constant from birth to death? What if the Earth, the entire solar system and the galaxy were, at least in some basic cosmic sense, organic whole with changing rates of growth?

What is Astrology For?

The most important fact, however, is not whether the basic rules of the old classical astrology are still valid today, but what it is they are valid *for*. In other words, to what can astrology be most significantly and validly applied today, and what is actually implied in the belief that there is value in astrology for twentieth century man, and that it fills a meaningful need in our scientific and technological society?

If I ask these questions it is because we fail too often to recognize that the knowledge of facts alone acquires "value" *only* in relation to the person and the society that knows these facts. What matters is *the relationship between the known and the knower,* not the knowledge alone. A kind of knowledge which may have been most useful under certain circumstances to a certain type of men may become valueless or meaningless in another period of human evolution and under different conditions of life. As mankind develops new faculties, other more primitive means of perception or adjustment to the environment often become mostly obsolete and atrophy — or they are reoriented and raised to another level. If one does not understand this, one has really no sense of what evolution — psychic and mental as well as biological evolution — implies.

Astrology was almost certainly developed originally by man as a result of his earliest experience of the fact that, while the mist-enveloped, hot, damp jungle where primitive man lived brought to him constantly unexpectable life-or-death encounters, the clear skies seen in deserts or on mountaintops presented an awe-inspiring picture of order and periodicity in motion — thus predictable, because cyclically repeated celestial occurrences (the phases of the Moon, the north-south oscillation of the Sun during a whole year, conjunctions and heliacal risings of planets and stars, eclipses, etc.). All religions have been based upon this contrast between the order, recurrence and grandeur of celestial phenomena, and the seemingly inherent disorder, chaos, unpredictability and danger of events in the biosphere where man lives struggling for survival — that is, the contrast between heaven and earth, between divine and human-animal natures. It is because astrology was, as far as we know, man's original attempt to formulate the order of the universe and to draw from it a sense of relative security that astrology has been called "the mother of all sciences." All sciences are attempts to predict what will occur when precisely measured factors come together under definitely stated and controlled conditions.

Science, however, does NOT oppose the order

of the sky to the chaos of the earth; for its claim is that there is order *everywhere,* that laws of nature operate everywhere in any environment. By knowing these laws man can transform his environment so as to increase his well-being and productivity. Science deals with causal relationships between entities and energies operating *within a particular environment.* Thus if science — as the term is used today — were to accept certain basic premises of astrology, it would have to do so on the basis of the recognition that the solar system as a whole, and eventually the entire galaxy, constitute *effectively* the environment of mankind; and we shall see that an embryonic "cosmecology" (the science of the cosmic environment as it affects the biosphere) is already being developed.

I feel certain that the astrology of the archaic ages did not think of the sky and the planets in this sense. It believed in two different worlds: the "formative world" of celestial Hierarchies and stellar or planetary gods, and the world of earth-nature. The former ruled over, and indeed had created, the latter. Divine and human natures were essentially different. Cosmic and planetary gods played the tune; all living things and all earth-phenomena had to dance to its inescapable rhythms.

Many of the devotees of astrology even today believe implicitly — though they may not like to admit it — in such a dualistic picture, even in spite of such statements as "the stars impel, they do not compel." However, during the first two millennia B.C., a few inspired men began to proclaim that there was in man a "divine spark," that he, as a Soul, was essentially an exile on this earth — sent here, either to gain certain experiences, or to work out some past *karma* — that this Soul could free itself from earth-bondage and either "return to its spiritual home" or realize even here its essential identity with an absolute divine Principle or Being. And Jesus taught: "The kingdom of heaven is within you." The Greek translation of his words uses the term *makarios* which means "the sky." This meant a great spiritual revolution. The duality heaven-earth, divine-human, order-chaos was transformed into unity. Order was everywhere. God was everywhere. Would not this mean that astrology had become useless?

It was so understood by most Christian Fathers and by the Church as a whole. Yet astrology persisted. Why? Because a new approach toward it began to evolve. This new approach was already implied in the old Hermetic axiom: "As above, so below" — that is, what occurs on earth *and in man* "corresponds" to what takes place in the sky, i.e., in the whole universe. The microcosm, man, reflects the macrocosm (i.e., the whole universe).

As astrology developed in Christianized Europe it mixed, in a rather ambiguous manner, the new principles of "heaven is within you" and occult correspondence with the old dualistic world-picture according to which creative celestial gods ruled over human nature from above.

By not recognizing that these two approaches to astrology are basically different, even if they can easily interact and interpenetrate each other, a vast amount of confusion has been produced. Old terms and concepts are still used which are no longer valid in terms of the new approach; and the confusion has become worse since man today thinks in terms of *heliocentric* (Sun-centered) and even galactic concepts, based now on the evidence of space-travel; yet the terminology still used by astrologers is mainly *geocentric* (Earth-centered). Thus, for instance, the astrologer speaks of "fixed stars," of the Sun "entering" a zodiacal sign or constellation, of the Sun and the Moon as "planets," etc. An equally confusing and ambiguous situation exists with regard to the meaning of "houses" and the new planets, of "planetary rulerships," of dignities and weaknesses.

The first thing astrologers should do, if they want to become "respectable" and see astrology academically and legally accepted, is to define clearly all the terms they use, and to agree on where the system they teach stands in relation to the whole astrological field, ancient and modern. A very difficult task considering that individual's opinions are often promoted with a nearly fanatic zeal, and that many astrologers present their findings on purely *subjective* grounds, viz., "In *my* experience with hundreds of charts, I find that. . . ." What is needed is a thoroughly *objective and historical* presentation of the various ways in which astrology has been and is being used — each way resulting from a particular approach-to-life or world-view and a particular temperament as well as cultural-social background. And the first thing to do is to accept the basic fact that there are indeed two basic approaches to astrology.

There is of course no absolute separation between them, and each takes much from the other; yet each is the expression of a fundamental way of looking at human beings and at the universe in general which colors every astrological concept and method of interpretation that is being used.

Astrologers may want to say at this point that what I am discussing here is nothing more than the difference between "mundane" and "natal" astrology, and that these represent merely two branches of the one art or science of astrology. But this objection deals only with the superficial aspect of the matter; for there are two very different ways of approaching natal astrology — and, even though it may be less obvious, various aspects of mundane astrology. What I am referring to is the fundamental attitude of the astrologer (and of his culture, historically speaking) toward the very purpose, meaning and function of astrology — as should be clear from what now follows.

4

The Event-Oriented Environmental Approach

According to this way of thinking (and feeling), astrology is understood to be *the study of forces* active in the cosmic environment of the Earth, affecting all living organisms and thus the life-events of human beings. The Sun, the Moon, the planets, the stars (individually and in those groups called "constellations") in some way exert a direct *external influence* upon all living organisms; they cause events and changes to occur. Such an astrology believes that it is dealing with actual, measurable energies. It believes in a world in which *force acts upon force*.

The idea of what "force" actually means has greatly varied since the dawn of human civilization. "Force" has referred to the will or formative power of gods or to the unbending power of Karma or Fate, or to some mysterious "influence" emanating from planets and stars (or sections of space). Today the scientific astrologer tends to think rather of the effect of solar winds, magnetic storms, cosmic rays, galactic forces upon the pulsations of the ionosphere surrounding the globe, and thus upon the whole biosphere and upon all human beings. But in all cases the situation is basically much the same; what has changed is merely the interpretation of the nature of the sources from which the forces to which man is subjected emanate. What is fundamental in this approach to astrology is that man, and every organized system of activities in the Earth's biosphere — his total environment — are *subjected to the impact of external forces.*

When these forces were thought to be the result of the will of celestial gods, there was very little man was able to do in order to improve his lot except pray to and propitiate these gods by means of religious rituals and sacrifices. The situation changed radically when man developed a growing feeling of being an "individual," no longer dominated from the very depth of his psyche by tribal taboos and by an inescapable feeling of unity with his kin and involvement in their welfare. Seers, mystics and prophets divinized, as it were, this newly found sense of individualistic separateness and ego-power by teaching these emergent individuals that essentially they were spiritual-mental beings — souls transcendent to social and environmental conditions. But then new problems arose; for the biological urges and emotional desires or ambitions of these actually ego-centered individuals most often indeed opposed or perverted the expression of this transcendent Soul.

The Soul — the "real man" — was therefore seen to exist most of the time in an inimical and dangerous *internal psychic environment,* i.e., an inner jungle. The new kind of religious leaders were thus particularly concerned with the teaching of ethical principles and rules of conduct which superseded or gave a new meaning to the old rituals. And as the important thing for individualistic man was to control what was now regarded pejoratively as his gross, unrefined or sin-perverted "human nature," this altered also the whole astrological picture.

In the archaic tribal world, man defined the forces acting upon his *external environment* as "favorable" and "unfavorable" according to their effects upon his crops, his livestock, and his projects for expansion or for mere survival. On the other hand, the new type of human individual, because of his belief in the Soul, came to think of the forces acting in his own nature as "good" or "bad." They were good or bad from the point of view of the Soul and he was supposed to rule over them. Thus, man had to deal with two kinds of environment; his external geographical-social environment, and his internal biological and psychic environment. The body and the psyche had become, I repeat, an inner environment for the Soul and even for the "rational" God-given mind which made a man a reasonable, self-conscious, self-reliant being.

By holding to the concept of the correspondence between the microcosm, man, and the universal macrocosm, it was possible to state that *both* environments were structured by planets and stars. Thus, the principle of force against force was operating in man's bio-psychic nature as well as in Earth's biosphere where all men lived. The same forces were operative, physically as well as psychically, causing events to occur. These forces, in cultures that had evolved beyond the archaic ages, were no longer regarded by learned intellectual men as the manifestation of the will of gods in the sky, but nevertheless they were forces, natural energies, which it was man's function to control by his will, his rational mind and his inventive intellect. Exactly how the motions of the planets were able to *exert force* upon both the myriad of events produced by the activities of billions of living entities swarming on the Earth's surface and the bio-psychic drives or social desires of human beings, was never made clear. It has not been made clear up to this day on the basis of the action of specific "energies" emanating from planets and stars.

There are today, and there have been throughout European history (especially during the Classical era between the fifteenth and the mid-eighteenth centuries), two types of astrologers. The great majority of astrologers deal with the forecasting of external events and the selection of the most "favorable" time to start a project; a minority are more specifically concerned with trying to advise their clients concerning their *interior* psychological problems and activities which result from them. *In both cases* the basic attitude is that the "real man" (the Soul, the will, the rational mind) is exterior to his birth-chart and that his duty is to rule, as well as he can, *both* external circumstances and the inner energies and biological or psychic urges of his more or less "unregenerate" — if not evil — human nature.

The question of whether the real "I" of a person is to be considered *exterior* to his birth-chart is one that can only be answered by an overall philosophy of existence, indeed by metaphysical or religious postulates which cannot be *proven* true or false. The answer must remain a subjective one, based on individual feelings, intuitions, beliefs and the allegiance to (or the repudiation of) an ancestral tradition. And there can be no meaningful answer unless one understands clearly what the alternative position is; and it has probably never been made sufficiently clear or presented in a consistent and all-inclusive manner, at least in terms acceptable to the modern Western mentality — though attempts have been made in recent years.

But what is important is first of all to recognize that when the astrologer speaks of "my" chart, "my" Jupiter or Saturn, etc., he takes implicitly for granted a transcendental position toward life and astrology. He accepts the idea that as a transcendent Soul, "he" was born in a body of earth-nature *subjected to* all kinds of forces beating upon "his" body and "his" psyche — and that he is in relation to the energies of "his" personality in the same position as an engineer-technologist sent to a tropical country to clean up swamps and build roads, airfields and cities.

This is a fine and quite challenging picture consistent with the technological mentality of our time; the difficulty with it is that, if we try to discover what these energies are, which the astrologers correlate with the ten planets (including Sun and Moon) and perhaps also with constellations or single stars, we find ourselves most embarrassed indeed. The scientist of our day realizes that variations in the intensity of magnetic electronic currents or modifications in the orientation of molecules of water (basis of all living organims) can affect every living thing, and, through the nervous systems, the mental-emotional responses of men or women and children. But to the modern scientific mind this acceptability of electrically and chemically detectable and eventually measurable energies acting upon *the whole biosphere,* does not prove the validity of the practice of astrology and of *predictions made to individuals* on the basis of a variety of traditional procedures, many of which seem to be completely outside of the field of such a scientific explainability. I shall only mention here such techniques or forms of inquiry as horary charts, all progressions and directions and Arabian Parts.

All these energies which could be accepted as causes of astrological effects ("influences") strike the whole biosphere and not merely this or that individual person. A sudden release of solar energies may affect not only the weather but subtler conditions which would react on the mentality of perhaps a large section of mankind. But the question of why the impact of solar, planetary and cosmic energies upon the newborn (or the ovum being impregnated) should result in the establishment of *a pattern of characteristics set for the entire life of a particular individual* is not easy to answer through the type of scientific explanations available today.

Why the conjuction of Mars and Saturn at the degree of the zodiac occupied by the Sun in Aries at birth should produce a barely avoided serious injury to the head, and a couple of days later a sudden case of jaundice cannot very well be explained on the basis of a science of cosmecology or "biospheric astrology." (These events occurred to me personally at the age of 42.)

What has to be explained in such a type of occurrence is why the conjuction of two presupposed currents of energies from Mars and Saturn should cause *both* an accident (the unexpected breaking of a string holding a heavy glass-covered painting hanging just above my head while sleeping at night) and a physiological illness — thus operating at two seemingly unrelatable levels. Astrological books say that Aries rules the head, and that a conjunction of Mars and Saturn on a person's natal Sun may affect his liver (and many other things); thus, the occurrence did "fit" astrological expectability;

astrology was proven to "work" in this case. Did the conjunction produce similar effects on all or even a "significant" proportion of persons born with their natal Sun on the third degree of Aries? This is what should be investigated.

The crucial difficulties in all statistical investigation is, of course, that astrology deals with many "variables"; so that even the most successful determination of a high percentage of correlations between an astrological occurrence and a certain kind of life-situation, event, or career can at best indicate only *a tendency.* That there is a strong tendency for a person caught in an insurrection to be hurt, needs no particular explanation. Likewise, if some strong release of energies from the solar system or the galaxy hits the entire Earth's biosphere on a certain day, it should be easy to accept the concept that individuals which for some reason are "more sensitive" to this kind of energy have a statistically significant probability of being affected by some kind of "event."

But is that all that astrology is meant to tell modern individuals? Is there not a far deeper, far more *personal* meaning to astrology — a meaning which can clarify basic issues concerning the very nature and purpose of an individual's whole personality by revealing the underlying patterns of his or her unique individual selfhood?

This is what the person-oriented astrologers believe implicitly, and in most cases merely on faith — a tradition-based, quite irrational and dogmatic faith. It should be the purpose of a humanistic, person-centered astrology not to be satisfied with a mere assertion of belief, but to provide a consistent basis of philosophical-metaphysical thinking as a meaningful foundation for such a kind of faith and such a psychological approach to the basic problems confronting a present-day individual person.

5

The Person-Centered, Harmonic Approach

For the last decades, atomic physics has opened to our conciousness a world of forces in which every concrete and seemingly solid object appears dissolved in whorls of fantastically rapid motion within a seemingly mostly empty space. Matter appears to us now only as a particular state of energy — energy operating under relatively enduring structural laws of Form. Most types of energy are polarized, positive and negative — and, in living organisms, anabolic (cell-building) and catabolic (destructive of useless forms).

However, the basic question is: "How does one *interpret* the relation of man to these forces," and, stated differently, "what is man?" Is man a small ephemeral organism fighting its way in the midst of mostly overwhelmingly superior planetary and cosmic entities — or is this world-picture, so much believed in by many last century thinkers, essentially false, in that it presents a totally inadequate evaluation of man? Is the universe to be seen as a scene of meaningless conflicts between blind unconscious forces all of which are inevitably to be levelled off under the pressure of the god of nineteenth century science, "entropy" — or is the universe in its totality a majestic manifestation of cosmic harmony, a great ritual in which a fantastic variety of fields of activity are interrelated in an immense polyphonic interplay of more or less conscious wills and meaningful purposes?

In picturing in the preceding pages the type of event-oriented astrology which purports to study the action of planetary and cosmic forces, we saw man individually and collectively *subjected to* the impact of these forces. Now, I am presenting a picture in which man appears as *the subject of* a complex play of energies objectivized in a concrete earth-born field of activities — that is, in an individual person. Every individual person is a complex existential whole of activities, the wholeness of which expresses itself as "I" — I, the real man — real, because this man includes, encompasses and is able to oversee and to give meaning to a harmonic group of interrelated and interdependent activities; and "reality" is, at every level of existence from the infinitely small to the infinitely vast, the harmonic interplay of multifarious activities organized according to a characteristic structure and within a self-perpetuating field.

What this means, in simpler language, is that every individual person is a relatively independent organic whole in which a multitude of forces dynamically interact according to an original and originating pattern which establishes its life-purpose and its basic relation to all other wholes in the universe. This organic whole — the individual person — is essentially no different from the almost infinitely greater and vaster organized Whole, which we call the universe. Indeed the individual person constitutes one particular aspect of the universal Whole. The individual person is this universal Whole, *focused* at a particular point in space and in terms of the particular need for it at the exact moment of its emergence into independent existence. This is the moment of the first breath because it is then that the individual's basic rhythms of existence are established within a particular environment.

All the forces of the universe are *latent* in this oganized human whole, the newborn baby. They are all there *in potentiality*. They are the same forces in every human being — indeed in every truly organized system of activities — but the arrangement (gestalt) of these forces differ, at least in some slight degree, in each newborn entity. This difference establishes the individuality and the particular purpose of this emergent human being. Likewise, every birth-chart contains the same planets; and it is senseless to speak of "my" Jupiter, "my" Saturn, etc. The *substantial* elements or basic drives in *every* organized existential system are the same. What differs is the structure or "form" of their arrangement. If a botanist endowed with superhuman vision were able, after looking at an acorn, to make a two-dimensional graph defining all the essential characteristic structures which will become actualized as an oak tree, he would do essentially what the astrologer does when erecting the birth-chart of a newborn baby.

The birth-chart defines the structure of the individual person. It is, in this sense, the blueprint of what *may* become the finished "temple" of the fully mature and perfected man. I say "may" become; for the birth-chart refers only to potentialities. It does NOT promise *anything* in terms of concrete, definite events, any more than a gardener planting an acron in a field can be certain that in a number of years it will have become a full-grown, healthy oak tree. Environmental circumstances, a poor soil, bad weather, storms, the interference of pests, animals or men, may blight the development of the oak; yet it will grow according to the basic structure of the oak species. It will not become an apple tree.

This means that man — the real man who says "I" — is not outside of his birth-chart. He is *the wholeness* of the chart. He is not in fundamental conflict with the energies of human nature — or of their planetary counterparts in the solar system — for he is their harmony. It may be a mostly "consonant" harmony (thus with a fundamentally *static* character), or it may be a predominantly "dissonant" (i.e., *dynamic)* harmony. It is always essentially harmony, because it represents the whole universe focused at a particular point in space and time.

Every human being is a particularized aspect of the whole universe — or, religiously speaking, of God. In a more limited but more realistic sense, every human being is a particularized aspect of "man"; he is born in answer to the need of humanity at a definite time and place. Because this "need" is limited, as it refers to a temporary situation, the individual person, whose life-task it is to answer this "need" — and some would use here the word, "karma" — must have a particular temperament or character. He is what he is, because that is what is needed at this precise time. His birth-chart represents the solution of this need. It is the *existential formula* of his total being — his "signature" (in the occult sense of the term), his sacred name.

If this be so, saying that, "the wise man *rules* his stars" makes little sense. The true Sage *is* the perfect harmony of all the energies which operate and exteriorize themselves through his total being at any particular moment. He totally fulfills his "dharma," his truth of being. Each moment of his existence is for him one phase of a total process which unfolds in beauty, significance, purposefulness and peace. The only will he knows and applies is the will to become and to remain fully, perfectly, what he is as a particular focal point for the activity of Man — or of the universe-as-a-whole, or of God. He is the Whole acting at a particular point in time and space *through* the focalizing structure of his total person; and he knows it, even though he is only one of myriads of aspects of this Whole.

If some individuals consider themselves separate and alienated from humanity-as-a-whole and from the universe, and if they think they have to rule over natural energies which they feel to be alien because they, as Souls, are exterior (and metaphysically superior) to them, this simply means that *they do not realize what they are.* Such a person has experienced a false kind of individualization. He does not want to recognize — out of a false pride — that the energies playing through his nature are the same as those operating in *all* human beings. He does not realize his common rootedness in the common humanity of all men. His mind reacts only to *local* conditions of family, culture and religion. He has no realization of what a *global* consciousness means.

If one lengthened the taproots of all the trees of the Earth, they would meet at the center of the globe. If all human beings were to stand erect at the same time all around the globe, the extended axis of their spinal columns would meet at the center of the globe; yet each one of these individual spinal axes would point to a different star of the galaxy. This is a symbolic picture worth meditating upon; it could change the course of human history if it stirred up powerfully the imagination of all men. It would explain at least one aspect of the meaning of the old Kundalini Yoga, which so many people talk about rather emptily these days.

"Man" is to be found, symbolically, at the center of the Earth-globe, not in the sky; and this is why a Humanistic astrology should be geocentric. But this is only one aspect of it; it should also be "person-centered" — each person having his own *real* (not merely "rational"!)* horizon, his zenith-star and his antipodal polarizing factor. Astrologically speaking, a man's unique function in humanity depends upon his exact orientation to galactic space — not, ultimately, in terms of a more or less mythological zodiac which refers only to the character of the basic energy powering his bio-psychic vitality, but with reference to single and mostly nameless stars of the galaxy. The star at the exact zenith of his birth-sky symbolizes, and, who knows, perhaps in a very real sense is — the man's *celestial identity*.

The task of astrology is to reveal to a mind still confused and usually perverted by the pressures of his social-cultural environment, the basic structures that characterize the particular manner in which the energies of human nature are organized within him, so that he can orient, polarize and re-order his activities (at all levels of his personal life) according to this *celestial pattern*. This celestial pattern is his true Name.

---

* The "rational" horizon is not the "sensible" or physical horizon, but is obtained by supposing a line drawn through the Earth's center parallel with the real horizon. What should be used is a "mean" horizon which would flatten out the relatively small variation produced by hills, valleys, etc.

It is the manifestation of his self in the realm of "form and name" (to use an old Sanskrit phrase). But what I call here "self" must be differentiated from "ego"; and it is because many modern psychologists fail to make such a differentiation and give to the term, self, a very ambiguous and over-extended meaning (actually the meaning of "person") that there is so much confusion in psychology — as much, indeed, as in the astrological field.

The ego is not the self. The self IS. It is the "fundamental Tone," the vibration which sustains the whole organism (body and psyche) of an individual human being. The self is power, not consciousness. It is the pure "I" unconditioned by concepts, or words. The ego, on the other hand, that *thinks* and *says* "I am," always adds to this assertion the conditioning features of "this particular person, Paul Smith, or Jane Strong." Thus, the ego can be described as the "reflection" of the self upon the socially and culturally conditioned field of consciousness of the whole person. The ego is, as Jung stated, the "center" of this field of consciousness. It develops out of the early years of human existence in a particular environment which gives to — and indeed forces upon — the newborn organism a name (personal and family), a language conditioning his mental processes, a code of conduct a basic way-of-life, and which even conditions (if not determines) his modes of thinking and his feeling-responses.

This is *not* to say that the development of

an ego is unnecessary and "bad." Just as the embryo has to develop its organs within the enveloping and narrow confinement of the mother's womb, so the mind (built by and operating through the nervous system) needs to pass a number of years within the matrix of his family and culture in order to reach a formed and "viable" state of consciousness which permits *emergence* from this social-cultural womb-like psychic environment. This process of formation of a potentially independent mind produces an ego. This ego is *not* the self; though without the integrative and sustaining power of the self, there could not be any ego.

What the family and social-cultural environment powerfully impresses upon the child need not be *in tune with* the Tone of the child's individual selfhood. Thus, when the teen-ager says "I am" and speaks of "doing my thing," what speaks in him is most often an ego that is not his true self. The basic vibration of this self has been so covered up by sheath after sheath of foreign material and unauthentic thinking and feeling (i.e., by "complexes" and automatisms, by biases, fears and sterile habits) that this vibration is not ordinarily perceived by the consciousness. Yet there may be rare moments, now called "peak experiences," during which the submerged tone of the self reaches the field of consciousness — moments when the ego-king, who ordinarily rules that field, abdicates temporarily its power. Then, because the real self is but one tone within the immense Chord of the Harmony of the universe — and of "Man" and of the Earth, the one home of the one humanity — the consciousness of the person is able to *resonate* to at least an aspect of this cosmic Harmony; and he may speak of an experience of "cosmic consciousness" and of unity — an experience of "light."

The ego bases its sense of value and its urges upon what makes it different from other egos. Ego-consciousness excludes everything that does not fit in with its patterns. To the ego, the foreigner or alien is always a potential enemy. It therefore lives in a world of perpetual conflicts — potential if not actual conflicts — a world in which "force meets force" and existence is a life-and-death struggle between "rugged individualists" greedy for power and wealth, trying to get all they can from other people. In such a world ethical and strictly rationalistic judgments are required for survival. This is good; that is bad. I love, I hate. I am right, he is wrong. Everything is *either, or*. Opposites are more or less irreconcilable adversaries.

The individual who has overcome the separative, dogmatic possessive and jealous tendencies of his ego can emerge into a different kind of world. It is this process of emergence which of old was truly called "initiation" or "the Path"; and today it seems that the whole of mankind is challenged to take a definite new step along that Path, or to perish. Those who cannot take it most likely will perish, in one way or another.

All this, needlessly philosophical and psychological as it may sound to many people who are merely interested in the set type of traditional doctrines which they call astrology, has nevertheless the most immediate bearing on the very practice of an astrology which could validly meet the needs of a New Age humanity — a truly humanistic, holistic and harmonic astrology. The purpose of such a type of astrology is, above all, to help the individual who is beginning to question his ego-attitudes and desires, to discover what his true *self* is — which means what he is as a total person and what his function in mankind is. Such a person wants to know the blueprint (or archetypal Form) of the individual that he is not yet, but would like to become. "What am I?" he asks. And the first answer the Humanistic astrology should give him is, "This whole sky, the whole universe." The second part of the answer should be, "This whole sky seen from *a particular angle of vision* which defines the purpose and meaning of your existence from birth to death." The birth-chart defines the potentialities, but also the limitations which result from its being only a particular focal point for the operation of the universal Whole (or of Man) — one focal point among billions of them.

The consequence of such an attitude to the individual person is that nothing is "bad" in a birth-chart. Everything concurs to define what the individual truly is as a self — his archetypal structure of being, or some may prefer to say, God's idea for his having been born at a particular time and place. *Everything is "good" in its proper place and in relation to everything else.* The humanistic approach to a birth-chart is a total Yes-saying to existence. It considers nothing worthless. Therefore it cannot accept ethical good-bad, fortunate-unfortunate judgments — unless these answers specific questions referring to limited concrete instances, such as, "Would this project be good for a particular purpose?" — or, "Would it contribute to my self-actualization?" In the latter case, the answer would have to be related not only to the chart as a whole, but also to the present phase of the questioner's development ("progressions") and to the conditions prevailing in his environment ("transits").

Ethical, either-or judgments apply to concrete situations at particular times; but not to the whole chart or the whole life of an individual. Every birth-chart is the "best" for the particular purpose of the individual to whom it refers, because he *is,* in structure and function, this chart. Every life is valuable in that it is a particular aspect of the whole universe; and all these aspects have to be actualized in concrete existence in order that the Whole should be a perfect, all-encompassing "chord" (or motet) of polyphonically evolving centers of *conscious existence.*

This does *not* mean that there are not catabolic as well as anabolic forces in *any* living organism, and in the universe as a whole. To call these forces "good and evil" in the ordinary ethical sense of these terms, is to fail to realize that both types are necessary — just as there would be no healthy metabolism in a living organism if there were not both a process of food assimilation, and one of evacuation of the unused material as waste products. Neither would there be assimilation of needed food if the teeth and digestive juices did not reduce the eaten foodstuff to a condition of absorbable chemicals.

The basic issue is whether one has a *partial* view of life-processes or one is able to reach a *whole-view* of the total process. Only such a whole-view can tell us what we are as "whole-persons," and what the meaning and purpose of life as an individual may be. But if we have only a partial view of life this can only mean that what we see are merely events — i.e., something that happens in the physical or psychic environment in which a mysterious, transcendent Soul (or "I") has been plunged at birth for mysterious reasons. It is only as one is able to envision the whole being and the whole life-cycle of an individual that one can see the *person that he is,* and that the rhythm of the self that is power, beating at the core of and throughout the total field of activity which this person encompasses, may be experienced.

Such a seeing-feeling requires — as I have repeatedly stated since 1934 when I began writing my book THE ASTROLOGY OF PERSONALITY — an *esthetical* approach to man and to the universe — a holistic or harmonic approach. If one looks at a painting, one would not merely examine certain colored bits on the surface of the canvas, and like or dislike this spot of red or that square of blue. One has to face the painting as a whole. Only then can one have a truly esthetical experience of the art work, and resonate to the meaning which it seeks to convey.

It is the same with an astrological chart. What a chart represents is the whole sky with all that it encompasses of energies *and of potential meaning*. True, it is only this whole sky focused at a particular time and place; but if the astrologer does not "feel" first of all the presence of the whole sky, and only after that determines the particular arrangement of the planets and stars at the time he does not have a whole-view. Moreover, if he does not even concentrate his attention on the entire planetary and house pattern, but merely reacts emotionally and "ethically" to this and that good or bad aspect, to a wonderful Jupiter or a "crystallizing" Saturn and an "aggressive" Mars in conjunction or square, then he cannot meet his client (or himself if he studies his own birthchart) as a *human person*. He perceives only *forces* trying to do him good or harm, and *events* resulting from the operation of these forces.

No planet essentially represents anything better or worse than any other. No aspect is inherently good or bad. No zodiacal sign or house should be valued more than any other. The negative judgments so often passed on the sign Scorpio, or the twelfth house, may indeed have most destructive effects on certain individuals. The attribution of most negative characteristics to some degrees of the zodiac (I quote, "a degree of suicide. . . . a degree of homicide. . . . a degree of insanity") on the basis of statistics which isolate only one somewhat more salient planetary feature out of many, and on a relatively small number of cases, can be almost criminal as to results.

Of course there are birth-charts which in the present state of society and mores suggest either a rather smooth or a most likely "difficult" life for the individual in question; but it is time that we go beyond the moralistic illusion that a normal, average kind of happiness linked with a minimal number of challenges and crises represents "the good life." In periods of history when every person had to struggle terribly hard for survival under conditions of generalized scarcity, Jupiter may have appeared to be "the great benefic" fulfilling the ambitions of the ego; but in our affluent suburban American environment, it may blot out deeper than ever the purpose of the self. Likewise, a dominant Venus may indicate, in our permissive society, a more than average indulgence in sensual satisfactions.

The astrologer who presents lists of good and bad features, favorable and unfavorable days or months in terms of expectable specific events, does not really treat his client as a human being, still less as an individual person, but rather as an object registering series of events. Besides, it remains to be seen, whether the expectation of danger or misfortune evoked by the more or less thinly veiled and ambiguous statements of so many astrologers will help the person to be "prepared" — or whether by creating anxiety or fear for the future it will not be a "self-fulfilling prophecy." The rugged individual type may rejoice in expected challenges, for he trusts in the strength of his will and the resourcefulness of his mind to ride the storm — a great adventure feeding his already dominant ego! But are we always dealing with rugged individualists with strong wills, and is a society where this type of individual predominates, the kind of society we want to live in? Will it, shoud it be the society of the new Aquarian Age?

Sociologists are now seriously concerned with this self-fulfilling character of social prognostication, and the result can be just as unwholesome if it is success and good fortune that is expected, for it may lead a person to relax in his efforts and to become careless or self-indulgent. The most basic psychological issue, is, however, whether crises should be avoided because they are "bad." The humanistic astrologer being concerned with the *fullest possible actualization* of the potentialities inherent in the birth-pattern considers that no significant step ahead can be taken except through some kind of crisis. It is not the predictable events which are important, but the attitude of the individual person towards his own growth and self-fulfillment.

Moreover, a harmonic picture of the universe implies that nothing occurs in a human life except for a purpose, and that this purpose is the purpose of the great Whole acting through one of its trillions of focalizing instrumentalities, the individual person. If this be so, any man has within himself the potential capacity to meet significantly whatever crisis occurs to him *at the time it occurs;*

but this does not mean that he would have this capacity developed two years or even two weeks before. Thus, if this crisis is announced to him when he is not actually ready to meet it with the whole of his being, the announcement may cause him an anxiety or fear which will act as an extraneous, man-made cause of failure in meeting the crisis — and this applies also to prediction of major good fortune.

6

Will and the Self-Maintaining Power of Form

The foregoing statements should not be taken to mean that a person should take a passive attitude of *laissez-faire* toward the drives operating within his body and psyche, and especially toward the cravings and reactions, or the automatisms and self-indulgent desires which are conditioned mainly by the person's environment and the examples it has provided since birth. The astrologer studying a birthchart will perhaps see that a particular function (represented by a planet) tends to be strongly accentuated in the nature of the person to which the chart refers. Such an accentuation defines a specially important aspect of the person's life, and serves the purpose of the whole life. Yet it can be at times *over*-accentuated, as changing factors (progressions and transits) stimulate it intensely.

Evil appears when the individual "I" who should be the wholeness or overall harmony of *all* the functions and drives of the total person *identifies himself* with a particular function which has become especially intensified and powerful. When a man says, "I am angry, I want you, I am depressed to death, etc." what actually happens is that the whole balance of functions has become disrupted. Analogically speaking, a "special interest" has managed to put such a pressure upon the legislative or executive body (to which belongs the task of keeping the State in a condition of dynamic yet basically stable operation according to its "Constitution"), that the power of the State has abdicated, at least temporarily, in favor of the special interest.

What can then be done? According to the dualistic and ethical picture of the human being which is traditional in our "Christian" society, the will of the individual should exert itself and "rule" the overpowering urge. But the question is, what is meant then by "will"? Is it really the will of the whole? In most cases it is the power which the *ego* has, as an autocratic king or the dictator in a police State, to rule over, confine or destroy the offending release of energy. However, what does this intensified energy offend — the purpose of the self, or some traditional social-cultural or religious standards? Is the willful control actually the result of the wholeness of the bio-psychic organism — the total person — struggling against the over-emphasis of one of its necessary and legitimate organic functions, or is it not rather the result of an arbitarary decision of the ego which has been conditioned by *external* pressures (family-indoctrination, traditional morality, etc.) or is fearful of losing its authority over organic energies? Is will the mobilized power of the whole individual seeking to maintain the particular character of his wholeness — his essential identity — when an explosive release of energy occurs within its boundaries, or is the repressive will an instrument to preserve the rule of the conscious ego and the traditional beliefs which have molded this ego *from the outside?* This is a crucial question and we should well understand what actually is the "mobilized power of the whole" — what is the source of this power.

When a contractor assumes the task of building a house according to the detailed blueprints of the architect, his basic concern is that the finished building should be a perfect actualization in concrete materials of the blueprints. I have stated that the birthchart of an individual constitutes what we may analogically call the blueprint for the building of a fully developed person. What does this actually mean?

We can follow the example of Free Masonry and call God "the Great Architect of the Universe." This is a most legitimate personalization, but for our present purpose we need only say that a person born at a particular time and place in the universe constitutes a focal point for the actualization of one particular aspect of the immensely vast harmony of the universal Whole. At this point in time and space an individual with a particular capacity is needed to fill a particular function in the all-encompassing field of activity which we call the universe — and in a more restricted sense, in relation to the Earth-field. This individual is charged, as it were, to play a role in the evolution of mankind.

His birthchart defines his role. It defines a set of potentialities. These potentialities are gradually actualized at the biological level by what we call "life" operating through complex formative processes and through bio-chemical drives and "instincts." The pattern defining all the operations of the human organism is apparently what is now named a "genetic code." It remains what it is throughout the life of this organism because it has the power *to maintain its integrity,* at least within certain limits. This means that it presents an inertial resistance to change, except to changes which are implied in this genetic code as necessary phases for the total development of the organism's innate potentialities.

The term, "inertia," means resistance to change. Inertia is a kind of will; and, in terms of this discussion, is the power to *maintain* the integrity of the original structure of the individual person. It has been said that when we speak of God's Will we should not think of the vacillating type of will related to a man's conscious ego, but to something like *cosmic inertia.* This cosmic inertia is the power that maintains the integrity of the original creative Word — that is, a particular type of *order* which is immanent in that particular universe.

Changes occur everywhere at all times, yet something does not change — an over-all internal structure or tone which remains what it is throughout the cycle of this universe. When we seek to analyze this cosmic structural (and structuring) order, we speak in scientific terms of natural laws and of universal constants; but laws and constants only refer to modes of activity. They are but parts of the workings of the universal pattern (the Word, or *logos*) which determined the over-all cosmic structure, and also the character and timing of the basic process of transformation, of which the universe (which we see it today) constitutes only one phase.

We have to differentiate clearly in astrology between birth-chart, progression and transit; otherwise, confusion is inevitable.

The birth-chart is simply the whole universe focused at one point in time and space. If we feel that some "scientific" explanation is necessary to explain why it defines the role of a person in the universe, and thus the pattern of his individual selfhood, it is because we have a fragmented and mechanistic view of the universe; that is, we fail to realize that the universe is and operates as an organized Whole of structured activities. It may not seem to operate exactly as a "living" organism — every cell of this organism enclosing within its nucleus the "genetic code" of the whole as well as whatever defines its particular function in this whole — but this depends only on what meaning we give to the term "living," and how restricted this meaning is.

Just as the structuring genetic code in a human body has inertia — i.e., it tends to maintain its structural integrity and the original schedule of transformation needed to pass from embryonic to fully mature existence — so a man's birth-chart has inertia and the chart's progressions indicate the way in which the viable newborn organism develops his *psychological potentialities* (his "intelligence," as I have defined this word — cf. PRACTICE OF ASTROLOGY, page 123) during the days following birth. A normal nine-month-long period of gestation is followed by some ninety days (three months) which refer to the development in seed of these psychological potentialities. This development can only occur *after* the newborn enters into relationship with his environment for a real person cannot be considered *only* as an individual operating *in vacuum*. He must be studied — as I have already stated — as an "individual-in-his-environment."

Once we realize that it is the relationship of the individual to his environment (a two-way relationship) which is the essential human fact, we can understand that a man is born to fulfill a function on this planet; but such a realization is difficult for most people because we live in an age of over-emphasized individualism, and this extreme individualism expresses itself in the belief that the "real man" is a mysteriously transcendent and essentially separate entity. In its most exaggerated aspect this attitude to man, the universe and God is expressed in the world picture of Descartes, the seventeenth-century French philosopher. According to this picture the universe is a huge machine — man and God being transcendent to it. By the use of his transcending "free" will and of his God-given reason, man can win over the mechanical forces of the universe.

The nineteenth century mechanistic, individualistic and materialistic approach to existence is still very much in evidence in the ordinary mentality of our day. But the most progressive physicists and a few philosopher-scientists have thoroughly upset this entire approach. A well-known physicist, Schrödinger, and several of his colleagues, think of the universe as an expression of mind. In his excellent book, ACCENT ON FORM, the great English scientist, Lancelot L. Whyte, emphasizes the fact that there are two basic attitudes in the pursuit of knowledge, the atomistic and the holistic, and he believes that science has largely failed so far to deal with the principle of form which refers to the holistic approach.

Of course, there are immensely complex energies acting upon the Earth's biosphere and making their impact upon men. They operate within the mother's womb and throughout the person's whole life; and in astrology these forces are taken into consideration under the name "transits." But the fundamental reality of man, as a living bio-psychic organism, is not a bundle of forces, but a *form of selfhood*. This form is the result of the focusing of the whole universe at the time and place of the newborn's first breath — the beginning of his relatively independent existence within a particular environment, the need of which he is "meant" to fulfill.

Any living form is a particularized manifestation of the universal principle of order, of cosmic Harmony. At every moment of the universe's existence, this principle of order and form takes

Will and the Self-Maintaining Power of Form

on a new meaning — an "overtone" of the fundamental meaning of *this particular universe*. There are no doubt myriads of universes in infinite time and infinite space, and each of these universes is a structured field of activity. Each begins with an implicit original "Word" (or formula of relationship) which becomes explicited and concretely actualized through a cyclic process of unfoldment. What is basic everywhere is the form (or "field-structure") of any particular whole, each of which plays a part in the total harmony of the universal Whole.

The Greek word, "cosmos," refers not only to a principle of order, but also to beauty (cf. the word, cosmetics); and today the mathematician insists that his mathematical demonstration should be "elegant." Lancelot L. Whyte writes: "Physics seeks to penetrate the music of the atomic spheres, biology the harmony of the organism, and neurology the melody of thought, and though they do not yet know it, these three sciences may be seeking to discover the same universal principle of elegance."

To this revealing statement, I would add that Humanistic astrology seeks to understand and to picture the movie depicting an evolving personality. The scenario of this motion-picture has its condensed and symbolic expression in the astrological birth-chart. The actors in this movie should play their role so as to make clear and convincing the meaning of the story. They should not try to hug the spotlight or to unbalance the interplay between the roles by acting as if they were each the "star" of the whole show. So should the cameraman conform to the spirit of the story in creating a pictorial atmosphere for its sequence. And the director should see that everything falls into its proper place according to the proper proportions, instead of indulging in spectacular showmanship and perhaps so imposing his will upon the actors that they lose all spontaneity and human convincingness.

We live in a universe of existential wholes. Any existent is a whole and everywhere there is order, purpose and meaning. But because we find ourselves immersed in a realm of life in which conflict and pain are ubiquitous features of the biological-social relationship between living wholes we tend at first to have only a "partial" or fragmented consciousness of existence. We are involved in our partial status. Our consciousness is not free because it is dominated by the *biological and social* pressures of the struggle for existence under the principle of scarcity. As a result our brains build up images of conflict and chance happenings — the kind of picture that a cell in the stomach or the duodenum might draw when trying to interpret what it is subjected to.

Metabolism is a harsh process; but to the healthy man the eating, the digesting and the assimilating of living substances poses no problem or concern. A consciousness which can encompass the entirety of such a process — of *any* process in the universe — realizes the *harmonic character* of all the activities which this process implies and requires. Our task, therefore, is to develop a holistic consciousness (whole-consciousness). It is to see the universe as a whole, the Earth as an organized system of interdependent activities within which humanity-as-a-whole fulfills a definite function, and ourselves as a structured whole-person unfolding through a cyclic process of self-actualization.

What we have to actualize are the potentialities indicated in our birth-chart; how this process of actualization should proceed at the level of the development of our conscious ability to relate to our environment (our "intelligence") is indicated by the progressions. What birth-charts and progressions reveal is not what *will* occur in terms of events, but the sequential steps which it would be *best* for us to take in order to gradually actualize our innate potential and to fulfill the purpose which is defined by our birth-chart. Everything in the chart indicates what the universe of God expects us to do. *Nothing* is superfluous or evil.

However, the "transits" can be considered in a negative as well as a positive manner. As they represent forces at work everyday in the entire biosphere, these forces could tend to disturb or disrupt by their impacts the essential form of our fundamental structure of being — the essential form of our individual selfhood. Transits, in this sense, tend to upset the pattern which the birth-chart represents; but whether we give to such upsets the meaning of "good" or "bad" depends on our biases and the mentaltiy of our society. On the other hand, transits can — and should — be seen as indicating the new contents of the experiences which every new day brings to us. As we assimilate these new life-contents, the form of our individual selfhood becomes *filled*. If this form is strong, it can contain these new experiences — and our mind can assimilate their messages to us. If it is weak, it may become distorted by the impacts from these forces. They may invade us, and we may lose our individuality. In extreme cases this means psychosis.

This is, I believe, the type of approach to life on which a Humanistic astrology can be most significantly based. The world-picture it implies has its roots in ancient vitalistic philosophies; but its formulation, and the practical approach to the interpretation of all astrological factors, are definitely new in that they refer to conditions of existence and possibilities of development of consciousness which did not normally exist in archaic times.

This humanistic attitude is an antidote against the poison of extreme individualism which has posed to our present society problems that are practically insoluble, unless a new world-viewpoint is very soon developed and it spreads broadly through the collective mentality of mankind. This does *not* mean that even "rugged" individualism and dualistic transcendental philosophies were wrong or accidental products of chance circumstances. They filled an essential historical need and they still do so partially for most people. But every trend becomes exaggerated and produces disharmonic results at one time or another. Then it has to be reintegrated in the whole process of evolution, and to become harmonized with its opposite. This is the Middle Way. It is the way of integration through form — the way of harmony, and beauty. Today a new humanity is emerging out of the pressures of "ethical" dualisms and is eager to follow this way.

At a time when astrology is becoming widely accepted and misused as much as used, and when conflicting tendencies are developing as to how it should be incorporated officially into today's social and educational Establishment, it is necessary to face straight forwardly the problems all this poses. There is no need to court favors from static minds or to bow down to a tradition pervaded with the type of Classical mentality which produced a Descartes. Great minds today are pioneering along a new way of understanding in physics and philosophy. They could show us a way to a complete reformulation of astrology based on a new realization of what man is and of his place in a harmonic universe.

THE ASTROLOGY OF SELF-ACTUALIZATION
AND THE NEW MORALITY

7

Event-Oriented and Person-Centered Astrology

In the first essay of this series, "Astrology for New Minds" two fundamentally different approaches to astrology were defined: the event-oriented and the person-centered approach. Let me briefly restate what these two approaches are.

In its most extreme aspect, the first of these considers astrology as an empirical science gradually built by men who in various countries noticed that certain definite types of events around them occurred at the time when they also observed celestial phenomena referring to the relative positions of the Sun, the Moon and the planets, and to the reappearance of some prominent stars at the horizon. These celestial phenomena recurred periodically, and so did the events on earth which had been observed to occur simultaneously. These men made careful records of their observations; and gradually through many centuries these records were codified into what we now call a science, i.e., a consistent body of knowledge dealing with observable phenomena.

Correlations between celestial phenomena and earthly events exist; and the scientifically-oriented astrologer claims that they are reliable — if not absolutely, at least in a very large (but so far not at all precisely determined) number of observed and observable cases — *provided* of course that the recorded data accumulated by past generations of observers are well understood and used as originally intended.

A question at once arises in the mind of the enquirer. Why and how should there be a correlation between a conjunction of two planets, or the reappearance of a big star in the West after sunset, and the fate of a battle, the occurrence of a serious drought, the illness or the falling in love of human beings?

The astrologer who is a strictly event-oriented empiricist admits that he does not know the how or the why of these correlations. He seems to take for granted that there is a causal relationship between the celestial and the terrestrial events; and he speaks of the "influences" of planets and stars upon human affairs and upon the character and well-being of individual persons, or even of nations. He might say that we do not really know how gravitation operates, but that we nevertheless are using our knowledge that it is to be reckoned with. Because we have measured the gravitational pull of matter upon matter we can *predict* accurately how much thrust must be applied to a missile so that it may escape from the gravitational field of the Earth. All empirical sciences are indeed means of predicting what will happen when this and that factor come together under definite conditions; and astrology is not different from all other sciences.

However, some serious problems arise. While it is true that empirical science bases its laws —

and therefore its "prediction" of events — on repeatedly observed correlations between two sets of factors, these two sets normally belong to the same order of phenomena. The correlation is seen to be one of cause and effect, and there is always some relevance or similarity of nature between the cause and the effect. If one speaks of "influence," then one assumes that there is a medium that is the carrier of this influence. How does this apply to astrology, *as it is used today?*

As already stated in the preceding essay, it is today quite acceptable, scientifically speaking, to believe that the positions of the planets at any time within the entire solar system refer to definable influences exerted upon the Earth and everything that lives on its surface. Powerful waves of energy stream forth from the Sun, and probably to a lesser extent from stars and regions of the galaxy. But what has this to do with astrology's claim that a certain section of a person's birth-chart refers to "possessions," another to illness or one's job, still another to death and legacy? Why is it that because Uranus passes in the sky over the degree of the zodiac at which the Moon was placed at a man's birth, this individual should expect without fail to experience some emotional upset, or some change in his relationship with his mother or his mistress? What causes this selectivity? What conceivable type of mechanism or process could explain the direct action of a particular planet upon a particular person, in terms of the person's meeting with another person who will change his life, or in terms of being run over by a car, or of taking a long journey which will prove successful because Jupiter is passing through a section of the zodiacal belt which occupied a certain angle of the sky when the person was born?

The honest empiricist-astrologer simply says that he does not know — that no one knows. But, he adds, these correlations have been empirically proven by numerous records, and so one can reliably expect that they will be repeated again and every time. To solve the problem, Carl Jung introduced the concept of "synchronicity"; that is, what happens at any moment of time carries everywhere the characteristic quality of this moment. But when one advances such a metaphysical concept one leaves the field of empirical science. Moreover, this does not really change one's basic approach to astrology — or more precisely to the meaning and value of astrology.

The approach changes only when one gives a different meaning to the purpose of astrology: what is astrology FOR? It is assumed by a great majority of the people that this purpose is to predict, according to the time and place of their birth, what is going to happen to them. This sounds simple enough; but is it really so?

Even if we take for granted that there are definitely known and *relatively* certain types of events occurring on the Earth and affecting the lives of individual persons when definite celestial events take place, this does not take in consideration the most basic problem, that is, the problem of *what this knowledge will do* to the human beings to which it is revealed. Moreover, if we look at this matter of prediction with intellectual honesty, we have to realize that when the astrologer predicts future events he is rarely able to pinpoint ahead of time (1) *exactly* what the events will be, (2) under *precisely* what circumstances they will take place, and (3) how they will affect the consciousness and the psycho-physiological health of the person.

Every so often we find in astrological magazines an author having made some prediction concerning world affairs congratulating himself for having "hit the mark" in so many instances. But we should look at what had been predicted; usually something rather vague which could have been interpreted in various ways. Let us say that an astrologer announces a ship disaster in the Atlantic Ocean during a particular week, or an insurrection in South America, or a scandal in Washington, D.C., or the fall of a European government. *What good* could such predictions have done, even if indeed what happened fitted into the broad categories of shipwrecks, revolutions, scandals or governmental upsets? Should all ships crossing the Atlantic remain tied up to their docks during the week in question?

When the prediction deals with an individual person, the situation is even more complex, for there is hardly any possibility of being certain of the level at which, and the actual circumstances in which "something" will happen that would fit the character of, say, a Saturn and Mars transit over the natal Sun, a solar eclipse on the Ascendant, a conjunction of the progressed Moon with the natal Uranus, or whatever it be. And, as I stated already in the preceding essay, prediction to human beings can be self-fulfilling; the prediction becomes a perhaps important factor in a developing situation, if only by generating some vague fear or an unwarranted optimism.

It is easy to take crucial events like the assassinations of the two Kennedys and show that they occurred exactly when a certain type of transit or progression did take place according to a particular system. But again would the foreknowledge of the possibility, or even the statistical probability, of some sort of catastrophe have constructively influenced the individuals who were to be killed? They might only have been hurt seriously and the shock might have had constructive results; and no astrologer could have been *sure* on astrological grounds alone that it would precisely be death. If President Kennedy had not known that Presidents of the U.S. elected close to the time of a conjunction of Jupiter and Saturn have died in office, he might not have had a kind of fatalistic attitude toward his death.

But this is not all. Were *all* people who were born with the *same* birth-chart as President Kennedy assassinated at the same time? To determine whether this was so or not would obviously be the test of the validity of a strictly event-oriented and ''scientific'' astrology; and I have urged astrologers for over thirty years to unite their efforts to make such a kind of test. If at that time, thirty years ago in large cities like New York,

London, Paris, Tokyo, the names and addresses of babies born with charts so nearly identical that no modern astrologer would have interpreted them differently had been taken — and if the lives of these children had been followed up year after year, we would have now indisputable proofs of the validity of astrology. I mean proofs of the extent to which this particular birth-pattern could have given a significant picture of the character of all these people and a reliable indication of the correlations between celestial happenings (transits, direction, progressions, solar returns, etc.) and the events in the lives of all of them.

It is obvious that the dozen or so babies which may have been born with charts practically identical to that of John Kennedy did not experience precisely the same kind of life-events. They most likely had different personalities molded by different surroundings and different hereditary backgrounds. Even if they married at the same time, had the same number of children, were promoted in the same year and died on the same day, the circumstances and implication of the *actual events,* and above all *the responses* of each of these individuals to the events, would have been different. How different? Would the fact that an astrologer could have predicted the dates of these events have added something very important to these lives? This is the important issue.

The person-oriented, humanistic and holistic approach to astrology changes the situation radically. It is no longer the prediction of events which essentially matters; for the basic purpose of studying a birth-chart and discussing it with the person to whom it refers is to help this person to *become more positively, more meaningfully, more creatively, more totally what he potentially is.*

The difference between the event-oriented and the person-oriented approaches is somewhat similar to that between laboratory Pavlovian psychology, and a most inclusive form of psychotherapy. The research psychologist is satisfied with recording events resulting from experiments and to analyze them statistically. The psychotherapist is preoccupied essentially with the health — psychic, mental and physical — of individual persons who seek his help.

Of course, the research psychologist experimenting with rats and monkeys, or attaching dozens of electrical apparatuses to the bodies of sleeping people or of men and women making love, may well hope that what he discovers will be "of use to mankind"; but will it necessarily be *valuable?* Might not this experimental psychological approach lead to a further dehumanization and mechanization of men and women? The possibility of tampering with the individual personality and of creating semi-human, semi-robot beings is certainly not to be ignored. Any true humanist should fight against such a purpose even if camouflaged under the attractive heading of "improving" human nature. The "improvements" which men have brought to the soil, the water and the air of our planet are a good example of what the intellectual and professional drive of knowledge for knowledge's sake can produce.

The basic justification for the technological, behavioristic and strictly event-oriented approach of our modern society is the proud belief that man's greatest achievement is the control and transformation of nature, that indeed he is godlike and in charge of the evolution of all there is around him. He can use his technology to do as he pleases, changing expectable natural events — including the events of his own life — to suit his intellectual and visionary purposes. Such an attitude is most likely to bring mankind to a catastrophe, because it is entirely one-sided. It makes of the intellectual mind a relentless and ruthless dictator. It enthrones the ego, whose authoritarian will and conceptual abstraction create laws which operate effectively because everything that does not fit in is cast aside as unwanted nonsense or as enemy of the realm.

These remarks may seem to be very remote from the field of astrology, but actually they are not; because the two approaches to astrology which I have defined refer to a fundamental dualism of attitudes which is found *in every area* of human thinking and human activity. They are related intimately to two basic human temperaments and to the general atomistic and holistic approaches to existence as a whole. No doubt *there is value in both*; and, when exaggerated and left unchecked, either can produce inharmonious and unbalanced results. But for centuries our Western society has so emphasized the atomistic, analytical-intellectual and event-oriented approach that it has become indeed tragically disequilibrated and near collapse — perhaps only after a frightened and dreadful hardening of its stance.

Man can change his environment to suit his proud craving for power, comfort, expansion, and self-glorification; but unless he changes his basic attitude toward himself and revaluates radically his capacities and his motives, this relentless expansionism can only poison or destroy this environment and eventually himself. What matters is not, man as an ambitious-restless individual, or as a group driven by a common lust for power or wealth, but the harmonious interplay of man and his environment; it is not the *quantity* and scope of measurable achievements, but the *quality* of the consciousness and of the relationships freely entered upon and harmoniously fulfilled — the quality of the purpose.

What is, I repeat, the purpose of astrology? Before any discussion concerning astrological technicalities is begun one should answer this question. For some astrologers it seems obvious, from their writings, that their implied purpose is simply to prove that future events can be predicted, and to show that they have the correct technical means and the skill to make correct forecasts — i.e., forecasts which, though usually quite broadly stated, spot the area in which the events occurred. The astrologer presents himself thus as a "professional"; he has done his job accurately for his client. How this will affect the total personality, the emotional life and the actions of this client is often not given any serious, careful consideration.

In contrast to such an attitude I think of astrology first as a *technique for the development of holistic thinking;* then, as a tool to help a person to face in a new way all life-situations — and first of all himself as an individual person. I consider astrology a discipline of thinking, a way of developing a new quality of consciousness. It is a method of "self-actualization"; and, as we shall presently see, a kind of *yoga* — a yoga with one's destiny; and by destiny I mean the process of self-actualization, i.e., the basic schedule of life-developments according to which a person can and should become what he was potentially as a newborn in a particular environment.

The purpose of astrology is not to tell a person what will most probably (or some astrologers might say, "inevitably") happen to him at this and that specified time; it is rather to assist him in relating everything that happens, inside even more than outside of him, to the total pattern of his life-development — to what he potentially is as a whole person. It is to help him *to accept himself wholly* so that he can meet consciously and openly all changes and opportunities, realizing as they occur their meaning and function in terms of the total character and purpose of his life.

To develop a capacity for holistic thinking — then, to assist the individual person in his process of self-actualization: these are two basic purposes. Let us see in greater detail what they imply.

Astrology as a Discipline of Mind

Not only the average person of our present time, but many people who are involved in activities regarded as "scientific," fail to recognize that the field of science is not monolithic and that a very basic difference of outlook exists among the most eminent scientists, especially among those who seek to understand the philosophical implications and the human value of the methods they use and the discoveries they make. Some of the most fundamental concepts and intellectual attitudes of science have become radically altered since the beginning of this century. The mechanistic picture of the universe which has been built since the days of Newton and Descartes is retained only by those men who are busy merely at the fringe of scientific enquiry and in terms of technological applications. A new world-view has been unfolding. Thus one should not be over-impressed by people who are brandishing the word "scientific" as a magic wand to do away with unfamiliar and perhaps "occult" ideas which in fact may parallel the latest concepts of the great physicists and philosophers of our day.

In his remarkable book, ACCENT ON FORM, the English scientist-philosopher, Lancelot L. Whyte, points out that "since the time of the ancient Greeks, thinkers have shown a tendency to fall into one of two camps which for convenience can be called the Atomistic School and the Holistic School." In the Atomistic School he places Leucippus, Democritus, Gassendi, Newton, Boyle, Dalton, Rutherford, Millikan; in the Holistic School Aristotle, Goethe, Bergson, the Gestalt psychologists, Whitehead and the Smuts. He says that "the classical atomistic doctrine asserts that the universe is made up of ultimate particles, each of which is simple, indivisible and permanent — that all observable changes are due to the reversible spatial arrangements of these particles resulting from their motions and mutual influences."

In the holistic view the universe is "a great hierarchy of wholes each following its own path of historical development. Each pattern, whether it is a crystal, an organism, a community, the solar system or a spiral nebula possesses its own internal order and is part of a more extensive order, so that the universe is regarded as a System of systems, a Grand Pattern of patterns. . . . The holistic thinker's model of the universe (is) an organism in which every part is harmoniously related to the processes characterizing the system as a whole." While the atomist finds perfection in analysis, precision and quantity, the holist seeks it in form, order and unity. The former tends to start with the detailed facts, the latter to think intuitively, using a direct sense of general situations and the relationships involved.

Another eminent scientist, a biologist with a remarkable vision of the universe, Donald Hatch Andrews, discusses extensively the concepts of wholeness, identity, form and synthesis in his recent book, THE SYMPHONY OF LIFE, and he likewise stresses the difference between the holistic and the atomistic approaches to every type of human experience and empirically ascertained fact.

He writes (page 91):

". . . At one extreme we have the philosopher and the scientist who say that reality resides only in the fundamental particles of which the universe is constructed. To this school of thought it is meaningless to say that man is any more than a little machine made up of these individual bits of reality. When life terminates, dust returns to dust and the particles go on their way in new combinations, but the illusory whole that was the personality has vanished forever. At the other extreme of this spectrum there are philosophers who maintain that it is only in the wholes that we have reality. Even with respect to matter it has been asserted that atoms exist only in the laboratory when, under very artificial conditions (as in the beam of the molecular mass spectrograph), we break matter up into individual atoms with controllable paths and make atoms really exist. These scientists maintain that the atom's existence in a mass of matter is just as illusory as the human personality is claimed to be by the atomist thinkers.

"How one feels about such questions is perhaps determined by the extent to which one emphasizes analysis or synthesis in thinking."

Astrology as a Discipline of Mind

and page 92:

". . . As we shall see in delving more and more deeply into the nature of matter, the new wave perspective shifts the emphasis strongly from parts to wholes, an emphasis of links. . . . I quoted Hermann Weyl earlier, pointing out that we must recognize in atomic physics that the whole is more than the sum of the parts. Whitehead also emphasizes this: 'But in all analysis there is one supreme factor which is apt to be omitted, namely, the mode of togetherness.' . . .

"Of course, it is all very well to talk of reality residing in the wholes, but is this a perspective in which we can do constructive reasoning? When we talk about parts instead of wholes we have the advantage of being able to count the parts and set up quantitative laws in terms of numbers. Assemblages of parts can be combined with the help of the laws of arithmetic. For the study of wholes we need an algebra of form rather than an arithmetic of numbers. So we have to study the relations that restrict putting things together and turn to combinatorial analysis.

"Coming back to the atom, we are more and more aware that we are dealing here with dynamic forms and that we have to study the relations of forms to one another. We have to see how these forms combine. Because we are dealing with vibrating wave patterns, these forms are dynamic, and this means that we are involved in a kind of combinatorial analysis far different from that involved in combining static geometric forms (though the relations in the latter process do have a most significant bearing on the combination of dynamic forms)."

and page 94:

". . . Our new discoveries reveal these unexpected aspects of the nature of matter and point emphatically to the need for revising our basic concepts of what is real. They tell us that reality lies not in the tangible, but in the intangible, in the unseen and the unheard. We have to think about the behavior of atoms in terms of dynamic form."

The dynamic aspect of these forms consists largely of vibration with harmonic relations that are in many ways similar to the harmonic relations found in music. . . ."

And he adds in his Preface (page 9):

"The familiar vocabulary of ideas based on the particle obeying the laws of Newton's mechanics in Cartesian space and time has been replaced by a syntax of dynamic forms operating in a space-time domain the nature of which is still largely a mystery. To sum up the nature of this scientific revolution in a single phrase, we are finding that the universe is composed not of matter but of music."

I could add many similar quotations, especially if some of the writings by prominent European scientists were mentioned; but these should suffice to show that the "scientific revolution" which has taken place should be understood and accepted by some of the persons who are so eager to approach astrology "scientifically." They might do well to read, for instance, many articles appearing in the magazine MAIN CURRENTS IN MODERN THOUGHT in which well-known scientists and philosophers often discuss new developments along the line of a holistic and integrative approach to the problems of physics, psychology, sociology and education.

"A universe composed not of matter but of music": how close to the Pythagorean Music of the Spheres and to the "planetary spheres" of ancient astrology! The main point in the context of this essay is that, more important than the *apparent* unit of matter moving around in a vertiginous dance, are the actual patterns made by such motions. As long as we concentrate our mind on "particles" — be they sub-atomic or cosmic — we think in mechanistic terms. We think of a world in which a vast number of infinitely small or enormously large billiard balls move in empty space according to the classical laws of mechanics. The new picture of the universe is one in which we are dealing with waves rather than particles, or more exactly perhaps with extremely complex wave-patterns within the boundaries of "fields" which have — in the abstract sense of the terms — "form" and "rhythm." We are dealing with one basic type of energy operating rhythmically (which means also cyclically) in terms of *significant forms* — forms which can reveal "meaning" to the mind able to think holistically.

The great Austrian psychiatrist, Victor Frankl, has emphasized, out of his own tragic personal experience in Nazi concentration camps, that men can stand almost anything except total meaninglessness. It is mainly on this fact that he bases his "logotherapy." John's Gospel states that in the beginning was the Word — the Logos. A Word is both a sound (i.e., a release of energy) and a form infused with meaning. In the beginning of every existing entity, whether cosmic or biological, there is form and order. A pattern, or formula, of relationship defining the fundamental arrangement of functioning parts within a whole system of activities — a cosmos, a solar system, an organism, a cell, a man — is *implied and inherent* in the original impulse to existence which produced this whole. The biologist is able to perceive such a pattern as a genetic code. The entire concept of astrology, if it makes sense at all, is based on the intuitive belief that the universe and, more specifically in terms of man's existence, the solar system are ordered and structured systems of activities in which meaning and purpose are inherent. Any astrologer who does not intuitively feel that there is meaning and purpose in the geo-cosmic pattern formulated in a birth-chart is at best merely a "fact-gatherer." The stage of fact-gathering could be said to parallel the phase of human evolution in which men were only "fruit gatherers." It is only as man began to *cultivate* the soil and became a "harvester" of the products of the process of seed-multiplication, both vegetable and animal, that culture and civilization developed.

Cultivation or culture requires not only the recognition of the presence of form and rhythm in the universe but also of a deep, at first unclear, feeling that man exists in a special and significant *relationship* to this natural environment which provides him with the possibility of agriculture and cattle-raising, and later on of industry. Man senses that there is a meaning and purpose in this relationship. Alas, in trying to formulate this meaning and purpose man, reaching the intellectual and egocentric phase of his development, often came to the conclusion that all nature is made for his sustenance and enjoyment. He proudly saw himself as the divinely intended master of nature; and he conveniently embodied such a conclusion in his religious "revelations"; God telling him that everything in the world was made for man, and therefore that the purpose of the whole universe is to provide man with food, raw materials, and experiences enabling him gradually to develop faculties so transcending the rhythms and the forms of nature that they can be called "divine."

Is it God's "Creative Intention" that earth-nature and what is more, the whole solar system, and galaxy, should be subjected to the proud will of man, doing with nature just as he sees fit, or is this concept, repeated today in various ways, a basic falsification of the meaning and the purpose of man's existence? We may think that this is a metaphysical or religious question which has nothing to do with astrology; but on the contrary, it has everything to do with understanding the difference between the event-oriented traditional Western astrology, and the person-centered humanistic and harmonic astrology which I have been developing for some thirty-five years. Should man try to "rule" his chart — to which he is external or is he intended to fulfill and actualize in every possible way this birth-chart and progressions, simply because the birth-chart is the seed-pattern, the *logos,* of his total being as an individual person operating within a particular and specific environment?

The Western Christian approach to existence implies that man is alien to the Earth, an angelic being "fallen" into this tragic and dark earth-nature and whose only valid purpose is to ascend to his original divine state. This approach gives a definitely negative meaning to the relationship between man and nature; and because it is so basic it has had and still has immense repercussions upon every human activity and every aspect of man's consciousness and personal development.

The humanistic, holistic and harmonic approach has a totally different character. According to it mankind belongs to the planet, Earth, as closely as the nervous system and the brain belong to the body. This nervous system has a definite function to fill in the total operation of this system of activities which we call a human being. In a somewhat similar sense, but of course *not literally so,* mankind is to fulfill a definite function in the total operation of this vast, yet closely integrated, system of activities which we call the planet Earth — provided we do not think of this Earth as merely a mass of matter. This function appears to be to *extract consciousness* out of all the activities within the Earth-field — a field which may extend at least to, and perhaps in a sense include, the Moon.*

The process of extracting consciousness, meaning and value from experience requires a specific

---

*These ideas are developed at great length in my forthcoming book:
THE PLANETARIZATION OF CONSCIOUSNESS
which should be available around June or July 1970.

type of mental faculty. It is one thing to deal with events analytically and statistically and to place them into various categories based on the exclusion of unduplicated individual characteristics; it is another thing to be able to envision the form and meaning of their relationships, thus to see them as functional parts of a larger whole. Astrologically speaking it is easy to list the positions of all the planets and the aspects made by two of these planets to each other, then to go to a textbook and to find out what each of these separate astrological factors are said to mean. But this is only a "fact-gathering" process, for these textbook meanings (theoretically at least) are also based on gathered single facts — the observed correspondence between celestial and terrestrial events.

Let me repeat here that these correspondences are never *exact* repetitions of *all* the facts to which they refer. A particular planetary position or a particular aspect between two planets in most cases may correspond to a particular trait of character, let us say, a tendency to have repeated accidents. But "accidents" may be of various types and have many causes. Will it help a person to know in advance that he is accident prone? Will this make him more careful? But careful of *exactly what*? An accident occurs under a complex set of circumstances; and even if there is in the person some psychological or physiological factors which cause him to act in an inadequate manner when he is faced by a potentially dangerous situation, these factors can be varied and complex. They will not be precisely the same in two accident-prone persons, because these persons are not only human beings but *individuals.*

Two individuals may have in their birth-charts a factor which is usually associated with an early divorce, but divorce may not only have many causes, it may *mean* very different things to different persons; that is, it may result in two entirely different inner attitudes, two different "harvests" of value. Because of this, in most cases it is unwise to tell in advance to a person that he will experience a *specific* event because the basic factor is not the event itself but the character and state of consciousness of the person *at the time* he meets this event. One may indeed say that it is not the event which happens to the person, but the person which happens to the event. An individual meets particular events because he needs them in order to become more fully what he is only potentially. The event occurs in order to bring out of his unconscious being and into the field of his consciousness his total individual selfhood.

This "bringing out into consciousness" is what the psychologist, C.G. Jung, meant when he spoke of the "process of individuation." In a circular written in 1932 entitled "Harmonic Psychology" I spoke of such a process as leading to the revelation "of the all-compelling Image of an individual's own Soul — the symbol that Life takes within his 'self,' the seed-Image of his destiny." I pointed out that in the ancient Mysteries the candidate to Initiation was confronted with this Soul-Image evoked by the magical power of the

Initiator. Today the situation is different because of the egocentric character of our culture, and also because it is possible for an individual to develop positively and by himself spiritual-mental faculties which will in time bring to him the concrete and effectual realization of the wholeness of his individual being.

Such a realization may take various forms; it may be brought about by various methods, among which is the ancient technique of "meditation," provided its purpose is correctly understood in the occult sense of the term. Astrology can also be a means to the realization of one's individuality inasmuch as the birth-chart can be considered the symbol or seed-Image of this individuality. But such a realization can never be reached through astrology *unless* the astrologer has developed a holistic faculty of perception — which means, at the very least, that he is able to see the chart as a whole, indeed as an Image of the universe focused in the individual person born at an exact moment of time and in a precise location on this Earth.

Because of this, one should consider astrology first of all as a *discipline of mind*. This discipline consists in learning to see and to understand all situations and all persons as wholes — that is, as patterns of interrelated and interdependent factors which become meaningful only if they are consciously apprehended in their structured totality. *Nothing really exists except through its relationship to everything else.* The individual and the environment cannot be separated; a human being has no truly significant meaning except in relation to the whole of mankind and to the planet, Earth — and of course, in an ultimate sense, in relation to the whole universe and to whatever "God" may actually be. Astrology dramatizes this fact when it brings to our consciousness the realization that every individual man or woman is the whole universe focused in an at least relatively unique manner. What the birth-chart reveals is the particular structural character of the focusing operation — which, symbolically at least, is the "first breath," the first moment of individualized existence within an environment in which the newborn can operate as a self-motivated organism.

Likewise, as I already stated, no planet has any meaning except in terms of its relationship to the entire solar system. The character of a zodiacal sign depends on its place in the closed sequence of signs which we call the zodiac, and the meaning of a House is derived from the fact that it is the first, the second, the third, etc. We might paraphrase the well-known words of John's Gospel by saying: "In the beginning is the Whole." A complex human being begins in *one* fecundated ovum. The totality of his being is there latent in seed potentiality. Then, gradually, this one whole differentiates into a multitude of parts. The process of differentiation occurs according to an inherent pattern which will persist, as a genetic code, inside of every one of the billions of cells of the human organism, even though each group of cells develops so as to fulfill the function

Astrology as a Discipline of Mind

it embodies *according to its meaningful place in the original whole* and its moment of appearance in the process of embryonic unfoldment.

If one understands these existential facts one should also understand astrology and its basic techniques, PROVIDED one forgets altogether the traditional concept that planets or stars cause events to happen to an individual person and exert a direct influence through the emanation of some mysterious "rays." Astrology is a symbolic language enabling us to interpret the interrelationships of all parts of any existential whole. It is a language based on the holistic perception of archetypal and evolving forms. The birth-chart is an archetypal form, and through the study of progressions and transits we can foresee its evolution, that is, the process according to which what is potential at birth becomes actualized *through* life-events.

Astrology informs us of the sequence of characteristic phases in the process of self-actualization — that is, of the individual timing and essential characteristics of turning points and crises of growth. It does NOT tell us anything *directly* about precise events. We can only infer the kind of actual events which will be needed in order to fit the character of the expectable turning points in the person's life. Such inferences are valid only because generic human nature tends to react in similar ways to similar needs and occurrences. If transiting Mars comes to the Venus of a woman one may assume that at this time it will be *natural* for the emotional nature of this woman to be aroused; but the *precise* events which will cause and result from this arousal are not foreseeable by astrological means. Essentially it is the character and inner needs of this particular individual person which will determine, or at least condition, the exact occurrences. These can only be deduced from the form or gestalt of the chart-as-a-whole through a holistic faculty which has to be trained. To train such a faculty is the basic *raison d'etre* of astrology.

But it is not only the chart-as-a-whole of a person which should be considered, for, as I said already, no individual person can be significantly studied except in relation to his environment — which means particularly in relation to other human beings with whom he closely associates, and to society as a whole. This obviously complicates matters, and therefore it is much simpler to believe that planets send rays which hit a person and cause him to fall and break his leg, to inherit a fortune, to marry or to take a long journey. However, we are living in a period of human evolution when a tremendous process of "complexification" (to use Teilhard de Chardin's word) is taking place. The seemingly naive conceptions of the past are being replaced by most abstract mathematical systems which exercise the holistic mind. Even young children are taught to think in terms of "sets" and group-algebra. As I wrote in my book THE ASTROLOGY OF PERSONALITY some thirty-five years ago, astrology should be considered an "algebra of life." It is a deductive, far more than an empirical science.

Astrology as a Discipline of Mind

The astrologer can, and to some extent should, use both approaches; just as the physicist uses induction as well as deduction. He builds mental systems (or "models") the validity of which he then tries to demonstrate by carefully devised experiments. Unfortunately these experiments are often so "carefully devised" that they already imply the kind of results which the scientist wants to obtain. The formulation of a problem already contains the kind of answer which, consciously or not, the mind of the questioner seeks to obtain. The essential question is always therefore: what do you really want? Science is said to be the search for knowledge; but what exactly do we mean by knowledge — knowledge in relation to what? This "what" is always and in any condition of existence, what the searcher *wants*.

If he — and his society — want comfort and material well-being, plus a sense of intellectual achievement fostering ego-pride, then a certain kind of knowledge is sought after which, through its technological applications, will bring these desired results. If, on the other hand, an individual and his society want above all things the harmonious fulfillment of the fundamental nature of man within an equally harmonious and wholesome global environment and the possibility for the individual person to actualize his innate potential of consciousness through experiences of love and sharing, then they will seek *wisdom* rather than what we call today knowledge. They will consider the welfare of the whole rather than the satisfaction or one-pointed development of some parts of this whole. It is this quest for wisdom which I consider to be the essence of "humanism" — a search for wholeness, for that intuition which succeeds in evaluating at once the value and meaning of any whole situation without having recourse to the self-defeating complexity of modern techniques of data-analysis.

Assuredly knowledge can produce amazing and exciting results, like a landing on the Moon; but what if the social processes and the intellectual emphases which led to such achievements result almost inevitably in a catastrophic ecological situation as well as in chaos in our cities and in interpersonal relationships replete with egocentricity and neurotic behavior?

If I bring here such questions which seem to transcend the field of astrology, it is because, to the holistic and humanistic thinker, no single field can be significantly isolated from the whole situation facing mankind. No human concern can be validly discussed out of the context provided by modern man's mentality and expectable behavior. What is at stake today is the transformation of the collective mentality undertoning our Western society. The great event of the second half of our century is not travelling to the Moon but a slowly expanding *revolution in consciousness*. This revolution demands a new approach to all problems; which in turn implies a new discipline of thought and feelings along holistic instead of atomistic lines, in terms of relatedness — mutuality, sharing, harmonization, love — rather than in terms of the glorification of the proud, aggressive and

Astrology as a Discipline of Mind

acquisitive egos of isolated and insecure individuals.

In subsequent essays I shall attempt to present more specifically and concretely procedures which represent the application of holistic thinking to astrology and to the interpretation of birth-charts; but the astrologer is first of all a human being deeply impressed and conditioned by the general mentality pervading the social and educational institutions of his day — even if seemingly he takes an unorthodox stand on the issue of the validity of astrology. This stand may be unorthodox and scorned by the people who control our official approach to knowledge, value and education; yet one may bow to the "spirit of the time" even while dealing with unorthodox concepts and "far out" occupations.

This is just what is happening today in the astrological field, as many astrologers busy themselves gathering data and working out statistics to prove their basic subservience to the scientific mind — alas, not to the scientific mind where it is most creative, synthesizing and integrative, but rather, where it is still perpetuating the mechanistic concepts and the psychological fallacies of the past. For this reason, the issue at stake had to be presented in its broadest outlines and in terms of what is basic in our present revolutionary condition of existence: that is, a choice between two types of mentality. The choice includes as well one between two nearly opposite approaches to the way in which a significant and valuable life is to be lived.

Astrology as Karma Yoga

The fundamental concept on which astrology is based is that everything that is "born" (i.e., that begins to operate as an individual factor in a specific environment) at a particular time and point of space is organized according to a particular seed-pattern or archetype *symbolized* by its birth-chart. This seed-pattern defines what that organism (or organized field of activity) SHOULD be if it fulfills its function in the universal scheme of things, or one might say according to God's Plan.

There may be of course not only a number of human beings but a great variety of biological organisms born at this same time and at least very nearly at this same place. They all have therefore the same time-space formula of existence. The same fundamental Cosmic Intention exists in all these wholes. Will this Intention work out *in actual facts and existential events* in exactly the same manner? Obviously not. What these facts and events will be will depend on, first, the nature of the organism — i.e., its genetic character and background — then, on the manner in which the organism is related, and will relate itself through its own effort, to the environment.

Such a relationship is almost exclusively determined by the racial type and heredity in biological species below primitive man. But with man the capacity to control this relationship to the environment appears. Man can transform his environment in order to fulfill a specific purpose. This is theoretically wonderful; but whether it actually is or not depends on what the purpose is. The purpose may be determined by collective-social factors and cultural values which have nothing or very little to do with "God's idea" for any *individual* entity born at this or that place and time. An individual human being may therefore live a kind of life in which the God-ordained structure of his total being is so overlaid by social, cultural and family determinants and collective Images of what should or should not be done that this life will turn out to be an expression of only superficial and collective aims, and a perversion of the "Creative Intention" of the universe. The archetypal essential character and purpose of the person's life will have been largely ignored, or at least they will have operated only through the distorting and darkening lenses of what family and society, but *not* the universe or God, thought to be the purpose of this life.

Several human beings may have the same birth-chart, the same seed-pattern, but Nature is prolific in its production of seeds; only a few acorns become full-grown oaks. Of these human beings who were born with the same seed-pattern only one or a very few perhaps will actualize the potentialities inherent in this seed-pattern in a conscious and significant manner. A genius and a madman may well have the same chart. This fact does not mean that astrology is without value, provided we realize that astrology does not tell us what *will* happen, but what would happen should the person act consciously and earnestly according to the *celestial instructions* represented in code by the birth-chart.

This is at least the attitude implied in what I call humanistic astrology. Humanistic astrology deals essentially with problems of consciousness. It is based on a philosophy of *conscious acceptation*. It asks of every individual that he accepts what he potentially *is* — the whole of it, without any ethical tag of good or bad, fortunate or unfortunate, being attached to it. This means that one should accept one's birth-chart as it is and be intent upon fulfilling its implications. But these implications must be seen in a totally new and untraditional light, in the realization that every birth-chart fills a significant purpose, all valuable, and that, as an embodied individual, *one is that purpose,* whatever it is and however society or parents may regard its value.

When one approaches life in such a manner one understands in a most vivid way what the Hindu philosopher means by *dharma*. According to the concept of dharma, every living creature has its own dharma, its "truth of being." It has what is often called today its "real identity."

Astrology as Karma Yoga

The rebellious youth of our day is often desperately striving to discover his identity, his "uniqueness of being," and it is because, in our culture, he has been given no traditional way of consciously searching for this identity and of discovering his "true Name" that he often tends to rebel wildly against every social-cultural-religious Image that has been stamped upon his mind during the early formative years of childhood, or else he wanders along paths of quasi-mystical escape in search of ever-evasive ecstacies.

Dharma, truth of being, identity: these and other terms all refer to what I have called the "seed-pattern" of an individual person's being. The spiritual life is one which is based on the conscious acceptance of this dharma-pattern. But how can one consciously accept that of which one is not aware? The first thing is therefore to come to a vivid, and if possible, clearly conscious, realization of what one essentially is *as an individual* — and not as a member of this or that race, family, social class, religion, culture and nation.

Astrology can become a method for such a realization; but if it is what is expected of astrology then obviously a great many of the traditional astrological concepts have to be utterly transformed. The birth-chart has to be understood as archetype or seed-pattern of one's individual being — as the symbolical "form" of one's individuality, and therefore also of one's destiny, for the two are identical. A man's destiny is the way following which he is able to fulfill his identity and to actualize what at his birth was only potential. Individuality is the *dharma,* destiny the *karma* of the human being. Dharma is the fundamental pattern, karma the specific type of activity to actualize this pattern of individual selfhood.

What the Hindu philosopher calls "Karma Yoga" is a process of total acceptance of the specific activities required to actualize and fulfill one's dharma. Karma does refer also to the results of past actions, but this is not the most essential, even if it is the popular, meaning. Past actions which were not performed according to the dharma of an individual leave residue or waste products; moreover what has *not* been done, but should have been done in order to fulfill one's dharma, remains as *unfinished business.* As existence is cyclic, the unfinished business left at the close of a cycle reappears during the next (or some new) cycle as karma. This "old karma" conditions and in most cases, determines, the character of the new dharma — that is, of the seed-pattern of the new birth. When the rigid concept of reincarnation is accepted, then obviously one must likewise accept that of karma being the results of the failures, the perversions, and the unfinished business of a past life.

Karma Yoga is "union" (i.e., yoga) with what needs to be done in order to fully actualize the characteristics and the potentialities of one's birth at a particular place and time — that is, in a particular environment and during a specific phase of the cyclic evolution of mankind. This means a total unconditioned acceptance of the chart as a means to fulfill the dharma which it symbolizes, but only when the chart is seen and understood as a focused image of the entire universe and of its rhythms as a whole of interdependent parts; and no part, *nothing* in the chart is considered essentially "bad" or evil.

Some forty years ago I wrote a pamphlet entitled: "The Will to Destiny." The phrase is in a sense a translation of the term Karma Yoga — but of course it is also an expression of the Christial ideal of surrender to the Will of God. However, all such phrases and what they imply become futile at our present stage of human evolution if one does not add that this identification with a cosmic pattern and attunement to the great rhythms of the universe should be the results of a *conscious* process. In other words, what is idealized is NOT a passive attitude of merely letting go, but a positive, dynamic *focusing of consciousness* upon the dharma. The consciousness is focused in a consistent and constant endeavor, first, to recognize the character of this individual "truth of being" — then, to understand its meaning. The end purpose is not only to fulfill one's destiny-individuality but, in the very process of this fulfillment, to realize consciously and clearly the cosmic-divine purpose of one's birth where and when it occurred — i.e., the *why* of one's existence as an individual person.

However, this purpose can never be truly understood unless the act of understanding is identical with the act of destiny-fulfillment. Dharma is revealed *through* the operation of karma, but only if there is a focusing of consciousness upon this operation as it happens — not before it happens. A birth-chart (plus its progressions and transits) has value only as it is seen as a background during the turning points, crises and decisions of the life of the person it symbolizes. It is, one might say, a kind of map upon which a navigator marks the path described by the past advances. The navigator faced with a possible change of direction asks: Considering what I have reached, what is the next step?

Nevertheless, such a question is not only futile but perhaps damaging, spiritually speaking, if the individual is not willing and ready to "perform yoga" with this next step, whatever it be. This means, if he is not able to realize that any step which is *for him* the next step ahead is "right," whether society or religion — and the usual astrologers — consider it good or bad, easy or hard, fortunate or unfortunate. The Karma Yogi will perform this act regardless of consequence if he "knows" — with a knowledge beyond reason, tradition, fear or anticipation — that it is for him the step just ahead.

The willing readiness to face any crisis and in general to live up to the hilt one's recognized and accepted destiny is not ordinarily found among human beings, especially in our permissive, hedonistic and comfort-oriented society. It has never been widespread at any time, and it is because of this that the Hindu *guru* has to play in the life of his disciples a role which the latter usually fail to understand and, even if they do so, rarely appreciate. The guru "precipitates" the karma of his disciple; he forces, directly or indirectly, the disciple to face the karma which this disciple would normally try to run away from, or to postpone by devious and clever mental subterfuges. But at the same time the guru remains close, psychically if not physically, so as to act as a kind of "magic mirror" on which the disciple can see consciously — perhaps not immediately, but sooner or later — *what* is happening and *why* it happens.

This is the "conscious Way"; and it is as well the way of the "symbolic life." The life is symbolic because every process and event in it is pregnant with meaning, and in some degree is an expression of the Will to Harmony which is the foundation of all existence, of microcosm as well as macrocosm. The birth-chart itself is a symbol. Astrology is a cosmic language. Every moment of time has a "message" to communicate to every point of space. The whole is constantly communicating with its component parts; but the parts cannot hear because they are mainly concerned with keeping their boundaries protected against any too disturbing communications. They should realize that the very form of the boundaries reveals their "celestial" identity. The universe is the outside of the form; the personality is the inside of it. The form — i.e., the individuality — does not separate; it *defines the meaning* of what it structures.

All of this can be applied to astrology. The birth-chart is the universe as a human individual sees it; but it is also the individual as the universe responds to him. The name given to a child by his parents establishes the character of the relationship of the parents (and of their community) to the child. The birth-chart of an individual is his celestial Name — the Name given to him by the universal Whole, i.e., by God. Will the individual accept this Name, accept this particular pattern of relationship to the universe? Will he accept it as a Karma Yogi accepts and wills his destiny with equal-mindedness — that is, without attachment to success or failure, to pleasure or pain, to joy or sorrow, to wealth or poverty?

In nearly four decades of familiarity with astrology I have remarked that so-called critical aspects seem to bring to a person astrologically aware of them sharper and often more upsetting confrontations than they did *before* he knew about astrology. The psychological explanation may be that, consciously or unconsciously, he expected and probably feared these confrontations; but this may not be deep enough an explanation. It may be that by establishing a conscious contact with his celestial Name (his birth-chart) the individual made himself more open to a downpour of the karma, held as it were in suspension in his unconscious, and more willing to accept it to the full without evasion.

I would indeed tell any person who seeks proficiency in astrological knowledge: Are you ready and willing to meet up to the hilt your destiny? Are you really intent upon discovering your true Name? If not, leave astrology alone. It might only

Astrology as Karma Yoga

bring you confusion. True astrology is "beyond good and evil," as these terms are usually interpreted in our supposedly Christian civilization. It is an approach to a philosophy of life which is demanding in a way with which you are perhaps not at all familiar. It is an application of this philosophy — a holistic, cyclocosmic way of attunement to the universe. To follow this way you have to leave behind many traditional beliefs. What you may achieve is simply the ability to qualify for a deeper participation in the process of birth of a new humanity.

10

The New Morality

There is much talk today about "the new morality," but the change from the "old" to the "new" morality is interpreted in a confused and often irrelevant manner. What usually impresses people is merely the fact that some kinds of actions which were not allowed and considered immoral are now regarded as permissible and in some cases valuable and truly constructive. The present revolution in interpersonal and social behavior is not, however, what makes the morality new. The new morality does not merely extend the permissibility of actions; it means, if it is at all significant, a change of attitude toward the concept of morality itself.

The "old" traditional idea of morality refers to the performance of actions: there is a "right" and a "wrong" way of acting. The term, right, comes from the Sanskrit word *rita*, which refers to the correct performance of actions in a ritual or ceremony; and in old India practically every act of daily living was involved in some kind of ritual. A divine Law-giver, Manu, was believed to have precisely defined how nearly every human action had to be performed; and this established the only "right" way to act in all circumstances. At the root of our Western civilization we find also God's Ten Commandments revealed to Moses, and the Hebrew society was, like the Hindu, rigidly ritualistic — with this very basic difference that in India the most valued human being was the Sannyasi, or Holy Man, who considered himself, and was accepted as being, beyond all the laws of caste and beyond the need to conform to most of the ritual of organized cults — a paradoxical situation.

In our Christian tradition morality has remained mainly identified with the performance or non-performance of specific actions, but an emotional quality was introduced into the nature of the moral action around the time of the birth of Christianity and, in India, of the development of Northern Mahayana Buddhism. It became not only the "right" action, but the "good" action. The inner motive for the action, the quality of the feeling within the person performing it and this person's state of mind or consciousness, entered into the picture. These elements may have been present in earlier days in the concept of ritualistic living, but around the first century B.C. they increased greatly in importance, at least in theoretical importance.

If we are to speak significantly of a "new" morality we have to refer to an attitude to life according to which the *moral value* of any action depends almost exclusively on the conscious meaning this action has for the individual performing it. According to such an attitude morality refers to consciousness, rather than to action. It is how an individual person sees and relates himself in thought and feeling to the action which makes it moral or immoral, good or bad — and to use terms emphasized by existentialist philosophers, authentic or unauthentic.

An authentic action is one which expresses the "truth of being" of an individual person — i.e., his fundamental nature, his dharma. The impulse to act in many cases arises "spontaneously" (vis. "of its own"); in any case it is not dictated or even deeply influenced by social custom, by parental wishes, by what has been impressed upon the conscious and/or unconscious mind by collective pressures, fear of social retaliation or religious sanctions. The action may fit in with social-cultural values, but if so this should not be due to a blind or compulsive kind of conformism, but to the conscious, objective and enlightened acceptation of such values. If a boy follows his father's profession *just because* it is his father's, and custom, financial convenience or personal comfort dictate this course of action, this is not an authentic choice. It may not be authentic either, if the child refuses to follow in his father's footsteps just because he is led by the example of many youths of his age to rebel in principle against what his parents wish.

This concept of "authenticity" was well understood, at least within certain social limits, in ancient India, where much was said concerning individual "acts of truth." In his remarkable book

The New Morality

PHILOSOPHIES OF INDIA, Heinrich Zimmer writes the following (page 160-162) quoting at first from the Bhagavad-Gita (3:35):

" 'Better is one's own dharma, though imperfectly performed, than the dharma of another well performed. Better is death in the performance of one's own dharma: the dharma of another is fraught with peril.' There exists in India an ancient belief that the one who has enacted his own dharma without a single fault throughout the whole of his life can work magic by the simple act of calling that fact to witness. This is known as making an 'Act of Truth.' The dharma need not be that of the highest Brahman caste or even of the decent and respectable classes of the human community. In every dharma, Brahman, the Holy Power, is present.

"The story is told, for example, of a time when the righteous king Asoka, greatest of the great North Indian dynasty of the Mauryas, stood in the city of Pataliputra, surrounded by city folk and country folk, by his ministers and his army and his councilors, with the Ganges flowing by, filled up by freshets, level with the banks, full to the brim, five hundred leagues in length, a league in breadth. Beholding the river, he said to his ministers, 'Is there anyone who can make this mighty Ganges flow back upstream?' To which the ministers replied, 'That is a hard matter, your Majesty.'

"Now there stood on that very river bank an old courtesan named Bindumati, and when she heard the king's question she said, 'As for me, I am a courtesan in the city of Pataliputra. I live by my beauty; my means of subsistence is the lowest. Let the King but behold my Act of Truth.' And she performed an Act of Truth. The instant she performed her Act of Truth that mighty Ganges flowed back upstream with a roar, in the sight of all that mighty throng.

"When the king heard the roar caused by the movement of the whirlpools and the waves of the mighty

Ganges, he was astonished, 'How comes it that this mighty Ganges is flowing back upstream?' 'Your Majesty, the courtesan Bindumati heard your words, and performed an Act of Truth. It is because of her Act of Truth that the mighty Ganges is flowing backwards.'

"His heart palpitating with excitement, the king himself went posthaste and asked the courtesan, 'Is it true, as they say, that you, by an Act of Truth, have made this river Ganges flow back upstream?' 'Yes, your Majesty.' — Said the king, 'You have power to do such a thing as this! Who, indeed, unless he were stark mad, would pay any attention to what you say? By what power have you caused this mighty Ganges to flow back upstream?' Said the courtesan, 'By the Power of Truth, your Majesty, have I caused this mighty Ganges to flow back upstream.'

"Said the king, 'You possess the Power of Truth! You, a thief, a cheat, corrupt, cleft in twain, vicious, a wicked old sinner who have broken the bounds of morality and live on the plunder of fools! 'It is true, your Majesty; I am what you say. But even I, wicked woman that I am, possess an Act of Truth by means of which, should I so desire, I could turn the world of men and the world of gods upside down.' Said the king, 'But what is this Act of Truth? Pray enlighten me.'

" 'Your Majesty, whosoever gives me money, be he a Kshatriya or a Brahman or a Vaisya or a Sudra or of any other caste soever, I treat them all exactly alike. If he be a Kshatriya, I make no distinction in his favor. If he be a Sudra, I despise him not. Free alike from fawning and contempt, I serve the owner of the money. This, your Majesty, is the Act of Truth by which I caused the mighty Ganges to flow back upstream.' "

This story, translated from an old Hindu text, presents in an extreme form, a very significant idea. The concept of total absorption in the specific function of a caste belongs to the past, but if we translate this ideal in terms of our modern individualism we can see what the "Act of Truth" can mean today in relation to the behavior of an individual person. The Act of Truth is the perfectly authentic action. Astrologically speaking, it is the act in and through which the total character and implications of a birth-chart are expressed, at the time when such an expression is attuned to the prevailing progressions and transits. This act carries the "Signature" of the whole-person. It is a "moral" act in terms of the new morality, whether or not it conforms to custom or a collective concept of ethics.

I spoke of morality, and now I mention the word, ethics. One may consider the two words identical in meaning, or one may restrict their use to specific levels of meaning. Perhaps arbitrarily I am using here the words, ethics and ethical, with reference to the traditional approach of a particular society or culture; the *ethos* of a culture identifies the basic character of its collective mentality and behavior or "way of life." On the other hand, I mean by morality the working out of *ideals* of conduct in the life of individual persons, and also the exteriorization of an ideal way of reacting and responding to the many types of everyday encounters and challenges.

The "new morality" actually has its roots in the ideals of Christianity, Mahayana Buddhism, and in its purest form Islam, for these religions are, in principle at least, "universal" religions.

They are universal in that they do not proclaim ethics that are the products of particular cultures and of collective ways of life. They bring the individual person directly in relation to what in him is essentially and universally "human." In actual fact, of course, these religions have not been true to their ideals; they have become "culturalized" and particularized. Ethics of race, nation, social class have been developed, and religious organizations have introduced intermediaries between the spiritual ideal and the concrete social facts. This is especially true of Christianity with its warring Churches, its priests, its sacraments, and its involvement in political and cultural-educational matters.

The Christian attitude toward sex and marriage, toward Church dignitaries or the Bible, toward a variety of "sins," and toward such procedural matters as the celibacy of priests, birth-control, etc., refers to the realm of collective ethics, but not to that of morality, as I defined this term. Ethical concepts and rules can be enforced by religious or social sanctions. Morality refers to the individual's capacity to live up to the ideal he has of his relationship to human nature and human possibilities of conscious spiritual development and, one may say also, to a God Who is truly universal and Who therefore cannot possibly take sides in human conflicts.

This discussion has a great deal of relevance to the defining of the meaning of a birth-chart in humanistic astrology, because, as I have stated repeatedly, a birth-chart is the whole universe focused at a particular point in time and space. It symbolizes therefore the *direct* relationship of a particular person to the most universal values he may be able to conceive and to exteriorize in acts. It defines the individual's relationship *not* to a particular society, culture or tradition but to God. It is God's idea of him and of what he *can* achieve as an individual. In the celestial code of astrological symbolism it gives to this individual a set of instructions. It symbolizes at the level of individual existence the meeting of Moses and God on Mt. Sinai in which God gave to Moses His laws — laws not for the collectivity of a people, but for an individual person.

As the individual lives *consciously and deliberately* in terms of this set of instructions, as he "performs yoga" with the celestial Message, his life becomes a constant "Act of Truth" — an authentic life, a self-actualizing life.

FORM IN ASTROLOGICAL SPACE AND TIME

11

What is Form?

Every important system of philosophy, metaphysics and esthetics has given to the word "form" its own definition; and of late the concept of form, structure or pattern has acquired a central importance in science, particularly among scientists who are discussing the basic philosophical meaning of the new ideas which have been the products of the great scientific revolution begun by Planck's Quantum Theory and Einstein's Theory of Relativity. In the preceding essays I have quoted from books of Lancelot L. Whyte (*Accent on Form*) and Donald H. Andrews (*The Symphony of Life*); and there are many other prominent scientist-philosophers who are now thinking along "holistic" rather than "atomistic" lines, and for whom the factor of form is perhaps the most important key to an understanding of the universe, of life and of man.

The traditional approach to astrology has been mainly in terms of "atomistic" concepts;

that is to say, astrologers have been dealing with planets considered as isolated factors, each with a definite character — and the same is true of zodiacal signs and houses. Relationships are established between planets and signs, and between planets and planets (i.e., "aspects"); but these are relationships between entities which are essentially considered as separate and independent factors. The character of each entity is affected by its relationship with another entity, but it always remains what it is. When "progressions" and "transits" are studied, what is considered is the motion of each separate planet and the individual contacts which this planet makes with another planet, or with each separate angle of the chart. Every astrological entity is like a particle in the current view on the construction of an atom. Each planet stands by itself as a cosmic particle in the vast "atom" constituted by the solar system. For most astrologers each planet is an individual center from which radiates a definite type of energy which affects individual human beings in various ways according to the particular components of their birth-charts.

The holistic, or humanistic, type of astrology which I have been promoting approaches the universe, man, and the relationship between both in a basically different manner. It leaves behind much of traditional and "classical" astrology just as modern physics leaves behind the picture of the world derived from mechanistic, force-against-force concepts and Newtonian ideas. It sees the universe as a continuum of operative energies, space as a plenum rather than as an empty container within which isolated material bodies move about, and the solar system as an "organism" (in the broadest sense of the term) in which moving planets are simply focal points for the operation of "systemic" forces and functions represented or defined by their respective orbits.

Humanistic astrology also considers man as an organic whole having its individual cycle of conscious existence, from birth to death — a whole in which every part is related to and affects every other part. It also attempts to view a human being, not as an isolated individual, but as a component part of larger wholes — that is, of a family, a socio-cultural whole, mankind, and the planet Earth. All these larger wholes provide the individual person with his *total environment;* and we do not limit this environment merely to its physical appearance, for it includes as well at least psychic and mental levels of activity. An individual person can never be fully understood if not related to his total environment.

In studying any manifestation of life, or any cosmic system of organization, the essential factor is "form." By form, I mean here simply the particular arrangement of the parts which in their togetherness constitute an operative whole. Instead of the word, form, we can use almost interchangeably, structure, or pattern. "Pattern" is usually more closely associated with a two or three-dimensional visual arrangement of points, lines, and areas; so we can speak of the pattern constituted by the angular relationships of the planets within the two-dimensional circle of the commonly used astrological chart — i.e., the "planetary pattern" of the chart. The term "form" has so many meanings at so many levels that it is often better to speak of "structure," in the abstract sense of the word. The structure of a thing is the way whatever it is made of is put together. It refers also to the manner in which all the component parts of the whole interact — that is, to the *functional organization* of the whole.

Form and structure refer not only to spatial arrangement, but also to dynamic processes in time: Musicians speak of the "Sonata form" or the "Fugue." These are forms in terms of a definitely structured sequence of musical events; for instance, the development of a theme, the successive "entries" in a fugue. Rhythm is form in time. In classical music a typical theme or melody was divided into a certain number of bars. In the Sonata form we hear first theme A, then theme B, in a related tonality; usually a development follows; theme B may reappear in the tonality of theme A, after which A is sounded again, and the whole movement usually ends in some sort of conclusion.

In music and as well in the universe and in all living organisms, we witness the principle of form guiding the sequential development of functional activities. The whole universe is like a symphony. Energy is released at every moment and at many levels of activity; but it is released according to law — i.e., according to a principle of order. A structuring or formative power is constantly at work *everywhere and at all times*. Humanistic astrology represents an organized attempt to understand and interpret at various levels the workings of this structuring power.

All astrologies and all sciences, as well as all philosophies worthy of the name, constitute such an attempt; but the *methods* used vary greatly. The atomistic approach concerns itself with the detailed analysis of outer events and symptoms — for which it compensates by the ambiguous because selective technique of statistics; the holistic approach tries to deal directly with form, that is, with the progressive unfoldment and disintegration of the structural interaction of the functional components of any organized whole which has a beginning and an end, and which passes through recognizable phases of growth, maturity and decay. The "holist" studies the dynamic transformation of an original set of potential relationships (in biology, the genes — in religious metaphysics, the creative Word — in astrology, the birth-chart). He deals *directly* with the innate original structure as a whole, and watches it being transformed moment after moment *also as a whole*. On the other hand, the atomist focuses his attention upon the precise behavior of the separate particles which he has analyzed more or less artificially (i.e., through standardized laboratory procedures) when these particles are subjected to equally standardized types of events.

Both approaches are, I believe, necessary; but

it is most unfortunate that for several centuries our Western society and its intellectuals have almost one-pointedly adopted the analytical, event-oriented, behavioristic and statistical way of thinking. It has led to spectacular "success" in terms of outer material achievements, but also to waste, destruction and perversion of human as well as natural resources and values. A fundamental reversal in the orientation of our society and of its collective official thinking is indeed necessary if our civilization is to avoid reaching the point of no return. If we have already reached it, then we should lay the seed-foundation for a new society and a transformed humanity astrologically associated with the Aquarian Age, the beginning of which is still in the future — I believe a century ahead.*

I do believe that mankind as a whole, and particularly our Western world — which includes European Russia — are at a time of fundamental decision: We must either accept an outlook on existence and a concept of social organization which is in many ways the opposite of the one implicitly accepted as valid by the "silent majority," or we will follow the quantitative and mechanistic trend of our modern technology — which controls our social, cultural and political systems of organization — to its inevitable end: Technocracy and Fascism on a very large scale. This second road can only lead, I believe, to the very same tradegy as befell the old Roman Empire.

---

*Birth Patterns for a New Humanity — D. Rudhyar, 1969.

The same situation exists in the field of astrology, and of course in many other specialized areas of study. Astrology is now highly "successful" in terms of its "Gross National Product" and its popular appeal — just as our Western society is. It could easily become set along quantitative, "atomistic," statistical events-oriented lines, especially if it is academically and legally regulated and licensed. It could then be used for purposes of a dehumanizing character, somewhat as biology and genetics may be used. *Fortunately* it does not seem possible that it should ever become an "exact" and quantitative science, *unless* the image of man is mechanized in such a manner that man may be thought of as merely an assemblage of interchangeable parts.

Man is a living, thinking, potentially self-determined whole. For Aristotle the wholeness of the man was his "soul" — and as well his (archetypal) "form." Humanistic, holistic astrology deals with this wholeness, which it certainly need not call "soul" — a very confusing term. It deals with the "form" of the individual person — provided that we do not mean by form merely the shape and outer appearance of the physical body. It deals with this form — I repeat what I stated in preceding essays — from an esthetical, not an ethical (good-bad) point of view. In that sense, astrology is art, rather than science; and moreover art with a purpose — not art for art's sake, but art for the sake of stimulating the actualization of still latent potentialities in a race, a culture or an individual person.

When science will learn to deal directly with form and is able to study, not analytically but holistically, the workings of the "formative Principle" within all existential wholes — be they microcosm or macrocosm — science too will take on something of the character of Art, in the broadest sense of the word. And may I quote again these words of Lancelot L. Whyte:

> "Physics seeks to penetrate the music of the atomic spheres, biology the harmony of the organism, and neuropsychology the melody of thought, and, though they do not yet know it, these three sciences may be seeking to discover the same universal principle of elegance. The principle must be simple and must define the character of change in complex systems. . . . It must surely express a natural tendency toward simplicity pervading all realms, . . . a formative tendency, or tendency toward simplicity of form, order and regularity." Accent on Form — p. 66-67.

Astrology's supreme contribution to human thinking and human search for order and simplicity is its ability to reduce all fuctional activities (physiological, vital-emotional, mental, behaviorial) to a few essential categories, each of which is symbolized by a planet. The picturing of an individual human being in a circular birthchart, including the cruciform lines of horizon and meridian and ten "planets" and related factors, is a triumph of simplicity and synthesis. It is a highly potent hieroglyph, a "magical formula," a *mandala*. Every potentiality or vital, emotional, mental, socio-cultural and metamorphic development is there, condensed and reduced to its essential outline and potency. But what is essential is the *organization* of these potentialities; it is their inter-relatedness, their interaction and interdependence. It is the "form" of the whole.

This form *is*; yet it also *becomes*. If one links all the planets of a birth-chart by intercrossing lines one obtains a geometrical pattern on the background of the twelve-fold sectioning of the circle. In a sense it is the "star" of the person's individuality — the original Word (or *logos*) of the individual, his "celestial Name." It is what the universe revealed of its creative intent at the moment when a set of universal potentialities became *focused* into the first inhalation of the newborn — his first opening to the Presence and Power of the universal Whole. What this first moment of individualized existence in an open environment conveyed is imprinted in the emerging *person* (which is more than a physiological organism with a specific parental heredity). It is indeed a "revelation." It is (to use a Medieval alchemical term popularized by Paracelsus), the "Signature" of the individual person.

This Signature is a *form*, a definite structure of potential development; but the *contents* which will fill this self-actualizing structure are only suggested by the birth-chart. They are absorbed by the structure from its psychic as well as social-cultural planetary and cosmic environment. Every child is born within an "ocean" of psychic and mental forces or human tendencies and memories, just as he is born within the biosphere and within a race and nation. The growing child and adolescent should "metabolize" and assimilate what this environment brings to him; but, alas, the environment nearly always *forces* psycho-mental and socio-cultural foodstuff into his unfolding psyche and mind. As a result the self-actualizing process turns negative. A state of tension, of unconscious conformism or impulsive rebellion arises which makes the harmonious development of the whole person very difficult if not impossible.

Yet the process of "becoming" — that is, the gradual transformation of the original "star of individuality" — goes on. The universe follows its cosmic rhythm; the planets move in their orbits regardless of what takes place in the biosphere and the collective Mind of planetary Man. The astrologer then speaks of transits and progressions or directions. All these astrological techniques refer to the constant transformations of the original Word; the "Word that was in the beginning" becomes a discourse — the pattern formed by the relationship between the natal planets changes its shape constantly, according to the syntax of the celestial language. Potentiality becomes actuality; but what is actualized are not "events," but rather "phases of growth," or we might say specific *turning points* in the individual's development.

The process of organic-personal unfoldment has a definite rhythm, but it is an unceasing process of change. What the astrologer notices and comments upon are the accented "beats" in the melody of change *not the change itself*.

What is Form?

Events occur at these beat-points, because the continuum of change then reaches "critical states." We call these critical states "aspects," and give them names and specific characteristics.

These aspects, however, reveal their meaning *in terms of the self-actualization process of individual unfoldment* ONLY if they are interpreted as "phases" of the several cyclic processes which refer to the organic functions symbolized by the ten planets (Sun and Moon always included). In order to understand what such cyclic phases really signify we have to consider first of all how the principle of formation of aspects operates. It is probable that the concept of aspects was the result of the observation of change in the Moon's appearance during a soli-lunar month, i.e., from New Moon to New Moon. But sooner or later the empirical evidence was generalized and abstractized, and the theory of aspects was developed by geometrically inclined minds. Actually, as we shall see, the theory is two-fold; and in order to understand this two-foldness we have to think of "form," not only in spatial terms, but primarily in terms of process in time, i.e., of cyclic "involution" and "evolution."

12

The Basic Structure of Cyclic Processes

In the Bhagavad Gita, Krishna, as embodiment of the creative God, states: "I am the beginning, the middle and end of all cycles." Many modern interpreters, Hindu as well as Western have taken pains to explain that the word "middle" referred to all that happens during the course of the cyclic process. This may be a "rational" interpretation, but like so many of the comments made in our day about ancient Scriptures, it is also superficial; indeed it altogether misses the point. Any cycle contains three fundamentally significant and "creative" moments: beginning, middle, and end.

The life of a human being is no exception. And one may add that when one deals with the unfoldment of a single creative Impulse (or *logos* at the universal level) there is also a fourth phase which occurs in a realm of "non-manifestation." The basic example is the cycle which we call an entire day. This cycle is defined astronomically by the rotation of the Earth-globe. In terms of *actual* human experience it is characterized by the rise, culmination at noon, and setting of the Sun; however it includes also a fourth cardinal moment, midnight. Depth in non-manifestation (the unconscious of modern psychology) polarizes culmination at the apex of manifestation, i.e., noon — just as sunset polarizes sunrise.

When Krishna says that he is the beginning, middle and end of cycles, he refers to cycles of manifestation, i.e., existential cycles. But Krishna also speaks of his non-manifested aspect — his "night" aspect. Man also has his night-aspect. In a daily sense it refers to deep dreamless sleep; in a more fundamental and spiritual sense, man's "midnight" occurs during his period of non-manifestation — i.e., between two "incarnations."

In astrology the cycles of the year and the cycles of the day are divided into four periods. We have two equinoxes and two solstices, and the four angles of a chart. But these cycles in traditional geocentric astrology refer to the cyclic motions of *one* factor, that is, to the *apparent* motion of the Sun in the sky. The terms "end and beginning" actually apply only to the manifested first half of the cycle. "Noon," or "summer solstice" constitutes the apex of only this first hemicycle.

The situation is different when we deal with the lunation cycle, from New Moon to New Moon. It is different because the lunation cycle is not a "lunar" cycle; but instead a "soli-lunar" cycle. What the cyclic process refers to is the *relationship* between the Moon and the Sun — a relationship whose character is constantly altered, because of the fact that the two "Lights" move at different speeds. The lunation cycle is a cycle of relationship. It can be considered as the "archetype" of all cycles involving the relationship between two celestial factors moving at different speeds — *all* celestial bodies move at different speeds. When, therefore, we speak of an aspect between two planets we are referring to one particular phase in their cyclic relationship.

In these cycles of interplanetary relationship the moment of culmination occurs at the midpoint of the *whole cycle*; thus, in the lunation cycle, at Full Moon. The entire cycle is divided also in two hemicycles, but *both* hemicycles refer to manifested existential activity — yet the type of activity in the first or "waxing" hemicycle is essentially different from the type in evidence during the "waning" hemicycle; or, more accurately, in each hemicycle the relationship between the two moving factors operates in a characteristically different manner.

This is true whenever the cycle of relationship between any two planets is the subject of astrological study, but the soli-lunar cycle is by far the most important and most easily interpretable of all such cycles of relationship because the changes in the relationship are made evident by the shape of the Moon in the sky. But let us not forget that what changes is NOT the Moon, but the *relationship* between the Moon and the Sun. This relationship, however, is made clearly visible by the change in the form of the lunar source of the light — a light emanating from the Sun and reflected by the Moon's surface, *as seen by an Earth observer*.

These italicized words are most important; for

any cycle of relationship between two moving celestial bodies exists only in reference to the Earth. The Earth is the third factor in the relationship. *Any* significant relationship implies, or should imply, a third factor as we shall presently see when discussing the trine aspect.

When an astrologer speaks of an opposition aspect between Jupiter and Saturn, he refers to a particular *phase* in the cycle of relationship which began when these two planets were in conjunction. An opposition is the culmination of a process which began some ten years before, as Jupiter and Saturn are conjunct every twenty years. If we use the lunation cycle as an archetypal pattern of significance, we can analogically speak of the period lasting from the Jupiter-Saturn conjunction to the opposition (in our present period from February 1961 to the years 1970-71; the opposition occurs three times) as the "waxing" hemicycle of the Jupiter-Saturn cycle. The "waning" hemicycle lasts from the time of opposition to that of the next conjunction (three times repeated during 1981, in early Libra).

Every aspect between the two planets should be considered as "phases" of the entire cyclic process. This means that no aspect can be fully understood except in relation to the character and purpose of the whole process. As astrology is indeed — as Marc E. Jones wrote long ago — "the science of all beginnings," it follows that the *seed meaning* of the entire Jupiter-Saturn cycle resides *in latency* in the conjunction which starts the cycle. At the conjunction *a new set of potentialities* is released with reference to the Jupiter-Saturn relationship. What is pure potentiality, but also intense dynamism, at the time of the conjunction should theoretically reach a state of *culmination in objective manifestation* at the time of the opposition. However, the process started at the conjunction may fail to take hold of the situation to which it refers; in other words, it may fail to overcome the inertial momentum of the past; it may be defeated in one way or another. If so, then the opposition aspect signifies the full evidence of failure, and, in the broadest sense of the term, divorce.

In our present instance February 1961 marked the beginning of the Kennedy Administration, and of a great wave of dynamic hope which swept over much of the world. We all know what subsequently happened. Immediately after Jupiter had moved sufficiently ahead of Saturn to reach a phase of septile relationship (51½ degrees — an aspect of "fate in action" or collective *Karma)* the President was assassinated in circumstances never satisfactorily elucidated, but which may have some relationship to the abortive attempt to invade Cuba in 1961. Just after the two planets formed a semi-square in July 1963, John Kennedy lost his newborn son, and our involvement in Vietman had at least potentially begun.

The two planets formed a particularly drastic square in July 1965; this is to be considered a "waxing" square. On the other hand the square between the opposition and the next conjunction — which in the lunation cycle means the "last quarter of the Moon" — is a "waning" square. Practically all astrologers consider these two types of squares identical in meaning. They do so because they simply do not realize that aspects have significance only in terms of the structure of a whole cycle of relationship. It is quite as senseless to believe that a waxing and a waning square have the same significance as it would be to say that the solstice of summer and the solstice of winter have an identical meaning in the seasonal cycle of the year beginning at the spring equinox. Even if we consider the shapes of the Moon at the first and at the last quarters we see that they are oriented in opposite directions; so are the Moon-crescent *after* New Moon, and the Moon-crescent (or de-crescent) *before* New Moon. Youth has not the same character as old age, even if one sometimes speaks of "second infancy." Likewise the two critical turning points in any cyclic process represented by the two square aspects cannot possibly have the same meaning. They operate in a somewhat similar manner, but at different levels. They mark *two opposite stages* in the relationship between the two celestial bodies being considered.

The reason why this is usually not recognized by astrologers is because their approach is not "holistic." They speak glibly of cycles, but actually do not think of cycles as *wholes in time,* i.e., as processes having a beginning, a middle and an end. They do not understand the structure of cycles, because they are hypnotized by geometrical and spatial concepts, and the idea that aspects represent angular divisions of a circle — division by two (opposition), by three (trines), by four (squares), etc. Such a process of geometrical sectioning of circular space assuredly is valid and significant, but it is not the only way astrological aspects are formed. There is form-in-time as well as form-in-space. The time factor dominates the first (waxing) hemicycle of a cycle; the space factor is mainly effective in terms of values related to the second (waning) hemicycle.

The reason why it is so should be very obvious, philosophically as well as biologically and psychologically. Every cycle of relationship begins in an act of mobilization of power — the power generated by the union of two factors. Something relatively new has been released, and this release means dynamic, concretely focused activity. It means the working out of an impulse to existence and the unfoldment of some sort of structural idea or archetypal form *seeking exteriorization through the impulse.* The creative Word-in-the-beginning is both energy and form; likewise any human word implies a sound-vibration (which is a release of vocal energy) and some kind of meaning, or feeling; and meaning and feeling refers to a particular kind of relationship between existing entities.

The first half of the cycle (for instance, from New Moon to Full Moon) is therefore essentially a period of building-activity. The new idea or feeling seeks to exteriorize itself in concrete and formed activity. In order to do so, as it is not alone in the world, it meets obstacles and other

The Basic Structure of Cyclic Processes

impulses-ideas-feelings which also seek full actualization. The future has to struggle against the inertia of the past. The *waxing* aspects during this first hemicycle refer thus basically to impetuous and spontaneous activity, to struggle, overcoming, building, and either to success or failure in the process of actualizing what was inherent and only potential in the original first moment of the cycle. I have described in detail the meaning of these aspects in my book *"THE LUNATION CYCLE — A Key to the Understanding of Personality,"* and we shall see presently the manner in which the sequence of such aspects unfolds.

When the opposition aspect is reached, as already stated, two possibilities are encountered: either fulfillment in a concrete form which successfully actualizes what was potential in the original release immediately following the conjunction — or a definite realization of failure, and the estrangement of the two factors — united at the time of this conjunction. Estrangement can mean physical separation, divorce, or a gradual withering of the relationship which remains only as an increasingly empty shell.

If the first half of the cycle has been successful — and to the extent it is actually a fulfillment of what was potential at, let us say, New Moon time — a new process starts in the Full Moon experience. It does not start suddenly in most cases, for it has been prepared during the phase of the soli-lunar cycle referred to as "gibbous Moon." Yet in many instances something definite happens; in a sense, it always happens, but the individual person may not quite realize the meaning of the occurrence. There is a "descent" of a spiritual factor which induces a transformation of the mind. Until the opposition aspect *mind* is subservient to *life*. At the opposition mind can, and should be born *as the power of objectively realized consciousness.* This is why Krishna said in the Bhagavad Gita that he is not only the beginning and end, but the middle of all cycles. *At the mid-point of a cycle consciousness is focused in a fully manifested and incorporated sense;* and this is also why the study of "midpoints" is so important in the interpretation of a birth-chart, for they focus the concrete operation of the spatial relationship between two planets — and also the relationship between the two axes of the chart, horizon and meridian.

What happens after the opposition — if it has meant success — is that a new process of consciousness unfoldment begins. Whereas during the first hemicycle activity was primarily (but not exclusively) biologically and physically spontaneous and seeking personal, limited self-expression, during the second hemicycle a *mental* type of activity pervades, or superimposes itself upon the physical-biological functions and seeks to dominate, guide or control them.

It is evident that such a characterization of the two halves of cycles must be taken in a most general and abstract sense if the principles it implies are to be applied to diverse cycles and various levels of existence. Yet if one can get a clear and basic idea of the principles involved, these can

The Basic Structure of Cyclic Processes **141**

be successfully applied to all cycles. But we should not forget that they are *structural principles;* they do not deal with *particular events*. They refer to the development of form in time. We will now see how this structural unfoldment of cyclic processes operates in greater detail.

13

The Aspects Formed During the Hemicycle of Spontaneous and Instinctual Action

It is very difficult actually to know *how* archaic man — say before 1000 B.C. — thought about many things. The few records we have of such ancient cultures can easily be wrongly interpreted by projecting our own intellectual thinking upon them and seeing the statements recorded on stone or clay in a rationalistic light. Why, for instance, do we divide a circle into 360 degrees? There are presumably scholarly answers to such a question. They may or may not be "authoritative." One important aspect of the problem rests, I believe, on the relationship between space-measures and time-measures; why, for instance, while there are 365 days in the year, do we speak of 360 degrees in a circle — the circle having been considered by all ancient people as the "perfect form," that is, the form of the ideal whole?

In this chapter we are dealing with time-values. Time is almost certainly the primordial frame of reference for the development of consciousness;

simply because the primary fact of consciousness is the alternation of waking consciousness and sleep, of days and nights. This alternation, then the cyclic succession of the seasons in temperate climates, must have been the foundation for the realization of "rhythm" in nature; and primitive man — hardly emerged from the womb of nature and with his nascent consciousness dominated by bio-psychic instincts — identified itself with these natural rhythms.

The soli-lunar month, from New Moon to New Moon — or probably from the first appearance of the Moon's crescent in the West after sunset to the next time this occurred — must also have been recognized as being most important, related as it is with the female rhythm of menstruation. As there are approximately 30 days within a lunation cycle and 12 lunation cycles within a year, this may well have been the first reason why man thought of dividing the year into twelve months of 30 days each. It is because the year includes actually 365 days that the difficult problem of making an accurate calendar had to be solved; and various solutions, none really perfect, have been advanced.

The point which I wish to make here is that the numbers 30 and 12 were obvious ones to choose in order to orient one's conscious activities in terms of a whole seasonal cycle. And it seems evident that the *solar* year was sooner or later recognized as the fundamental whole of time, at least as soon as man became cultivator of the land, and agricultural societies were born. Nevertheless, the *lunar* (or soli-lunar) month may have been the dominant time-measure earlier, especially among matriarchal, cattle-raising and nomadic tribes; and there are records, particularly in India, of a long struggle between Lunar and Solar Dynasties. There must have been an even more general struggle attending the change from matriarchy to patriarchy.

The type of astrology which we have inherited from Chaldea, Greece and Alexandria is evidently the product of a patriarchal system of organization. It is basically solar; yet it is also soli-lunar because it speaks of the Sun and the Moon as "the two Lights," and these Lights are related to the day and the night periods. Our astrological tradition is therefore based on the fact that, within the great time-whole determined by the solar year, there are approximately twelve soli-lunar periods of about 30 days each. From this the concept of a twelve-fold zodiac and of zodiacal degrees is derived.

In other words the perfect whole of the year contains twelve successive "steps," each constituted by 30 days. Each step is then seen related to the beginning of the cycle; *it forms an aspect to it*. As each step covers 30 degrees, the primary aspect is the 30-degree aspect, which we now call semi-sextile, for reasons soon to be elucidated.

We have thus a series of aspects, or rather of "steps," which encompass 30, 60, 90, 120, 150, and 180 degrees. I have called this series an "involutionary" series because it refers to the progressive involvement, or rather incorporation,

The Aspects Formed During the Hemicycle.....

of an ideal form into concrete materials. Each "step" represents a further stage of differentiation and complexification of the energy released at the beginning of the cycle — a deeper advance of the creative will and idea into matter. This series of aspects or steps constitutes an "arithmetical progression" — i.e., a progression resulting from the addition to itself of a single number; for instance, 1, 2, 3, 4, 5, etc. is an arithmetical progression, while 2, 2x2, 2x2x2, 2x2x2x2 constitutes a "geometrical progression."

Astrology and music were closely related in ancient cultures, especially perhaps in China, and later on in the doctrines of Pythagoras which owed probably a great deal to the more ancient Orphic Mysteries. The first instruments which man used were presumably the taut string of a bow, the flute (originally a tube of bamboo) and resonant material (wood, stone, stretched skins) for rhythmic percussive effects. When one uses a taut string or a pipe (the "pipes of Pan" are a good example), it is evident that, if one increases the length of the string or of the air column within the tube, one obtains a progressively lower sound.

Now, a most important fact — to which musicologists strangely enough give so little importance, if they mention it at all — is that what we call today musical scales were long ago considered to be *descending series* of tones. For many centuries now man has been thinking of scales as starting with the low note (tonic) and rising to the octave-sound above; but it is very clear that in archaic times the general feeling was that a chant would normally begin with a high tone — a shout most likely; then the voice would fall to lower tones. We could still see this operating in the tradition of the Basques (on both sides of the Western end of the Pyrenees mountains between France and Spain), a very mysterious people of unknown but very ancient origins.

Music in these archaic times seems to have expressed the "descent" of spirit into matter, the progressive conquest and involvement of man into the physical realities of the earth. Since the sixth century B.C. and the days of Pythagoras and Buddha — which marked an epochal turning point in human evolution — an inverse sense of direction slowly developed after a period of confusion and uncertainty. It became definite some five centuries later, at the time which I consider to be the starting point of a Great Year (precessional cycle) of some 25,868 solar years — thus the beginning of what we call today the Piscean Age.* Since then, and particularly since the late Medieval period and the development of *Ars Nova* (the "new music" of the thirteenth century and the beginning of counterpoint) the natural "slope" of music has been most definitely upward, from bass to treble.

With Pythagoras, geometry became a most important object of study, and was used as a *symbolical key* to the understanding of universal processes. Space, more than time, occupied the attention of the leading thinkers. Man being

---
* cf. Birth-Patterns for a New Humanity.

The Aspects Formed During the Hemicycle 147

now completely "incarnated" in the substance of the Earth began increasingly to want *to master* space and his environment. On the contrary, archaic man sought rather *to adapt* himself to the rhythms of time and of the unfoldment of life-processes; thus the dependence of music upon time-factors is evident all through Asia, especially in India where each time of the day and the year had its own melody or "mode" (*raga*) which could only be sung or played at that time. Adaptation to the rhythm of nature and of the seasons means following, as it were, step by step the unfoldment in time of natural processes — the growth of plants, for instance. Growth means increase in size. The bamboo tubes grow longer and bigger, and the sounds they generate become deeper and deeper.

Likewise during the first half of a cycle — any cycle — gradual expansion is experienced. Astrologically speaking the aspects increase in size, and we have the involutionary series of aspects from the conjunction of the opposition; that is what we call today (from the opposite Pythagorean and geometrical point of view) semi-sextile, sextile, square, trine, quincunx. With the conjunction and the opposition we have thus *seven* aspects — a very significant number in all occult traditions. We can also say that six steps are taken: that is, from 0 to 30, from 30 to 60, from 60 to 90, from 90 to 120, from 120 to 150, from 150 to 180. The crucial steps are the third and fourth steps, especially the third.

If we think of the life-span of a human being,

the length of which was said to be 70 years (3 score and 10), but which, in the case of a fully individualized human being is rather 84 years (the cycle of Uranus: twelve times seven) we reach interesting and psychologically very significant conclusions. The first half of the human life lasts 42 years, or six 7-year periods; and the third of these occurs between the ages of 14 and 21. At twenty-one man is theoretically and legally "coming of age": this is the "square aspect" of the involutionary series. The period 21 to 28 leads to the trine aspect; and it is around 28 (from 27 to 30) that an individual can experience what I have called (in my book *New Mansions for New Men,* soon to be reprinted) the "second birth," or birth in individuality. During the period 21 to 28 a young person should gradually build his own approach to life and society together with his or her chosen companions, and as the result of such a process should reach a conscious realization of his own identity and his work of destiny.

The first half of a human life ends at 42; and it normally is a period of waxing vitality and strength of purpose. As the second half begins the "dangerous forties" are reached — the symbolical Full Moon. Then the vital processes begin to be reversed. The opportunity to "change gears" presents itself. The "change of life," psychological as well as physiological, is soon to occur. The physical body and its energies may begin to "wane," but a new beginning may occur at a mental-social level. And as the once famous book stated, it is possible that "Life begins at 40." But it should be a new kind of life; realization of the meaning, value and purpose of existence; life in a new dimension of consciousness; a truly mature life based on individual experience and the development of the mental faculties through the play of interpersonal and social relationships.

If we examine the involutionary series of aspects — i.e., of steps in the unfoldment of vital and personal energies, and of will and purpose — we see that three aspects stand out: the sextile, the square and the trine. Each one has a definite character, and the sextile cannot be considered at all as a "weaker trine" — as is often stated in astrological textbooks. In a human life the sextile aspect corresponds to puberty (around 14). When two planets form a *waxing* sextile something happens to their *relationship* which brings out its potentially creative significance, but also which — at least in terms of progressions and transits — can be the cause for a subsequent crisis in reorientation. This crisis is implied in the square aspect. It should become resolved into constructive harmony and productivity in the trine aspect.

The 30 degree aspect is, in a sense, a preparation for the sextile, and the 150 degree aspect for the opposition. The conjuction is a release of energy, but everything toward which this release is directed exists only in a state of *potentiality*. This means pure subjectivity, and, often in terms of external circumstances, some confusion. It is for this reason that I cannot accept systems of symbolization of each degree of the zodiac in which the symbol for the first degree of Aries describes some very positive and forceful male figure. Neither do I believe in the cosmological "Big Bang" theory as an explanation of the beginning of the universe. *Nothing* begins in a spectacular show of power — at least as far as human experience goes. This must be so because nothing begins in empty space. The past — or at least the "ghosts" (the unfinished business) of the past — always surround the new beginning. The first phase of a process therefore consists in the effort to overcome the pressure of the past, and in doing so gradually to discover the limits and the special character of one's being.

In terms of the relationship between two planets, a conjunction represents the initial release of the *possibility* of bringing such a relationship to a new level of value, or of expressing it in a new field of activity. For instance, in most cases every New Moon occurs in a new sign of the zodiac: and this means that every new "fecundation" of the receptive Moon by the active Sun operates according to a new mode of existence, or a new quality of vital response to the ever-altered challenge of life.

If Venus and Mars form a conjunction, some new form of emotional-personal self-expression is starting to operate. Because it is only *starting* to operate, the person born with such a conjunction is usually over-concerned with emotional self-expression; and this may mean an over-focusing of attention upon the problem of "transmuting" emotional energies or giving them a new value.

Quite a few "occultists" were born with such a conjunction, because the development of occult powers normally requires a basic repolarization of the instinctual emotional drives.

A conjunction of Jupiter and Saturn likewise refers to the reorientation of the social and/or religious faculties, i.e., to the potentiality of a transformation of one's relationship to society and traditions. Men and women born at the time of, or just after the three conjunctions of Jupiter and Saturn in 1940-41 have been, during the last few years, at the forefront of the social-religious-ethical revolt of youth — often a rather confused and instinctive revolt lacking a clear consciousness of means as well as purpose. Persons born in 1951-52 when Jupiter and Saturn were in opposition will no doubt take, generally speaking a more objective attitude — or else will emphasize their eagerness to "divorce" the society and the traditions within which they were born.

People born at the time of the Uranus-Neptune conjunction of 1821 became the ardent followers of the Romantic and Revolutionary Movement which made history in the fields of human activity some 23 to 28 years later. The Industrial Revolution began then to affect large numbers of human beings; and when these two planets of reformation, rebirth and transcendence came to their long lasting opposition from 1906 to 1910 the potentiality of a total transformation of mankind became very much clearer and more objective, with the spread of depth-psychology, the Einsteinian and electronic promise of new powers, and also with the break-up of the old feudal-national *status quo* at the level of international and interclass relationships.

The semi-sextile theoretically implies the "descent" of the focal point of the new relationship into the actual physical or personal realm of experience. In a human life, this corresponds to age 7 — the formation of permanent teeth. The child is potentially able to "chew" his experiences as a more individualized center of activity. Rudolf Steiner followed an old religious tradition when stating that what he called the "ego" becomes really embodied at that age — the "age of reason," or of spiritual responsibility in the Roman Catholic sense. This focalization of an actional ego-center leads to the next step: puberty. The focus now is in the field of interpersonal relationship as a result of the exteriorization of the sex-force through specific glandular activity.

The sextile therefore sets the stage upon which the "crucial" (i.e., cross-like) phase of the square aspect will operate. Thus we have this sequence: semi-sextile — *self-focusing;* sextile — *focus in relationship;* square — *the working out* of a relationship between individual selfhood and interpersonal relationship on the basis of a social tradition and a set type of "Establishment" — first at school, then in the whole of society. Then comes the trine which provides the means as well as the opportunities needed to integrate self, relationship and social traditions into *a workable and productive way of life.*

The quincunx (150 degree aspect) brings

means and opportunities to a more specific focus, and prepares the final step of the first hemicycle of activity, the opposition aspect. It theoretically marks the possibility of relating in and through a work the various forms or modes of activity already experienced. This can be achieved also through the challenge of providing one's children or one's employees with a personal example of human maturity, or through "sitting at the feet of a Teacher."

Before I undertake to discuss the geometrical principles of formation of astrological aspects, I should make it clear that the meaning I have attributed to the involutionary series of aspects represent only one of two sets of meanings. They are meanings which refer mainly to the time factor, and which are particular value when one studies transits and progressions, that is, the successive phases of unfoldment of a process begun with the conjunction of two (or more) planets. They are the products of a *dynamic* approach to existence; they refer mainly to self-exteriorizing outward activity — activity focused at the vital-emotional and largely instinctual level. This does not mean that other factors do not enter into the picture of the first-hemicycle-type of development. These other factors *surround* this development, because no cycle begins in a vacuum. Every whole is "born" *within* a larger whole which completely envelops it.

Every child is born in a community with a specific system of social behavior, which is rooted in an ideological, religious and cultural tradition

— a mental and objectively institutionalized tradition. The child's growing mind is stamped and moulded by traditional ideas and feeling-responses, even while he strives to act "on his own," and to "do his own thing." The self-assertive attempts operate at the dynamic level of the involuntary series of astrological aspects, because they are rooted in his natal act of original self-utterance — his first cry. But the development of his *mind* is in most cases far more an expression of the great variety of family, social and educational pressures to which he is subjected.

Thus, two types of forces operate through childhood and the teen-age period, and still later on: the dynamic force of self-exteriorization which operates in "spontaneity" (literally: "of its own"), and the moulding pressures of the collective mentality and the basic way-of-life of the community. It is to the second type of force that the geometrically produced and mentally objectified *evolutionary* aspects refer. And it is these aspects which I shall now consider.

14

The Geometrical Principle of Formation of Aspects

When on April 12, 1962, the first man to orbit the Earth — the Russian astronaut Gagarin — saw our globe from a distance he was able to perceive the planet as a whole. He saw it as a spherical object. He, and through him mankind, had gained an objectively conscious, direct and visual experience of the wholeness of the Earth and, as a result, of mankind as a whole. One can never gain a truly objective awareness of that within which one is still enfolded. One needs to be distant from it, even if only for a moment, in order to gain a true perspective on its existence — and gradually to understand and evaluate it dispassionately in clear consciousness. One can then return to it with a new and realistically concrete image of what it really is.

Consciousness — as we understand the term in the Western world — begins in separation. It may be fulfilled in eventual identification, but *only* at the end of a process made possible by the gaining of a sufficient perspective. The development of consciousness begins with the realizaton of duality. The whole to which a man belonged by birth and which enfolded him like a womb must be sundered. The circle of unconscious prenatal wholeness must be divided into two halves; and this division must be directly perceived, felt, experienced: I and the other, I and the world.

This experience may be long in coming, even if it may be foreshadowed by intellectual realization and temporary emotional feelings of loneliness. Its meaning is never *fully* realized until the instinctual-emotional drives of the physiological and social natures of man have reached either some kind of fulfillment, or have led to a total breakdown of one's relationship with the society and culture which had enwombed the first part of one's life. These two alternatives are characteristic of the astrological aspect which we call an "opposition," and the Full Moon is the archetypal symbol of such an aspect. The opposition aspect at the same time ends a period of growth and starts a new process of objective conscious realization. It is essentially a mental process — indeed a process of rebirth at a new level. The physical organism (or any kind of relationship) may begin then to disintegrate; but *in counterpoint* to this disintegration, consciousness develops and slowly matures at the ideological level.

The beginning of the Sixth Century B.C., particularly in the person of Pythagoras marks "the end of the archaic ages." The Greek civilization brought to this present mankind — there may have been other mankinds very long ago —

The Geometrical Principle of Formation of Aspects

a capacity for objective and rational consciousness. It also developed a worship of the human form as a symbol of the wholeness of Earth-existence. Pythagoras and other Greek philosophers of his time stressed the symbolic and indeed sacred meaning of geometry, inasmuch as geometry is the science of form-in-space. The perfect cosmic form being thought to be the circle, other basic forms were seen to be derived from it. They were derived through a process of division and differentiation.

The fecundated ovum, origin of human existence, likewise divides itself into many cells, through a process of self-multiplication. The whole becomes the parts, which nevertheless in their togetherness remain the same whole in a multitude of differentiated aspects.

This is the process which today is usually considered to be the basis for the generation of astrological aspects; yet such a process does not account for the quincunx (150 degree) aspect, which only belongs to the "involutionary" series of aspects, as we saw in the preceding chapter. Dividing the circle into two accounts for the opposition. Dividing it by three produces the trine — by four, the square — by five, the quintile (72 degrees) — by six, the sextile — by seven, the septile (51 degrees, plus an endless series of decimals) — by eight, the semi-square (45 degrees) — by nine, the novile (40 degrees) — by ten, the semi-quintile.

Actually if we consider the characteristic meaning of this process of dividing a whole circle into equal sections we come to the conclusion that only three operations are basic: dividing by 2, by 3, and by 5.

Dividing by two produces aspects which are considered "unfortunate" or "bad" (the square, the semi-square and the semi-hemisphere, 22½ degrees). Dividing by three produces the "good" aspect *par excellence*, the trine — and if the dividing goes a step further, the novile (40 degrees, the third part of the trine) an aspect which, perhaps unfortunately, is not usually considered important. Dividing by five gives us the quintile aspect which I think is very significant, even if it operates characteristically in a birth-chart only when the human being has reached a degree of positive individualization.

Why should the process of "dividing by two" be considered unfortunate or bad? To understand this we need only refer to myths and concepts which seem deeply rooted in man's consciousness. The "Fall" out of the state of unity and into duality, which implies a sort of "descent" into embodied, concrete existence, has been considered in all religions a tragic event. "Liberation," in the Hindu sense of the term, means becoming free from duality, and a "return" to a condition of unity; and this implies, at the emotional-biological level, freedom from the compulsion of sex and the experiencing of a "unitive state" — a mystical experience of union with all there is, and with God.

Number 2 is the symbol of actual, substantial and polarized existence. Dividing-by-two therefore refers to a process of exteriorization and concretization. Is this process "bad"? It is so only from the point of view of the single entity, or (in Christian terminology) of the Soul that loses its "purity" and in a sense its wholeness when it "falls into matter"; which means, when it becomes involved in relationship.

The OPPOSITION aspect refers to *the conscious facing of existence,* and therefore of relationship; for there is no existence without relationship. Most individuals rush into a variety of relationships without consciously facing them; they are drawn into them by biological and psychological needs and wants, by "Karma," by complexes and illusory dreams. It is only after many things affecting a relationship have occurred that finally the individual *faces up to* it and discovers its real meaning and value. This confrontation in full awareness may result either in fulfillment or in an eventual breaking-up. In other words, the opposition exteriorizes and makes actual a capacity for consciousness which was only latent or unclearly expressed in the participants in an existential relationship. The relationship acts upon its participants; it may transfigure their lives, or separate them. It may produce illumination in consciousness, or frustration and bitterness.

The SQUARE aspect is produced by dividing-by-two the two halves of a whole circle. It refers thus to a further stage of exteriorization and actualization; it carries the process begun by 2 to an even more evident and concrete phase of operation: What this may mean is that, if number 2 (the opposition aspect) represents a confrontation, number 4 (the square aspect), symbolizes a condition of existence in which the results of this confrontation have become either set into a definite form or have led to a clear-cut crisis impelling or compelling action of a definite type.

We can think of an opposition as an international conference in which the diplomats of two nations face each other trying to resolve a basic conflict in policies. If the conference leads to an agreement — caused by a realization of the interdependence of all groups of men — a treaty is signed which sets down, or crystallizes, the good will having been generated, and embodying it into some plan for action. If, on the other hand, the conference breaks up and the conflict of interests or ideologies cannot be resolved, the next move may be mobilization for war.

If we are considering an entire cycle of relationship, from one conjunction to the next, and if we compare the "waxing" square of the first hemicycle to the "waning" square of the second hemicycle, we should realize that while these two square refer to moments of crisis, the meanings of the two types of crises are basically different. The waxing square represents essentially a crisis in spontaneous, self-exteriorizing, impulsive, body-building *action,* while the waning square refers rather to a crisis in the building of a *form of consciousness* which would be the foundation on which a new cycle of activity can start. The waxing square deals with the process of establishing oneself and one's basis for action in the community within which one was born; the waning square refers to the process of giving — as the result of a confrontation is relationship — a more or less permanent form to an experience of meaning.

Let us consider the Jupiter-Saturn cycle which began in 1940-41 as the United States under President Roosevelt was preparing for a nearly inevitable participation in World War II. When the waxing square of these two planets occurred in 1945-46 our nation was triumphant and trying to establish its new leadership in the international community on a definite military and financial-economic basis. This of course polarized a similar attempt by Soviet Russia, and the "cold war" was the result. The *waning* square occurred in 1955-56 and it referred to a far different social and international situation. The McCarthy era was closing. The U.S. Supreme Court had ruled school-segregation unconstitutional and that event — an ideological decision — led to a series of physical actional developments which were to be characteristic of the next Jupiter-Saturn conjunction beginning in 1960. A new type of consciousness was, as it were, triggered into being by a revulsion against McCarthyism and the old failure to assimilate the Negro people as first-class citizens. A comparison between Soviet Russia in 1945-46 under a victorious Stalin, and the same country under Khrushchev's process of de-Stalinization would also be significant — also between the defeated and bitter France and Germany of 1945 and these two countries beginning to cooperate in terms of the idea of European unity.

The SEMI-SQUARE is the result of a further process of dividing-by-two. If there had been "mobilizaton," then comes "action." If one considers an electro-magnetic field it appears that the 45-degree angle refers to points of maximum dynamic intensity. We are dealing here with an eight-fold pattern, and the number 8 has been in many mythological and Gnostic systems related to the Sun. The semi-square should not be considered as a "weaker square"; it exteriorizes within definite limits the dynamic quality of the square. At the waning semi-square of Jupiter and Saturn, Fidel Castro was on his way to establish a new government in Cuba — an event which deeply affected the future Kennedy Administration. The old cycle of social-political and economic developments was breaking up, and revolutionary forces were released in preparation for a new cycle.

The number 3 symbolizes all modes of expression and activity which have polarity as a basis, but in which *polarity is transcended through understanding* and often through some kind of "vision." No conflict can be resolved harmoniously unless a "third factor" is present which, because it can encompass the two poles of the struggle from another "dimension," is able to see the *meaning* and the *value* of the confrontation. This is why when a man and a woman unite in matrimony according to a truly religious ideal they are expected to realize that a third factor is pres-

The Geometrical Principle of Formation of Aspects

ent in their union. In a transcendent sense this invisible "third" is God, or in more mundane sense society or the human race as a whole. It is also the potential child which will in due time bring the *conjugal* relationship to the level of a *family* relationship; and at that level, social and cultural forms are basic. The coming of the child involves the two participants in the conjugal confrontation and interaction in the well-being and the future of their culture and society — and, in some cases, even if there is no child, the third factor may be a social, cultural or spiritual work undertaken in a community of understanding, efforts and goal.

Real consciousness is always *awareness* (the opposition aspect) *plus* understanding and the sense of value; the TRINE is an aspect of growth in understanding. What has been "seen" in the opposition phase, is now understood because it is related to a larger frame of reference. The vision or intuition becomes related to the collective mind and to the values of the culture; it can then be expressed and formulated by appropriate symbols and words.

When the trine is reached during the *involutionary* first half of the cycle, what is being established in concrete substance reaches the point at which it can be felt or comprehended as a whole; the general purpose of the instinctive impulse born of need and desire begins to be realized; an appreciation of beautiful proportions is emerging. The technician or mason can become, to some extent at least, philosopher and artist. Interpreted in terms of the *evolutionary* second hemicycle, the trine refers perhaps to the formal systemization of an intuition, or to the final harvest of a truly fulfilled relationship.

It is because the trine refers to a process of growth, expansion and understanding that it is considered usually the most "favorable" of all aspects; yet an abundance of trines in a birth-chart often means an over-idealistic or dream-like nature or a type of mind which is too satisfied with pure abstractions or generalities and not enough focused upon practical applications. The 40-degree aspect, NOVILE, is the further expression of the dividing-by-three process. It should be considered to deal with a *process of gestation* by means of which the idea or the beautiful form is brought to a condition of organic viability. The 40 weeks of pregnancy, the 40 days in the desert, or 40 years in captivity refer actually or symbolically to such a process. However, if this aspect is used — and I believe it certainly should be in Humanistic Astrology — it has to be exact within one or at most two degrees.

The SEXTILE aspect, if considered in terms of the geometrical formation of aspects, has an ambiguous character; for it is a trine divided in two. In the sextile therefore two processes are combined: division-by-three and division-by-two. The latter refers to the exteriorization and practical application of the results of the former. The sextile has a character entirely its own. It is the most "constructive" or organizational of all aspects, and the most practical. In the zodiac Fire signs

The Geometrical Principle of Formation of Aspects

are in sextile aspects to Air signs, Earth signs to Water signs; these two categories of signs are in a much more constructive relationship than those belonging to the same "elements," because the relationship is a *productive* one.

The SEMI-SEXTILE brings the process of dividing-by-two still a step further. A masculine sign is linking a semi-sextile relationship to a feminine sign, for instance Aries to Taurus. The principle of productivity is brought down to its most basic components, polarity and sexuality. We saw that the 30-degree aspect represents the fundamental step in the involutionary series. According to Greek philosophers the universal Whole was symbolized by a dodecahedron inscribed in a sphere. Here we find the basis for the concept of twelvefold internal bio-psychic and universal or occult organization, in its most intimate manifestation.

With the QUINTILE aspect (72 degrees) we come to the process of "dividing by five." The number 5 stands for the creative mind which is the truly "human" principle in Man (in Sanskrit *manas*). The five-pointed star is traditionally the symbol of Man, who is able to transform his environment — for better or for worse! — according to an "idea" or an impulse to action. A quintile aspect between two planets shows that the relationship between them can become a source of personal or social-cultural transformation.

As this power of creative — and negative or essentially destructive — transformation is not operative in the majority of human beings, content as they are to conform to what is around them or in them, quintile aspects in a birth-chart may refer only to latent, never really actualized, powers in the individual person. However, by the term, creative, I do not mean "artistic." A person is creative to the extent to which he can impress his essential individuality upon that with which he comes in contact. A statesman who successfully imparts his ideas or purpose upon a nation is far more creative than a second rate artist or novelist who only "produces" forms according to the standardized procedures of his society. The quintile may refer to "genius," but one can say that every man has potentially a genius of his own, or a certain type of creative imagination — thus, a strictly individual way of meeting life situations and interpersonal relationships. But he may be afraid of using it, or too lazy to do so.

The SEMI-QUINTILE aspect (36-degrees) theoretically refers to the operations by means of which genius exteriorizes itself — thus, in a general sense, to "talent" — i.e., to the technical ability to give a concrete form to creative impulses.

With the SEPTILE we reach the first mode of division of a whole 360-degree circle which does not produce a "rational" number — i.e., 51.42 85714 etc. Because of this it has been associated with irrational processes, compulsions of fate, sacrifice. If two planets in a birth-chart form an aspect of 50 to 53 degrees, the bio-psychological functions which these planets represent *may* serve as channels for the performance of actions which either are not acceptable according to the definite norm of social-cultural behavior in the person's environment or class, or else which can be interpreted in a super-personal sense as acts compelled by a collective need, an occult power, or fate; and these may lead to "sacrifice" and a symbolic life. For instance, President F.D. Roosevelt was born under a septile of Mars retrograde to Saturn, and one of the Moon to Neptune and Jupiter; Lenin, under a septile of Jupiter to Uranus (a fine symbol of revolutionary activity, upsetting the traditional Jupiterian social order); Edgar Poe, who was the source in America of fantastic, drug-inspired literature, and of the murder story, has in his birth-chart a septile of Sun-Mercury to Neptune.

In concluding this all too brief and sketchy study of astrological aspects, I should stress again in a somewhat different way what I regard as a most important point. In Humanistic Astrology one should approach aspects *in a birth-chart* in a manner different from that required for the study of transits and progressions. The reason for this is, of course, that a birth-chart represents an "archetypal form" — a space factor — while transits and progressions (including solar and lunar returns) deal with time-sequences.

This basic distinction can be illustrated by comparing the portrait of a person made by an intuitive and talented painter, who has sought to evoke by his painting what he feels to be the individual character of the person, with a motion-picture taken of the same human being as he goes about the business of daily living. This illustration, for many reasons, is far from adequate but it may have some value in stressing a basic fact. A birth-chart is a static factor. It refers to whatever it is in an individual person which remains permanent from birth to death; we may call it man's "identity." Because it is a static archetypal factor it should be studied from the perspective of space. It is a geometrical pattern; but one which has a very specific meaning. I have spoken of it as a *mandala* — a hieroglyph basically constituted by a circle divided by a cross, and with planetary symbols scattered through the chart, or concentrated in some section of it in such a manner that a basic over-all design emerges from the whole figure.

When, however, we deal with planets and/or "angles" in motion, year by year, or day by day, we are studying something that belongs to a basically different level, i.e., to a constant process of change. This process is cyclic. Planets return by transits to their natal places; the progressed Moon returns to its natal zodiacal position in less than 28 years. Solar and lunar returns — and also the return of conjunctions of Jupiter and Saturn, of Mars and Venus, etc. — mark the beginnings of various cycles. But these beginnings merely outline patterns of wave-interferences, nodal points in the continuum of ever-dynamic, ever-changing existence.

It should be obvious, at least from the point of view I am presenting in these essays, that we cannot think of interplanetary relationships in a birth-chart in the same way as we interpret them in terms of cyclic changes; and this is the basic reason why astrological aspects should be interpreted as parts of two series: one which represents a series of *steps* in the development of the life-process from potentiality to actuality, the other which refers to *a mental and objective picture of totality* — which means to the "meaning" of the whole chart.

The opposition aspect represents, symbolically at least, the moment at which such an "objective structure of totality" is most likely to appear in terms of the relationship between two planets. It is particularly important in case of the soli-lunar relationship, because the two Lights refer to the bi-polar life-force which sustains and feeds the whole organism, psyche as well as body. In a most general sense, and if we think of the entire life-span of a man, he who has experienced much of life and has enjoyed and suffered through a variety of endeavors and attempts at self-actualization should come at his life's mid-point (a symbolic Full Moon) to "see" vividly the picture of his own totality and identity — what I have called his "celestial Name." He should apprehend this entire celestial picture in an "esthetical" (i.e., holistic) act of perception, thus in terms of meaning and purpose.

Astrological interpretation is, in this sense, a process of "revelation." It certainly should not begin with the analysis of separate features, even less with the listing of data taken out of the ancient aphorisms or modern textbooks. The Buddhist monk *meditates* on mandalas in which are symbolized various processes of consciousness-unfoldment, various complex relationships between dynamic forces within organic wholes, be they human or cosmic. What one meditates upon is "Form." Meditation thus partakes of the nature of the truly esthetical experience. The Form "speaks" to him who faces it with an open and alert mind, a mind able to "see" even more than to cogitate.

It is difficult to teach this language of Form. One can only gradually develop the special ability to understand it by constant practice, and above all by maintaining a "holistic" attitude to any and all experiences. This implies the development of a new type of mind-perception and of a "resonance" of whole-being to whole-being. But resonance does not mean identification, anymore than empathy implies union! What is primarily involved is, I repeat, a sense of Form, and a capacity to respond to the totality of any life-situation, rather than to study analytically and piecemeal various particular characteristics. Yet some of these characteristics may give essential clues to the whole situation, *provided* they are referred at once to this whole situation rather than perceived as things in themselves, i.e., as unrelated individual factors.

The essential study is a study of relationships, a study of the structural character of the interrelatedness of all the components of a whole — whether it be a whole life-situation or an individual person. And this is why the study of astrological aspects is essential in a holistic interpretation of a chart. What is to be learned, however, is to apprehend at once the total pattern of interplanetary relationships, and to respond mentally and intuitively to its meaning in terms of the fourfold and twelvefold structure of astrological space defined by horizon and meridian.

I shall leave to the next essay in this series a more detailed discussion of "planetary patterns" and their general meaning in the interpretation of a birth-chart.

FIRST STEPS IN THE STUDY
OF BIRTH-CHARTS

15

The "Signature" of the Whole Person

FOCALIZATION IN SPACE

As we approach the interpretation of a birth-chart we should never lose sight of the fact that the chart is a two-dimensional projection of the whole universe in relation to a particular "organism" which began its individual existence at a particular time and on a particular locality on the Earth. And I use the word "organism" to define any steady system of organization of inter-related and interdependent functional activities.

Obviously the contents of the birth-chart are selective, and they refer in modern practice almost exclusively to the positions of the "planets" of our solar system — the term, planets, including the Sun and the Moon — and to secondary points or lines such as Nodes, Parts, etc., which refer to the interactions of these planets or of their orbits. Modern astrologers make a minimal use of the stars in our galaxy; and I perhaps need not repeat that, from the point of view of Humanistic Astrology the zodiac does *not* refer to actual groups of stars (vis. constellations), but to the constantly altered relationship of the Earth to the Sun through the cycle of the year — a relationship which can be expressed in twelve "modes," each constituting a *sign* of the zodiac, with Aries as the first phase of the cycle.

The fundamental concept in astrology is that the first moment at which an organism begins to operate as an at least relatively independent unit *within its total environment* is to be regarded as the "seed moment" of the complete life-span of this organism. As here we are dealing almost exclusively with human beings this "seed moment" is the exact time of the first *inhalation* made by the newborn. The exhalation (first cry) which follows marks symbolically the start of the "germination process," that is, of the active existence of the organism as it responds to its environment.

A seed is a small entity within which the power of the life-species is focused. In a much broader sense, at every moment the entire power of the universal Whole is being focused into whatever attains the status of independent organic existence, according to (1) the relation of the precise birth-locality to this universal Whole, and (2) the genetic and social-cultural capacity of the new organism to respond to that power. Again let me say that by "universal Whole" I mean, for all practical purposes, the solar system and to some extent our galaxy. By genetic and social-cultural capacity I refer to the *limited* possibilities of existence *defined* by the life-species, the race, the family heredity of the newborn organism, and also by the society, the culture and all the crudely or subtly operating factors in the total (psychic as well as physical) environment.

The occultly inclined person may want to speak also of "spiritual" factors, i.e., of the character and evolution of the "individual Soul" incarnating in this organism; but actually astrology does not deal *directly* with such a transcendent factor. Obviously "something" selected the genetic arrangement from a vast number of genetic possibilities and presumably likewise "selected" the exact moment of the first breath. In astrology the term, *karma,* combines all these various factors determining the seed-moment of birth. And karma simply means that any new cycle of existence is *conditioned* (and in some cases entirely determined) by a past cycle, or a combination of the "seed harvest" (positive or negative) of a number of past cycles.

All these above-mentioned points are as basic in astrology as, let us say, the concept in modern science that every law and "constant" in the universe applies as well to any part of space and — which is far less certain and logical — to any period of time, or that a "simple" solution using known factors is preferable to one which brings in as yet not adequately known elements. If we are not clear in our mind concerning these points — and a few others which will emerge as we proceed — our approach to the interpretation of a birth-chart can hardly be not only consistent, but, from the Humanistic point of view, valuable and constructive.

In the preceding essay I discussed the meaning

given to the term, form (or structure), with reference to an astrological chart. I stressed the importance of seeing the chart as a structured whole, of making use of the "esthetical" and holistic capacity to see and feel directly the meaning of the whole, if possible before attempting a detailed analysis of the parts. I spoke of the birth-chart as representing, as it were, the "Signature" of the whole person. I spoke of the "planetary pattern" formed by the angular relationships linking all the planets, a pattern which had to be referred to the framework defined by the natal horizon and meridian, and also to the zodiac as a whole.

What I now propose to do is to discuss the few characteristic planetary patterns which can be easily identified as one looks at a birth-chart. Identifying them is, I believe, the first step in the study of a birth-chart. The second step is a consideration of *which planet fills what place* in the over-all pattern. The first refers to the factor of structure; the second to the contents of this structure.

To say that there is meaning in the fact that one single planet stands alone in the lower half of a birth-chart while all others are located in the upper half (i.e., above the horizon) is obviously not enough for a total grasp of the whole situation. One must know which planet is the isolated factor — and its zodiacal and exact house position. Yet the knowledge of such a type of over-all planetary pattern of itself *predisposes the mind* to approach the problem of interpretation of the chart in a holistic manner. It forces one to think of the

The "Signature" of the Whole Person

chart as a whole, and to bring to the study of it a type of faculty which no analytical listing of separate planetary positions and aspects could *induce*.

We are dealing here with psychological factors. But psychological factors indeed do condition not only the interpretation of what is being observed and studied, but even the *kind* of knowledge obtained — a fact which modern science only recently has begun to recognize. One's attitude toward knowledge conditions what one will know, and the questions one asks conditions the answers which experiments organized in terms of these questions will give. If we want to know a person as a whole, we must therefore approach his birth-chart in a whole act of perception. What strikes us at first is the *gestalt* (or overall configuration) of the chart: i.e., how it looks as a whole. If we learn to look intently enough the chart-as-a-whole may "speak" to us.

How can we learn? First of all, by focusing our mind upon the basic form made by all the planets. What we will learn is not so much any trait of character in particular, but something more general, yet all-encompassing and structurally significant — something within which, or with reference to which, all particular planetary data will organize themselves quite naturally as we proceed further in our study.

Pioneer work in the establishment of basic types of planetary patterns was done nearly forty years ago by Marc Edmund Jones in his book THE GUIDE TO HOROSCOPE INTERPRE-

TATION (1941). It is a very significant work, and it is no doubt valid in terms of the author's philosophical background. I feel nevertheless that the entire subject of defining, naming and interpreting these basic types of structural arrangements should be reexamined, and that a new list of classes of patterns has to be made and differently interpreted in accordance with the basic principles of the holistic thinking I am formulating in this series of essays.

Before we come to this part of our study a few preliminary points should be at least briefly touched upon.

Form — in the sense of *internal* structure — arises out of the specific arrangement of the elements constituting, in their interdependent state of togetherness, a definite whole. If the component factors in a structured group are found evenly distributed throughout the whole we are facing an un-accentuated situation. If the distribution were absolutely even we could hardly speak of any internal "pattern," but instead of a "plenum," i.e., a fullness of interrelated activities. Pattern emerges when the distribution is uneven, and one or more zones of concentration is found, balanced in some manner by zones of emptiness.

There are times at which all the planets of the solar system are, as it were, bunched within a relatively narrow section of the zodiac. This is perhaps the most obvious type of patterning. Marc Jones called it appropriately the "Bundle type." Such a picture of planetary concentration, however, raises a problem. The planet might be scattered within several signs of the zodiac, yet they may be found concentrated within one of the four quarters of the birth-chart, perhaps within two houses, leaving the other houses empty. This could easily happen in northern latitudes. What then, is to be considered as the significant feature, planetary distribution with reference to the twelve houses, or with reference to their positions in the zodiac (i.e., their celestial longitudes)?

In view of what has been said concerning the need to be able to "see" the chart as a whole in a single act of perception it should be obvious that what matters here is the *immediately perceptible form* presented by the chart on paper; and this means the arrangement of the planets in terms of their House positions, and especially with reference to horizon and meridian. One might object to this in that astrologers use different House-systems. But what counts is the particular situation as viewed by a particular astrologer using a particular system. The client has sought this astrologer, and the relatonship of this client and this astrologer at a particular time and in a particular place sets the stage for the interpretation of the chart and the possible solution of the client's problem. Astrology deals with strictly individual and unique situations and this differentiates it essentially from science which is primarily intent upon establishing classifications which exclude the non-generalizable facts or features, and "laws," which are postulated to be valid everywhere and at all times. Psychology, at the level of its application in psycho-therapy or counselling, refers to the same situation as natal astrology — and so does any really valid type of medicine, especially when functional disturbances are the causes of ill-health. What is tragic in our modern civilization — worshipful of quantity, norm and statistical averages — is that it fails to recognize that all truly "human" values are individual values, and that everything is to a person as this person sees and meets it at a particular time and place.

Thus when I speak of *any* astrological factor in interpretation I always refer to what this factor means to the astrologer as he is aware of it in a particular situation and according to the technique he or she uses. If the astrologer uses the "equal House" system the zodiacal and the House frames of reference for the distribution of the planets, in a sense, are the same; but the planetary pattern should still be referred at least to the horizon. An ambiguous situation exists in such a system, because the meridian is no longer a line of reference. Consciousness is thus deprived of its "verticality" — which means, of a basic spiritual and social dimension.

While the disposition of the planets of a chart in terms of the frame of reference created by the Houses is the basic fact to consider, the distribution of the planets in the zodiac is also important in another sense. If all the planets are located in spring signs or summer signs or one planet in a winter sign and all others in the summer sign, this too is very significant, for any deviation from an ideal norm or from an even distribution of factors within a whole, produces an *accent* and therefore some kind of stress and disequilibrium. When this occurs, two possibilities always arise: the situation can be used constructively as a means to focalize some type of activity and the consciousness emerging from this activity — or else the situation may lead to unresolved tensions and crises. However, everything which refers to the positions of planets in zodiacal signs belongs to another class of interpretative judgments — the class which refers to the relationship between planets and the four "Elements" (fire, earth, air, water), to rulerships, etc.

I should also mention, in answer to a probable objection, the evident fact that the planetary pattern presented by a birth-chart would change in many cases if new planets were added to the ten ordinarily used in present-day astrology. Here again I shall simply state that what counts is what the astrologer uses as his or her tools. In the case of the charts of people who died before Uranus, Neptune and Pluto were discovered the situation should be clearly understood. If we add these planets in their birth-charts, what we are seeing in their planetary pattern is *our present ability* to understand what these persons represent in the evolution of their society and culture. Their contemporaries presumably would not have understood these individuals in the same light, because we have gained a *historical perspective* on their lives and works. It is to this historical perspective that *our* understanding of the symbols, Uranus, Neptune and Pluto refers.

Of course, these planets "were there" in the solar system, whether or not man knew of their existence. But if they had a *direct* influence, it was an influence upon the Earth as a whole — and thus upon mankind as a whole — but *not* on the consciousness of human beings or individuals seeking to understand themselves and their experiences. There are many radio waves filling the space of the room in which I am writing this; but if I have no radio able to tune in to these radio waves they do not affect my consciousness. A series of crimes committed a few blocks from my house does not affect me if I do not hear about them; but if the facts are brought to my consciousness, I may become fearful and my daily actions may be thereby altered.

Astrology — at least as I am considering it — deals with consciousness. It should enable us to become attuned to, and thus aware of, a new and more universalistic environment, and of our relation to all that takes place in this environment. The environment in which human beings operate, feel and think has gradually expanded from strictly local to a provincial, then national, and now global and eventually solar-systemic and galactic level. Changes in the tools used in astrology must naturally follow this expansion process. But the process is not only a quantitative one; it is also, or it should be, qualitative. If a human being brings to a larger environment the kind of consciousness, feelings and thoughts, which were the natural products of the narrower field of activity, confusion and indeed serious troubles are nearly inevitable. The vaster the new environment, the deeper should be the change in consciousness. If men were ever able to function in a galactic environment, moving from star-system to star-system, it would be tragic if these men were not able to meet their new experiences with a "cosmic" consciousness. Unfortunately, science-fiction writers and the social-political organizations which are trying to train astronauts are totally unaware of this basic fact.

16

Planetary Patterns

As already stated, if the ten planets used today in natal astrology were absolutely evenly distributed, that is, if each planet was separated from the preceding and following ones by at least approximately the same space, there would be no accentuated function or area of activity. As there are twelve Houses (or Zodiacal signs) such an even distribution would still leave at least two Houses (or signs) unoccupied by planets, yet this fact could hardly be considered significant in a structural sense; and eventually man may discover two more planets. Indeed, some astrologers, even today, use such as yet officially undiscovered planets on the basis of the testimony of clairvoyants, or of deductions made in order to account for what they consider the absence of indicators for specific types of events — a most questionable procedure.

Actually, it is very difficult to find a chart in which *no* planet is found to be less than 30 degrees from another planet. I personally have not seen any during the fifty years I have studied birth-charts. Marc Edmund Jones in his already mentioned book speaks of what he calls the

Splash Type of pattern, but he defines it by saying that "any individual with his planets rather well divided around the wheel is said to belong to the Splash type"; and to find what he calls an "outstanding illustration" he had to go to the highly speculative chart of the visionary occultist, Jacob Boehme. In this chart we see a very exact conjunction of Mercury and Saturn only 17 degrees away from the Sagittarian Sun. In the Campanus House system, the three planets would be in the eighth House. This certainly cannot be called an even and unaccentuated distribution. The other examples of this Splash type are no more truly characteristic.

The perfectly even distribution seems to be an ideal, rather than a reality. The charts in which an *approximation* of this ideal is revealed belong in my judgment to a type which should be defined and evaluated in a different way. The planetary pattern in such charts fails to conform to a *harmonic* kind of distribution. It presents a picture of *relative disorder*. As we shall see presently there can be a highly creative type of disorder or disharmony; but in order to place this type properly in the series of pattern types we have to consider it as the last of the types.

THE HEMISPHERIC PATTERN

As we have seen in the preceding essay in this series, the simplest way in which a whole can be segmented is by dividing it into two equal parts. Dividing by two produces the "opposition" aspect.

As we are now dealing with the grouping of ten planets within the celestial sphere, which is projected in two dimensions as the birth-chart, the dividing-by-two operation refers to a planetary pattern in which all the planets are gathered within one half of the birth-chart — that is, within six contiguous Houses. This leaves the opposite six empty. The meaning of such a pattern is particularly strong and clear-cut when the planets are all on one side of either the horizon or the meridian, i.e., below or above the horizon, or East or West of the vertical axis of the chart.

The meaning of such a pattern seems rather obvious, for this type of distribution establishes an opposition between the two halves of the chart — between the empty and the full sections. But what should we understand here by empty and full? Everything depends on how we interpret these terms.

Planets in a chart represent modes of functional activities within an organized whole. Where a planet is, there we should find *a focus of activity*. If we consider a birth-chart from the point of view of "consciousness," it is clear that where there is activity there is also normally consciousness; i.e., the person's *attention* is drawn to the type of circumstances and the conditions which call for such an activity. When a planet is located in a House the person's attention is drawn to the matters — the type of experiences — symbolized by this particular House. When several planets are found in one House the "native" (the person represented by this chart) will face the various types of confrontations related to this House in a number of ways; that is, several of his functions will be involved — at one time, or in succession — in such experiences. The consciousness which he will draw from such experiences is likely to be complex.

Here again, however, we are confronted with one of the most basic concepts in astrology. Every astrological indication can have a negative as well as a positive meaning; and the potentiality of both is, indeed, always present, even if one seems totally to blot out the other. If several planets are in one House, the experiences referring to this House may be *rich in their diversity;* but they may also be *confusing,* or even bewildering. An individual's attention tends to be drawn to an area of his life which presents to him definite problems. He may solve successfully these problems, and as a result his experience will produce a rich, spiritual, conscious harvest of values. But the person may be unable to solve the problems and they may draw out much energy and over-focus his attention at the expense of other matters that also should be attended to.

Thus when all the planets are located within one half of the wheel of Houses he should expect that the native's attention and consciousness are drawn to all that this section of the chart represents. Yet the situation may not be as simple as that, for the "empty" section certainly does not need to mean a "blank space" in the life. To understand accurately the situation we have to look at it from a point of vantage which embraces both the occupied and the unoccupied halves and *evaluate their relationship.* This relationship can be interpreted as one between what is being actualized, and what remains still in a condition of potentiality, or even more between what needs an effort of conscious attention and what operates automatically without there being the need for willful or deliberate effort.

A divided life may be one of unresolved conflict leading to a more or less definite type of "schizophrenia," that is, to a break between conscious objective activity in the outer world, and subjective dream-consciousness in an inner world. But, if the consciousness of the person is able to reach a higher level of realization from which both the full and the empty, or the objective and the subjective, can be experienced as complementary parts of the whole, *then* a very positive situation may unfold. The full-empty and objective-subjective duality would be understood to mean a constant state of dynamic interaction, just as, in a doctrine of Lao Tze, *Yang* and *Yin* are interacting within the circle of the Chinese *Tai Chi.* This parallels what I wrote previously concerning the opposition aspect; for this aspect can mean either fulfillment and illumination, or a "divorce" or breakup of the relationship linking the two planets in opposition.

When one tries to apply such concepts to the chart of a particular person, especially of a person of whom one knows only the public image — which often does not reveal the real personality — one finds oneself always in a difficult and embarrassing position. How can one know how successful this person is, or has been, in reaching this integrating over-view of the rhythmic interplay of objective and subjective, of actuality and potentiality? Especially in the case of a public figure like England's Prime Minister, Harold Wilson, such a person's life is deeply involved in the circumstances affecting his nation — just as his personality affects at least some of the main phases of the nation's collective welfare. We can only surmise how the specific character of such a person somehow fits in with the destiny of the nation, the latter having called for just this type of individual as a leader.

Harold Wilson's chart provides a perfect example of what I call the Hemispheric Pattern: All planets are located East of an opposition between Mars retrograde in Leo and in the third House and Uranus in Aquarius. Every House and zodiacal sign East of this opposition contains at least one planet; and the Ascendant in Cancer is surrounded by Pluto and Saturn. It is a clear-cut situation.

The Ascendant refers to the pole of individual selfhood, while the Descendant represents the capacity for relationship and the characteristic way in which a person enters into relationship. As the planets in Wilson's chart are mostly on the hemisphere controlled by the Ascendant, and moreover as the ruler of the Capricorn Descendant (Saturn) is just rising a very strong emphasis is placed in this chart on the individual factor — on self-reliance perhaps to the point of obstinacy.

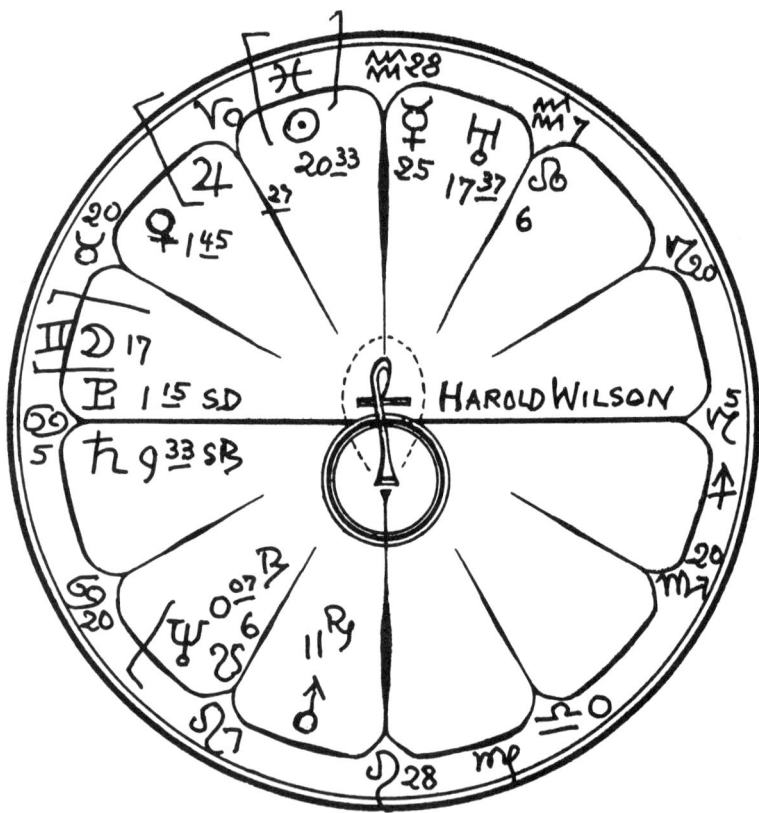

The Moon is very important in the twelfth House in that it mediates (by sextile and trine) the one opposition which defines the chart's pattern. Wilson seems to have a "karmic" task to perform, and he is doing what he can with great self-determination. This "doing" refers to the conscious *actualization* of his purpose of destiny; but it is polarized by the area of emptiness in the western half of the chart which refers to the *potentiality* of his life-situation. The "open"

potentiality in this chart refers essentially to whatever belongs to the realm of relationship — relationship with partners, allies, and as well, enemies. The ex-Prime Minister's problem is how to integrate the ideas and personalities of other people with his own rather relentless and ambitious drive — and how to keep open to what human relationships may bring while carrying on the purpose he has set for himself.

We find another typical example of Hemispheric pattern in the chart of Abdul Baha, the son of the great Persian Prophet, Baha'u'llah (1817-1892) whom the Baha'is all over the world regard as a "Divine Manifestation" and as the Law-Giver for the New Age. Abdul Baha guided the growth of the Movement after his father's death. He was born May 23, 1844 in Teheran, Persia around 0.43 a.m. with early Pisces rising. An opposition of Saturn retrograde at 7°17' Aquarius to the Moon at Leo 2° 50' divides the chart, linking the twelfth and sixth Houses. All planets are below the horizon except Saturn and Neptune (Aquarius 23°42') in the twelfth House. The Moon is at the entrance of the sixth House (he was called "The Servant"). The Sun at 1°48' Gemini is in trine-sextile to the opposition. Other positions are: Jupiter rising at Pisces 28° *18'*, Uranus at 5°18', Aries, Pluto at 23°15'. Aries, Mercury retrograde at 10°39', Gemini, Mars at 24°27' Gemini, Venus at 16°54' Cancer.

In such a type of Hemispheric chart, the midpoint between the two ends of the opposition is important. It may be considered the "center of gravity" of the hemisphere of conscious activity. In this case it is the fourth degree of Taurus, which interestingly enough is the degree of the Part of Fortune, the point of greatest ease of happiness in the personal life. I should add here that while the Part of Fortune (or any Part) and the Nodes of the Moon and the planets do *not* count in determining the type of planetary pattern, their positions in relation to this entire pattern can be very significant. In the case of Abdul Baha the Moon's Nodes are practically identical with the chart's meridian, with the North Node in the Tenth House, thus in the unoccupied half of the chart.

The opposition of Saturn to Moon as the dividing line in this chart is very symbolical, and the position of Saturn and Neptune in the twelfth House is significant for a man who was more or less in prison for 40 years of his life (in Acca, Palestine). The polarization full-empty refers to the inner life vs. the outer, public life. The inner life of personal activity is defined by Abdul-Baha's relationship to the past, to his parental or spiritual inheritance or karma. In a sense he may be said to have absorbed the karma of his culture and religion; and he could do this because he could see this past in the light of the future Age of mankind. In him future and past interacted, as the unconscious and conscious realms interact in the individual who is truly open.

Another typical instance of a Hemispheric pattern is the chart of Claude Debussy (August 22, 1862) who gave a new direction to music around 1900. A broad conjunction of Saturn and Jupiter in late Virgo opposes Neptune (often referring to music) at 3½ degrees of Aries. As I do not know the birth-moment, it is impossible to determine which half of the chart is occupied by planets (Mars at Aries 19°, Pluto at Taurus 12°, Uranus at Gemini 21°, Moon in Cancer, Venus and Sun in Leo). Another case is Alice Bailey's chart (June 16, 1880 — Manchester, England at 7:32 L.T.) which reveals, like that of Wilson, an occupied eastern half of the chart, most likely with a Leo Ascendant.

I believe that the term "hemispheric" is appropriate and particularly significant today when the world of Man is divided into two basic camps: the Have's and the Have-not's. The division is nearly hemispheric even if it does not follow the equator. It may well be that there is also in fact always a fundamental polarization between the northern and the southern hemispheres. The focus of the process of actualization of human potential may be in one of the hemispheres, while the other represents more the area in which the future potential is to be found in a latent state. "Global integration" can only be achieved significantly when potentiality and actuality are harmonized in a dynamic *yang-yin* type of interplay.

THE FUNNEL PATTERN

This is one of the most striking and interesting planetary patterns. All planets are gathered within one half of the celestial sphere (and often within an even less extensive area) — all *except one*. This one stands therefore isolated and constitutes what is called a "singleton." In the most characteristic cases this isolated planet is found separated from all the others by either the horizon or the meridian.

I am giving here two examples in which the same general disposition exists — that is, where one planet isolated in the fourth House broadly

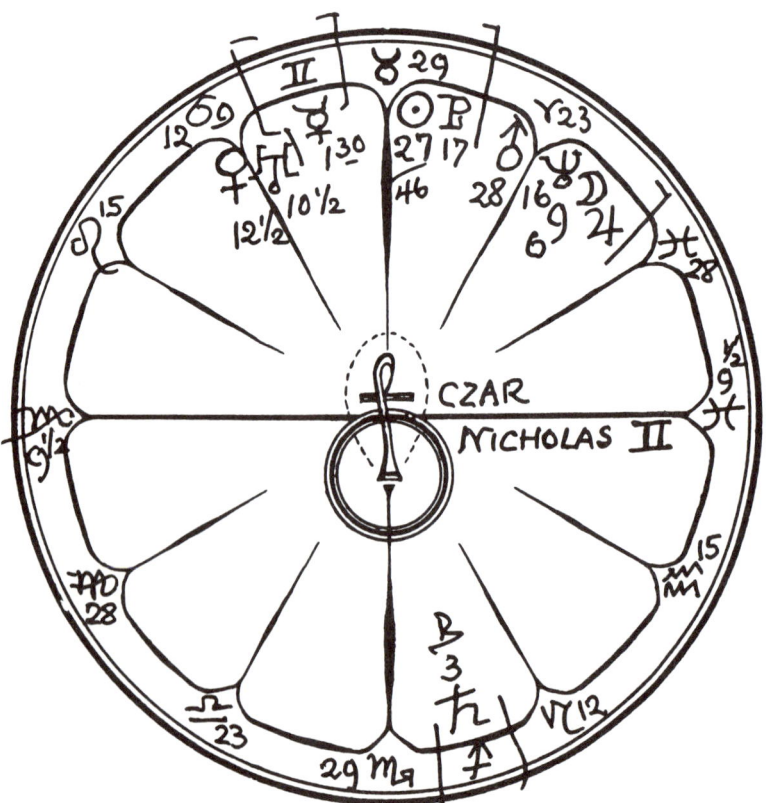

opposes all the other planets well above the horizon. These examples show most clearly that the basic factor in such a type of chart is the nature of the isolated planet. In the chart of the unfortunate last Russian czar, Nicholas II, this planet is Saturn retrograde in Sagittarius. In the chart of Sigmund Freud, it is Mars retrograde in Libra.

One can, of course, interpret such a gestalt in several ways, but it seems to me most significant to think of the pattern as a *funnel,* or in some cases a *wedge.* Obviously the symbol is most adequate when the isolated planet is in at least broad opposition to the "center of gravity" (or mid-point) of the group of all other planets. It occurs also in the chart of Clara Barton (Dec. 25, 1821), founder of the American Red Cross, where Mars is also the isolated planet, but in the sixth House and in the zodiacal sign, Virgo, in very broad opposition to a twelfth House Venus (the group of planets extend between a ninth House Mercury at Sagittarius 18° and a conjunction of Saturn and Jupiter at Aries 20°).

What I wish to convey by the symbolic image of a "funnel" is the idea that the power generated within the grouping of the nine planets is brought to a focus in a thin stream which is released through the narrow opening of the funnel. In the above-mentioned charts in which Mars is the isolated planet, this Mars is to be seen as a particularly intense focus of activity because the power of all the other planets is concentrated and released at the point where this Mars stands in the chart.

198 PERSON-CENTERED ASTROLOGY

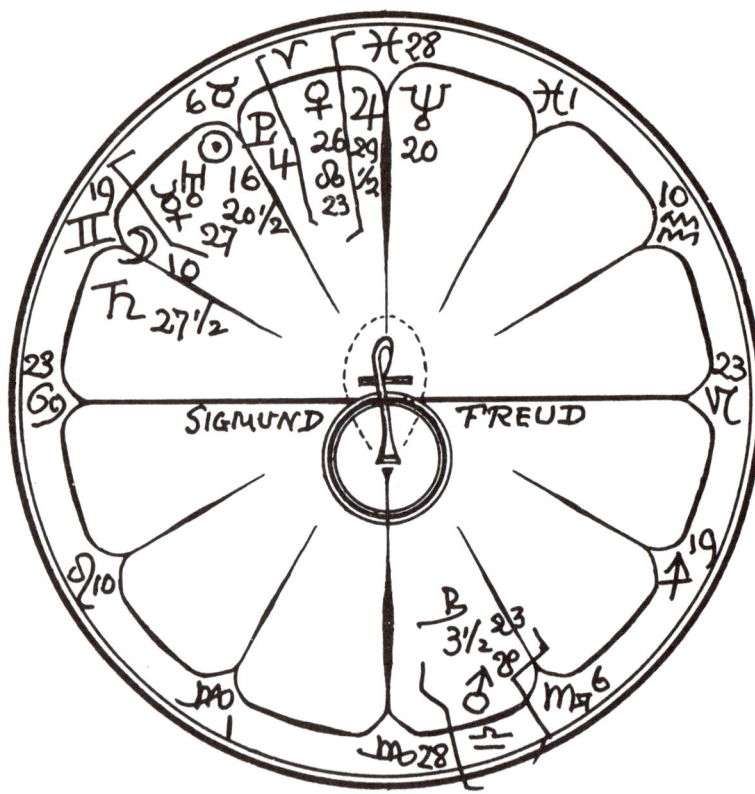

In Freud's chart the release is through the fourth House,* which signifies not only the home, but the very roots of the personality and the basic feeling of security and identity; and Freud's psychoanalysis poured a stream of sharply focused revolutionary and cathartic energy into these roots and upset deeply the traditional sense of personal

---

* A chart with Scorpio rising is also being circulated in Europe; but I do not know on what birth record it is based. A Scorpio Ascendant is, of course, not at all impossible, considering Freud's work and his features.

Planetary Patterns

integrity of modern men and women. In Clara Barton's chart everything is focused into the field of service and health (Sixth House). The fact that in Freud's chart Mars is retrograde simply stresses the revolutionary meaning of the planet; that is to say, the power is turned inward.

When there is such an emphasis on a Martian release of energy, one can think of the planetary pattern as a "wedge"; the power distributed upon the wide surface of the wedge is focused at the sharp end.

In the case of the murdered czar, Saturn retrograde is the isolated planet in the fourth House. In him the karma of the old tradition of the Russian imperial power became focused. His life assumed the character of an expiatory ritual. It was a symbolic life. The ruling planet (Virgo rising) is the tenth House Mercury and Saturn is in opposition to it. The Sun is conjunct the Pleiades, traditionally an ill-omen. His Moon is conjunct Jupiter, but is squared by a conjunction of Venus and Uranus.

In the Czar's chart the planetary group is concentrated within some 96 degrees. In Freud's chart is similar condensation within a little more than a square exists. In none of the charts mentioned does the grouping of planets cover 180 degrees; but in some instances it may extend a little over such an area. It is essential, however, that there should be a nearly even distribution of the planets within the group, otherwise one should deal with another type of pattern. Preferably there should be no empty House within the group, and in no case more than one. Instead of one planet isolated there may be two planets in very exact conjunction. This is the case in President Eisenhower's birth-chart; a close conjunction of Neptune and Pluto around Gemini 7° opposes Venus, strong ruler of the chart and in square to Saturn and in sextile to a tenth House Jupiter. The conjunction here acts as a single planet.

THE SEESAW PATTERN

I am using the name given to this type of chart by Marc Jones because it is graphic. However, one should not think of the symbolic image of a seesaw as implying necessarily a constant shifting of activity from one end to the other, though it may be what takes place within the consciousness of a person born with such a type of planetary pattern. Much depends, of course, on how the ten planets are divided. Two planets may be found more or less separated in one half of the chart and eight in the other; but it may be that the planetary "load" is evenly divided, with five planets in each hemisphere.

The pattern is shown most clearly when the two groups of planets are almost evenly distributed on either side of an opposition aspect, or of a line linking the centers of gravity of the two groups. These two groups may be close aggregations of planets, or the planets in them may be more widely spaced; but each group should be separated from the other by no less than two empty houses, and there should be no more than one empty House within each group.

The chart of the Declaration of Independence, when Neptune and Pluto are included in it, is quite a good example of the Seesaw pattern. In the chart with Sagittarius 13 rising (which is by far the most significant one if one considers the character of the American people and the typical American way of life) Pluto and the Moon oppose the grouping of planets located within the trine of Uranus to a tenth House Saturn (our paternalistic Executive and our worship of the Constitution!). The pattern is not absolutely symmetrical, but the focalizing aspect is the opposition of Pluto in the Second House to Mercury retrograde in the eighth. Pluto here, of course, refers to the power of Big Business in opposition to the investments of the little man and small shop-owner (The eighth House is the House of business, for all business depends on contractual agreements, and various kinds of relationship — relationships represented in our heavily tenanted seventh House of marriage, divorce, installment buying, *and wars*).

When only two planets are found at one end of the Seesaw configuration, they tend to operate as a counterweight that may act as a brake, or as a deterrent, if one considers the progress of the action signified by the larger group. It can also be a means to achieve a deeper, more objective realization of what is being aimed at. If the two planets are relatively close but not in exact conjunction one can even consider them as the two-fold opening of a funnel. In the U.S. chart with Sagittarius rising the power of the planets in the larger group can be said to be released through two openings, represented by Pluto (Big Business, and also gangs and organized crime syndicates) and by the Moon (the common people).

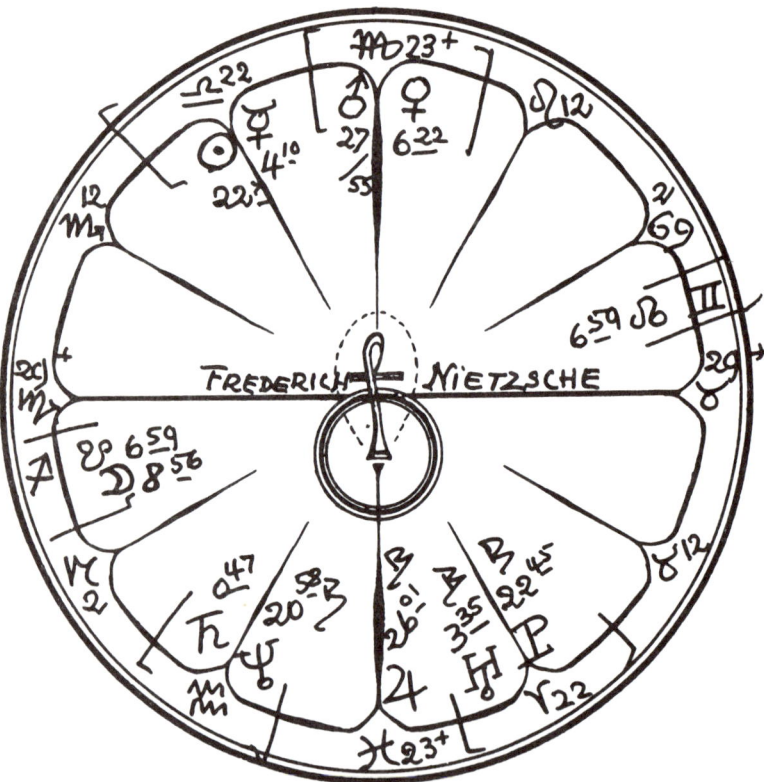

The birth-chart of the revolutionary thinker, Frederich Nietzsche (October 15, 1844 around 10:08 a.m., Rocken Thuringea, Germany) whose influence has been so wide-spread fails in some ways to be an exact Seesaw type; yet in terms of House distribution it belongs to the type, as each of the two groups is located in one hemisphere, and there is a strongly focalizing opposition of Mars near the Mid-Heaven to Jupiter. There are also nearby oppositions of Mercury to Uranus and the Sun to Pluto. The characteristic features of the opposition aspect are thus strongly marked, and Nietzsche's life ended in an insane asylum. It is interesting to note that in his case the Sun and the small planets (Venus, Mars and Mercury — all "rising before the Sun") were near the zenith, while the Moon (intercepted in the first House, in Sagittarius and close to its South Node) and all the larger planets were below the horizon, placing too great a pressure upon his inner life. The chart contained several quintiles and bi-quintiles, and an ominous septile between the Moon (Sagittarius 8°56') and Saturn (Aquarius 0°47').

Sometimes we find a Seesaw type in which the planets are disposed on either side of one strong opposition — let us say in Pisces and Scorpio while the opposition links two planets in Aries and Libra. This suggests a teetertotter in motion, an often repeated attempt at readjusting an uncertain equilibrium. The characteristic genius of the Seesaw type is as Marc Jones stated "a tendency to act at all times under a consideration of opposing views or through a sensitiveness to contrasting and antagonistic possibilitites. The Seesaw temperament has its existence in a world of conflicts, of definite polarities." President Nixon's birth-chart belongs to this type: its three retrograde planets (Saturn, Pluto and Neptune) in the ninth, tenth and eleventh Houses "balance" all other planets in the fourth, fifth and sixth Houses, with Pluto opposing a conjunction of Mars, Mercury and Jupiter.

TRIANGULAR PATTERNS

So far we have dealt with planetary patterns which were an expression of a dualism of factors: i.e., the contrast between a full and an empty hemisphere — between one planet opposing an aggregation of all other planets — between two opposed groups of planets. Now we are to deal with patterns implying a triangular or trinitarian principle of formation.

The most obvious and ideal pattern is, of course, one in which we find the planets divided into three groups, each group occupying a House, which would be leaving nine Houses empty. Such a disposition is undoubtedly quite rare, but many charts can be found in which, for instance, six planets are bunched within two or three consecutive Houses, two planets are in a broad trine to the center of gravity of this group, and two more planets form trines to the larger group and the pairs of planets. Such a type of pattern is found in the birth-chart of the great Indian philosopher, poet, yogi and seer, Sri Aurobindo.

Then there are two other types of planetary patterns which, in a less obvious manner, belong to this category of patterns based on a trisection of the celestial sphere. In one of these types which has occurred fairly often in the recent period all planets are bunched up within a more or less exact trine, leaving the rest of the chart empty.

This is Marc Jones' "Bundle" pattern. The complementary pattern is one in which a third of the chart is empty, and the other two-thirds are occupied by planets. Marc Jones called it not too convincingly the "Locomotive" pattern.

THE TRIPOD PATTERN

The foundation of such a pattern being the trine aspect, this type of distribution of the planets around the chart normally emphasizes all the characteristic features of that aspect. Sri Aurobindo's chart is most characteristic. It contains two grand trines: one, in fire signs, links the rising broad conjunction of Jupiter and the Sun in Leo, to Neptune in Aries (ninth House) and to the Moon in Sagittarius (fifth House) — the other, in earth signs, links Mercury in Virgo (second House) to Saturn to Capricorn (sixth House) and to Pluto in Taurus (tenth House). Six planets are clustered around the Ascendant; the two remotest planets, Pluto and Neptune, are on either side of the Mid-Heaven; and the Moon and Saturn retrograde — symbols of the past, of karma and of the relationship to the parents — are located on either side of the cusp of the sixth House.

The three interrelated groups deal thus, one might say, with the power of the present personality — a typical Leo-type of guru and leader — the mystic future to which the public life is dedicated, and with the past, conditioned as it was by the special temperament of his parents and of his country. (He was one of the first radical champions of total independence from England).

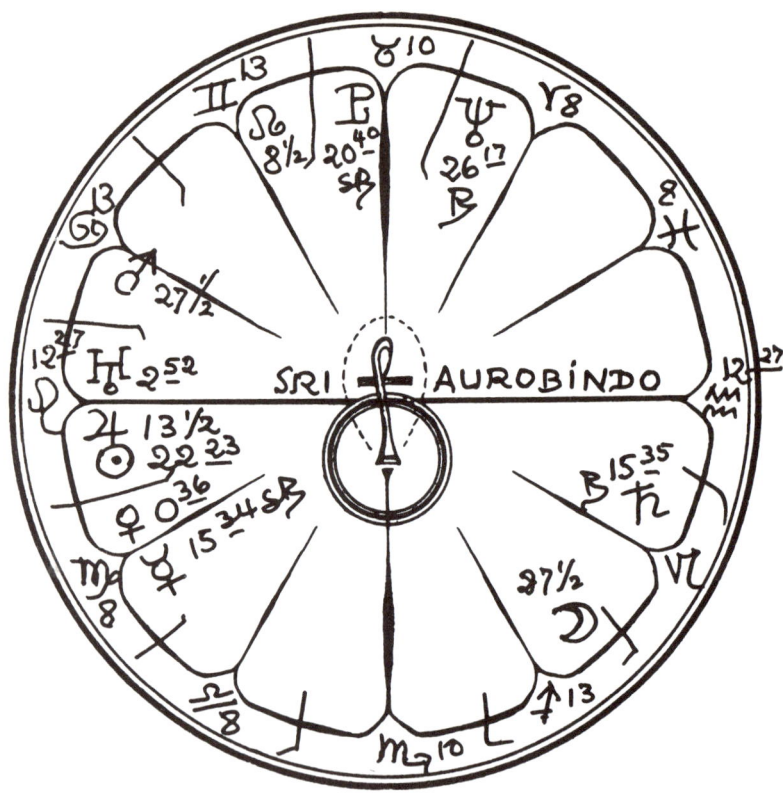

As I wrote in the preceding essay, the number 3, symbolizes all modes of expression and of activity which have polarity as a basis, but in which *polarity is transcended through understanding* and often through some kind of vision. "Life" is bi-polar; but the formed consciousness (mind) adds a new dimension to the dualities of life, the dimension of meaning and value — also the symbolic dimension. The trine is an aspect of growth in consciousness; through it the life-experiences are related to a larger frame of reference; they are seen in their functional relationship to a greater whole — whether it be a social, all-human or cosmic whole."

All of this applies perfectly to Sri Aurobindo whose intense life — outer at first, then inner — has been totally dedicated to the bringing down into concrete manifestation of a new and "supermental" level of consciousness and activity oriented toward a future condition of mankind.

Another great Indian personage, Sri Ramakrishna (born February 18, 1836 at 5:25 a.m.) who was the inspiration for the Vedanta Movement operating now in several American cities and retreats was also born at dawn (Aquarius 8° rising) with eight planets congregated between Neptune at Aquarius — and Pluto at Aries 15°; and with Saturn retrograde in the ninth House, and Jupiter retrograde in the fifth House, both planets being in "grand trine" in water signs. Ramakrishna was a pure mystic in the great Hindu tradition.

Pope Pius XII (March 2, 1876) had eight planets below the horizon in the third, fourth, fifth and sixth Houses, except a just risen Jupiter in Sagittarius, and a ninth House Uranus; but the "grand trine" in fire signs is too broad to be really effective. The great pianist and composer, Franz Liszt (his chart is used as an illustration in my book THE LUNATION CYCLE) had eight planets grouped on either side of the nadir point of the chart, with Jupiter in the eleventh and Pluto in the seventh Houses (an imperfect "grand trine" in water signs).

An unusual chart is that of the French poet, Charles Baudelaire (April 9, 1821, 4 p.m.) in which a Hemispheric and a Tripod pattern are combined. The Moon in late Cancer (eleventh House) opposes a close conjunction of Neptune and Uranus (both stationary retrograde) in early Capricorn and the fourth House; and the seven other planets are in the seventh and eighth Houses, massed within twenty-two degrees. The Moon is in trine to Mercury, but the Uranus-Neptune conjunction is in square to Mars and Venus. The pattern is disharmonic, and hardly fits in the Tripod category, yet it presents three sharply defined centers of emphasis and of stress. Baudelaire's genius was indeed disharmonic and his main book is the well-known "Flowers of Evil."

THE CLUSTER PATTERN

In this pattern all planets are found in not more than four contiguous Houses — and generally within 120 degrees of the zodiac. A very typical chart is that of Benito Mussolini (born July 29, 1883, 1:10 p.m.) which I discussed in my book THE ASTROLOGY OF PERSONALITY (1936). All planets are located within the exact trine of Neptune in the seventh House to Uranus in the tenth. Two Houses contain four planets; the two others, one planet each. The emphasized section of the chart is the south-west quarter. The chart of the Czech statesman, Eduard

Planetary Patterns

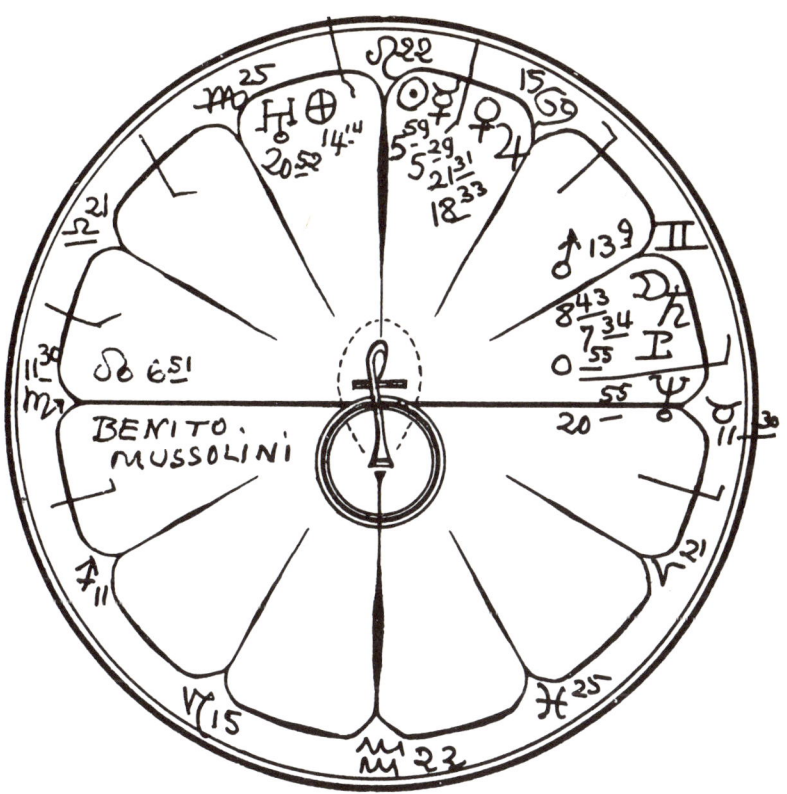

Benes, is less condensed in terms of House distribution, yet all planets are gathered within a nearly exact trine of Neptune to Uranus, from the twelfth to the fifth House. Five planets are in the "karmic" twelfth House.

Obviously such a pattern denotes a concentration of the native's attention upon a definite area of operation. Whether it is correct to assume that the individual "takes a little central point in self and makes a vital impact upon the entire world around him" (Marc Jones) is rather questionable.

A person like Mussolini was the focal point for socio-political forces of great moment. He gained power by playing on the fears and insecurity of the middle class, and by a one-pointed determination to have his way, regardless of consequences, that is, without much concern for the whole situation of mankind. What is essential in this Cluster pattern is the fact that there are no opposition aspects, even a remote one. There is therefore very little objective awareness of the great issues at stake. The native may be driven by a highly focalized purpose, or a great Image (with Mussolini, that of the Roman Emperor), or some Power concerning whose nature he has little objective knowledge. This can be all to the good; but at best it is a limiting situation.

This Cluster pattern often appears in the ephemeris at certain times of history; but it does not seem too frequent among lists of "notable horoscopes," perhaps "success" often requires more than a somewhat blind concentration of activities; both a somewhat larger perspective and a certain type of inner tension may be needed. In such a Cluster pattern much depends on its center of gravity. In Mussolini's case Venus is at the mid-point of the exact trine between Neptune and Uranus; and Venus rules the seventh House with its Taurus cusp. What is interesting in this case is that the planetary pattern is defined by two universalisitc planets and focused by Venus in the ninth House. This means that Mussolini's concentration was defined by large social issues with an ideological character.

Fascism, in the modern sense, is an answer to the fear of Communism — or in general of any kind of chaos out of which a new order *might* emerge. Fascism is based on the worship of a simple, traditional "safe and sound" image of order — whether the order is political, religious, social or cultural. Venus is the Image-maker, the factor of value. In Mussolini's chart Venus is conjunct Jupiter in the House of religion, philosophy and law — and in the Zodiacal sign, Cancer, which limits and possesses in order to insure early growth of selfhood and security. The only square aspect is a broad one between Mars and the tenth House Uranus; and Neptune forms a quintile with Mercury and the Sun. Of course, the chart symbolizes primarily Mussolini as an individual rather than Fascism. Considering the environment he rose from, his life constitutes a tremendous "success" — even if one thinks of it in a purely negative sense. Nevertheless, as long as the ideal of Fascism is held as a vital social-political concept the image of Mussolini and of the type of man he embodied will remain in the collective Mind of mankind; and this is "success" however tragic the end-results.

THE OPEN ANGLE PATTERN

This pattern is the polar opposite of the Cluster. It is also based on a threefold division of the circle, but now the planets are scattered through two-thirds of the chart, and the remaining third is empty. While in the Cluster pattern there was focalization in terms of activity and a concentration of the attention upon a limited area of experience, in the Open Angle Pattern the focalizing factor is *a particular type of openness* to "transcendent" elements in the life situation; and in this connection the term, transcendent, is not to be considered as relating solely or even mainly to spiritual or mystical realizations or occult forces, but to whatever transcends the normal or traditional factors in any situation.

In other words, such a type of planetary pattern suggests a person who is busily engaged in well distributed activities, but who keeps within himself an area of openness to wider and, in a sense at least, more-than-personal or trans-personal influences or spiritual realizations. Through this open area of consciousness inspiration may flow, unless it is blocked by personal tensions or fears which the relationship between the planets should indicate. In such a pattern the planets should be as evenly distributed as possible in the occupied two-thirds of the chart. There should be no more than one unoccupied House. Two successive planets should not be at more than 60 degrees apart.

A good illustration of this type of pattern is the chart of the occultist, philosopher, creative artist, educator Rudolf Steiner (February 27, 1861 11:16 p.m. — Kraljevic, Austria). In this chart the "Open Angle" is defined by the trine of the Moon in Libra to Venus in Aquarius, and the planets are well distributed in the occupied sector, only one House being vacant. There are quintiles, and the Moon is in bi-quintile aspect to the Sun.

Planetary Patterns

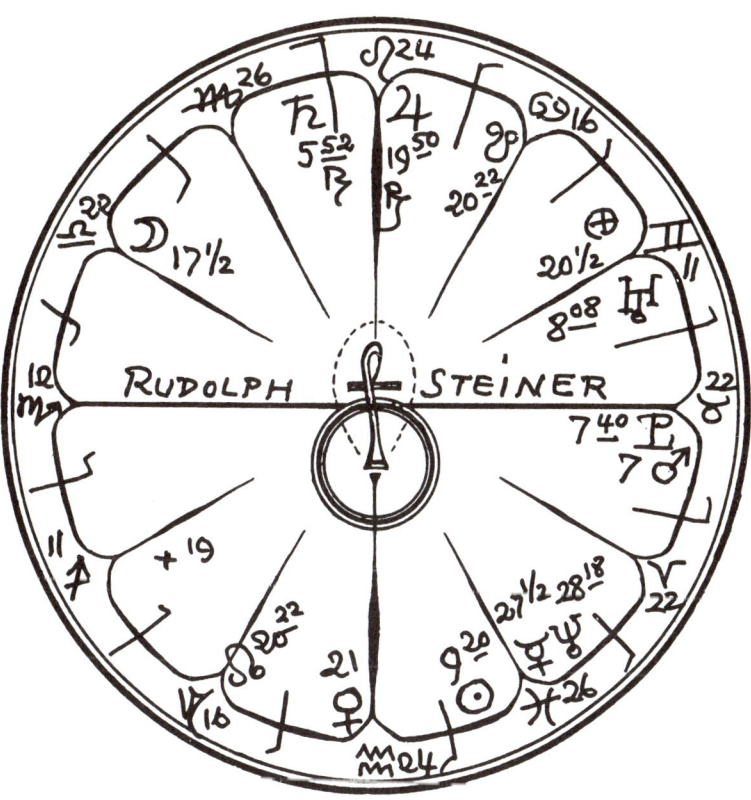

The "grand trine" in Air signs is very broad, yet noticeable, and there are two oppositions, one of which becomes a T-cross in mutable signs. The Mid Heaven is surrounded by the only two retrograde planets, Jupiter and Saturn — suggesting an inward directed search for fellowship and for principles of organization. The mid-point of the empty Moon-Venus trine is about Sagittarius 19° which broadly completes the T-cross (Sun opposition Saturn, squared by Uranus). This point is thus, symbolically, the source of the transcendent inspiration which flooded the remarkable creative genius of this "universal" man. Being in the second House one could deduce from this that Steiner's genius had been "inherited" from the past — for the second House refers to whatever capacities or gifts (i.e., innate possessions) an individual person had within his total being at birth. Legacies or grants received during the lifetime should be referred to the eighth House which symbolizes the fruits of relationships. (Thus you could be disinherited by a parent to whom you have related in a negative manner.)

The chart of Henry Ford (July 30, 1863: 2:22 p.m. Dearborn, Mich.) is interesting in relation to that of Steiner because the empty trine is also between Libra and Aquarius, and the Moon is involved in it; and the chart's Ascendant is also Scorpio. Henry Ford was two years younger than Steiner, and the lives of the two were obviously most different — and so were the Sun-signs and the Moon-signs. Ford had a powerful T-cross in Leo, Aquarius and Taurus; and he had a Full Moon type of personality. In a sense, he had his "vision" of what could be done industrially to alter the way of life of mankind, and he was successful in actualizing through work this vision.

Ford's chart includes also two oppositions; but these are linked by sextiles and trines; thus we have here a fine example of the organizational possibilities related to a *rectangular* configuration — one which, at a time, I have called (not too validly) the "mystic rectangle." There is really

Planetary Patterns 215

nothing "mystical" about it; it indicates rather a capacity for integrating two sets of conflicts (the two oppositions), so that out of this integration power of a sort is made available. The opposition of Saturn to Neptune reveals a potential conflict between individual-traditional and collective-utopian elements in the personality. Ford was a strong individualist, who affected radically the patterns of life of his collectivity, and indeed of the whole world.

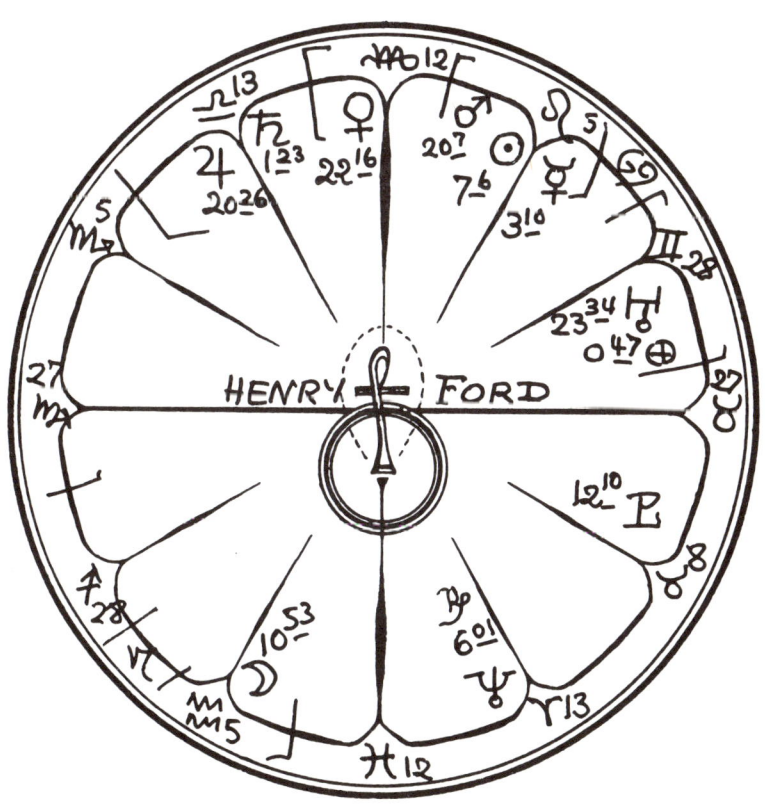

The Moon in the chart is in practically exact trine to the mid-point of the Jupiter-Saturn pair (Libra 11°). In such a case, the mid-point may be more important than either of the planets. Thus the mid-point of the empty sector of the chart could be said to be Sagittarius 11° — or Sagittarius 16° if one counts from Jupiter. In any case it is located in the first House and it broadly opposes Uranus. Henry Ford was a strong authoritarian and a self-made man in the American manner.

THE FOURFOLD PATTERN

In this type of planetary pattern the planets are divided into four groups, or into one group and three isolated planets (as in the case of governor Nelson Rockefeller), or into two groups and two isolated planets (as in the case of Lyndon B. Johnson). There are cases in which all planets are disposed quite precisely in a four-armed cross formation, but this is rather rare and the concept of a fourfold patterning of planets should be broader. Nevertheless, without at least a clearly defined T-cross one can hardly speak of a fourfold pattern.

The case of Nelson Rockefeller is quite graphic in that the fourfold distribution of the planets follow closely the pattern of horizon and meridian. The T-square is in cardinal signs; Saturn at 10° Aries (sixth House) squares the opposition of Uranus in Capricorn (third House) to a bunching of plan-

Planetary Patterns 217

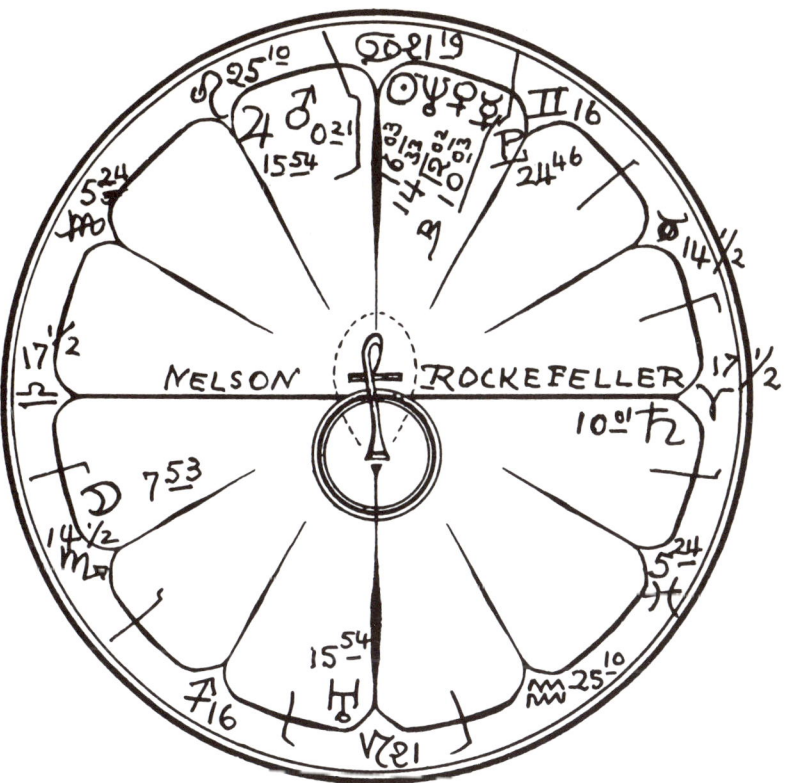

ets in Cancer and in the ninth House — Mercury, Venus, Neptune and Sun. The fourth angle (Libra Ascendant) has the Moon soon to rise in early Scorpio in square to the mid-point of the Mars-Jupiter pair in the tenth House. The zenith grouping occurs within a septile of Pluto to Jupiter — a very interesting and challenging situation.

The chart has many squares but there are also two strong trines and one sextile. It denotes ambition and the will to face life "squarely" and to make one's presence felt. There is personal activity and Leo pride, yet the grouping of planets in Cancer, the rising Moon, and the predominance of planets in cadent Houses — particularly the ninth House — show a complex and sensitive mind. The situation is rather different in President L.B. Johnson's chart with the massing of planets in the first House and the rest of the planets in succeedent Houses. The T-cross is in cardinal signs (Aries, Cancer and Capricorn) but the only two retrograde planets are in the Western hemisphere (which often correlates with definite psychological complexes) and the first House planets are not too closely related to the T-cross which is not even very exact. In other words, the individual ego is shown to be intensely self-assertive, and the personality not too well integrated and beset by confusion. One could well speak of aggressiveness and self-inflation. But of course there is strong personal power and the Leo will to use it.

The birth-chart of Carl Jung (July 26, 1875, about 7:20 a.m. near Zurich) is another example of fourfold planetary distribution. It has a strong T-cross in fixed signs, and four groups of planets are found. The larger one is centered in the Western half of the chart and bounded by the square of Mercury-Venus to Jupiter; a triple conjunction of Neptune, Moon and Pluto is in the third House; and Saturn and Mars are isolated respectively in the first and eleventh Houses.

THE STAR PATTERNS

If it is rather rare to find a chart in which four groups of patterns occur on the basis of a perfect cross, it is presumably even more unusual to find a chart in which the ten planets would form a five-pointed star — or a six-pointed star. However, there are charts in which planets indicate four of the points of a five-pointed star, or five or six sextiles in a series are shown. What is more significant, the planets may be distributed in six Houses in alternation — or in some instances one of the four quarters of the chart may include four to six planets and the others may be evenly divided between the remaining Houses, but not in two successive Houses.

What I mean can be illustrated by the birth-chart of Dr. Roberto Assagioli, founder of Psychosynthesis (February 27, 1888, noon, Venice, Italy). The tenth, twelfth, second, fourth, sixth and eighth Houses are occupied; and there are three separate opposition lines (Sun-Moon, Jupiter-Pluto, Saturn-Venus). These planets are linked by sextiles and trines; and a strong and highly integrative rectangular pattern is formed. A conjunction of Uranus and Mars in the fifth House disturbs the sixfold pattern, adding another point to the star. What we actually have is a group of four planets within a sextile in the Northwest quarter of the chart, and five other fairly evenly spread out centers, at least in terms of House positions.

Such a type of chart, even if it does not show a perfect five-fold or six-fold distribution of the planets, reveals an especially well-integrated or creative nature with broad interests — or at least the potentiality of it — provided the distribu-

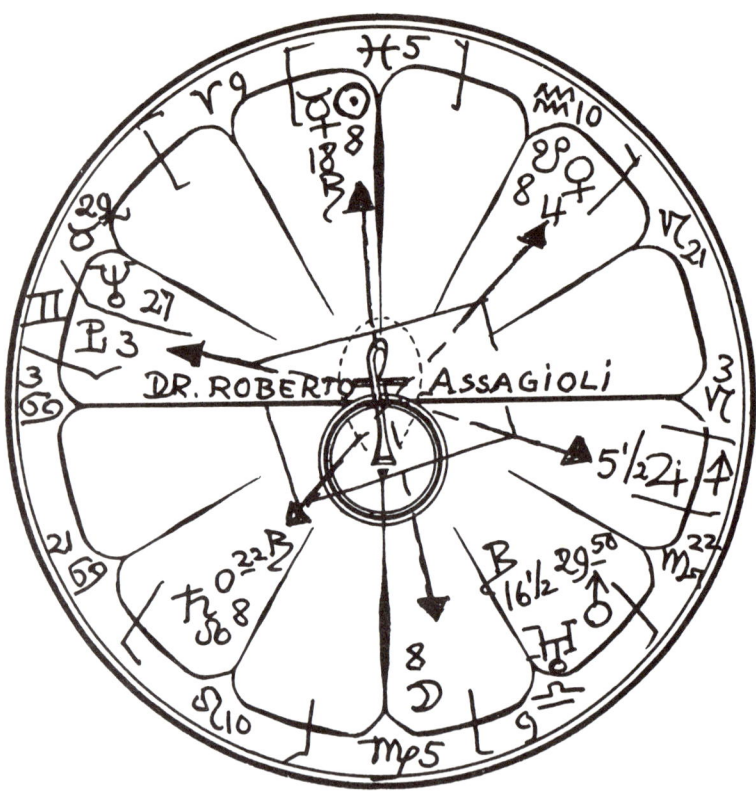

tion is well balanced, or I would rather say "harmonic." Any pattern of distribution produced by the regular process of dividing-by-two, dividing-by-three, dividing-by-four, etc., fits into this harmonic series of geometrical patterns. At the limit we have, of course, what I spoke of at the beginning of this study of planetary patterns, the perfectly even case of a tenfold pattern in which each of the ten planets is isolated and separated from the rest by about 36 degrees of empty space. But this is to be considered as a theoretical limit-situation; and I repeat that the situation depends on how many planets the astrologer uses.

There are however many charts in which the planetary pattern does not have a "harmonic" character. One can speak in these cases of a *non-harmonic* distribution of the planets. By non-harmonic I simply mean a pattern which does not fit in any harmonic classification, though it may approximate it in some respect. A situation also frequently occurs in which the chart could belong to two different types. In some instances both these types may be considered relatively valid; in others it may be better to think of a non-harmonic type. In all cases the situation reveals a basic ambiguity.

You may have, for instance, a clearly marked Hemispheric pattern, yet the planets within the occupied half of the chart may be sharply divided into two groups, separated perhaps by an empty square. If one of the groups is above the horizon, and the other below, the pattern could well be thought of as an unfocused Seesaw pattern. In this case the characteristics of both classes could be somehow combined. And there are several other possibilities of indefiniteness, each of which has to be approached as a special case.

NON-HARMONIC PATTERNS

Any form manifesting a harmonic or rhythmic type of organization falls easily into a particular group or class; but when one deals with non-harmonic patterns and with unclear rhythms, the situation has to be considered as if it were unique. This evidently means, astrologically speaking, that one is confronted with a relatively unusual individual case — a case that does not fit into even the broadest categories of organization. What such a type of pattern suggests is therefore a person with a temperament, or a karma, stressing a rather unique way of responding to life and to society — a very special "destiny." One could speak here of non-conformism, but this might be misleading. The individuality of the person may be strong and accentuated yet able to operate effectively with a relatively normal type of life; but one may deal also with an eccentric character. And there is often no way of telling whether the individual may be a genius or a criminal. The House and sign positions of the planets and the aspects they make should give some clues, yet *every* astrological factor can be either positive or negative; thus one can never be *certain* of what the existential outcome of a particular pattern will be.

I shall present here two charts which illustrate two extreme cases, not mentioning at first the names of the persons to whom they belonged: the first reveals a very complex planetary organization which hardly fits in any harmonic classification. It has a particularly intriguing rectangular figure linking two oppositions: Saturn (and Sun) to Pluto, and Mars to Jupiter. The oppositions are very close, and there are quintiles between Saturn and Jupiter, and Mars and Pluto. There is also another quintile between Moon and Saturn.

Planetary Patterns

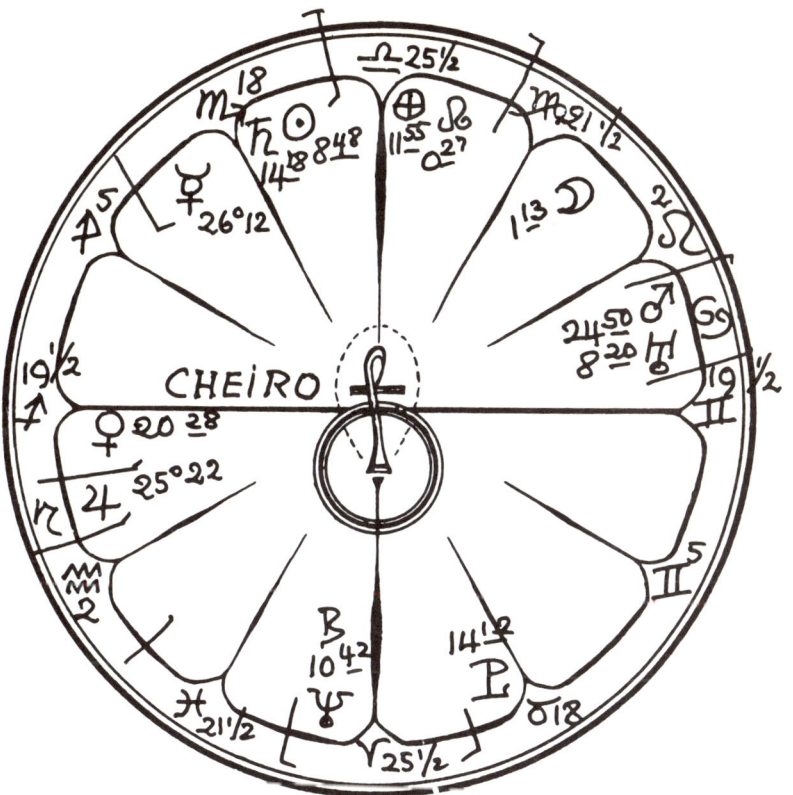

The above-mentioned rectangle has therefore quintiles (of about 71 degrees) for its smaller sides; and it has bi-septiles (110 degrees) for its longer sides. Then there is a trine of Sun to Uranus and one of Mercury to Mars, plus sextiles made by the Moon. This is quite a fascinating chart, with Venus just rising and Jupiter in the first House; and a ninth House Part of Fortune in Libra opposed by Neptune which is squared by Uranus.

But now consider the other chart with its very strange pattern — even more unbalanced with Campanus cusps. Six planets are in Aries, intercepted in the twelfth House, and squared by Uranus in Cancer — but forming a "grand trine" with Mars and Saturn retrograde. Pluto rising in Taurus squares Mars in Leo. Jupiter is conjunct the Part of Fortune. One cannot classify this chart as an Open Angle type, in spite of the empty third of the chart. In a sense it shows a fourfold group-

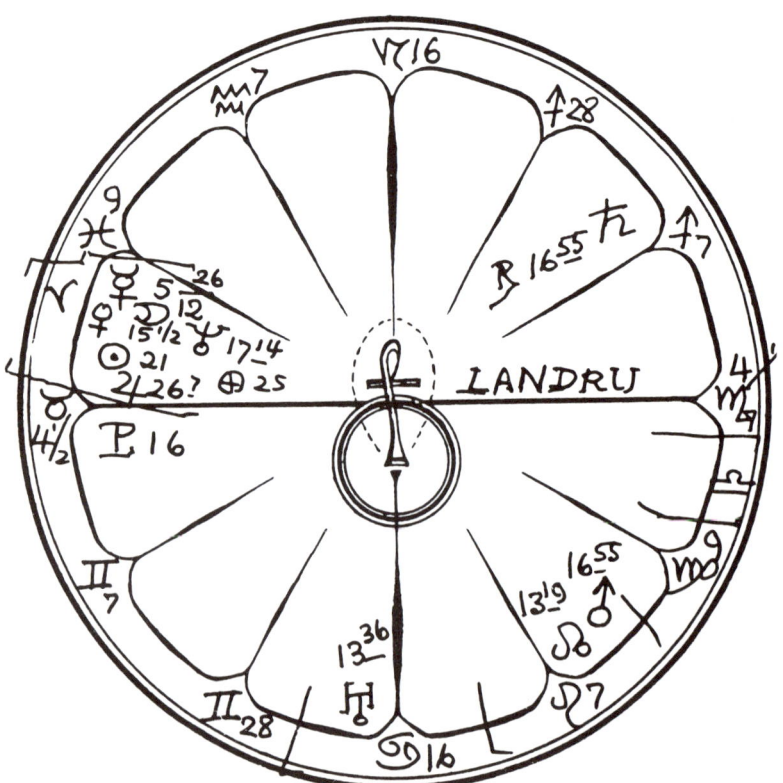

ing of the planets, yet there is no T-cross and no opposition. The three isolated planets are too far from each other to define, in contrast to the Aries cluster, a Seesaw pattern; yet in a sense this twelfth House group stands apart, challenging the three isolated planets, or *vice versa*.

This strange chart is that of the French murderer, Landru, who killed a number of women he had attracted to his home, supposedly with promises of marriage, and disposed of the bodies by burning them. The other chart is that of the Irish nobleman who, under the name of Cheiro, attracted international attention as a reader of hands and as a prophetic seer, and became associated in this role with kings and famous people all over the world. Two interesting charts to study both nonharmonic and referring to "unique" individuals; yet what different types of individuals!

Of course, in studying these various classes of patterns I did not pay much attention to which planets were located in which parts of the pattern. But it should be obvious that even while the holistic astrologer is seeking to grasp the meaning (or shall I say the "message") of the form as a whole, he should be aware *at the same time* of the positions in the zodiacal signs of at least the Sun and the Moon; this, with reference to horizon and meridian. There is no living structure without its contents, and the main factors in the living organism are the two "Lights."[*]

---

[*] For a holistic study of the signs of the zodiac, the reader is referred to my book, THE PULSE OF LIFE. The cyclic relationship between the Moon and the Sun, is studied in another volume, THE LUNATION CYCLE. A general approach to all the factors used in astrology is discussed in THE PRACTICE OF ASTROLOGY, and in the earlier and far more extensive work, THE ASTROLOGY OF PERSONALITY.

17

The Moment of Interpretation

FOCALIZATION IN TIME

The birth-chart, considered as the seed-pattern of of the human being just being born within the Earth-environment, is a focalized expression of the state of the universe in terms of this precise moment and location; this seed-pattern outlines the particular set of potentialities which should be actualized in the life of the individual person if environmental pressures at the socio-cultural level do not interfere. There is, however, another moment, or category of moments, in the life of this person which has or may have a profound significance. This is the moment when this person, either by himself or through the intermediary of an astrologer, becomes conscious of his birth-chart and interprets it, or has it interpreted for him.

This "moment of interpretation" may be repeated any number of times. Yet, however often it recurs it has a definite character, the meaning and implications of which are usually not clearly understood. A person who, at this moment, has developed both a more or less individual consciousness, and personal needs, life-attitudes, expectations or complexes, comes face to face with his relationship to the universe. He faces this relationship at two levels: the "archetypal" level of his first moment of individualized existence — what he potentially "is" and is meant to be as an individualized human being — and the "existential" level of his development as an evolving personality. This development in a specific geomorphic and social-cultural environment almost inevitably gives rise to various problems or at least questions. There may be internal problems of growth referring to the need to understand better his nature at the threshold of some decision-making or during a crisis; there may be more specifically problems of interpersonal relationships. But, in the broadest sense of the term, they are problems which somehow have intruded upon the consciousness and which therefore demand to be met and know what an astrologer could tell by studying one's birth-chart is the manifestation of a problem — a socio-cultural problem; i.e., how to evaluate the possibility that astrology might be a significant and valuable tool for man, and not a superstition.

Here, I would like to deal primarily with the case in which a person, who has but the most superficial knowledge of what astrology is about and who does not know at all his birth-chart, comes to an astrologer asking for a "reading." This evidently the most common situation and is much more sharply defined than the case in which a person painstakingly tries to calculate his birth-chart from textbooks and ephemerides and to interpret it. Thus, in the situation which I am now to discuss, a client in some phase of his personal development and presumably with some general or precise problems, comes to a professional astrologer. He gives him or her his birth-data; and let us take for granted that they are precise and accurate. What is implied in such a situation, and what is the astrologer's best way to approach it?

Again let me state that there are two factors to be considered: the birth-chart and the time at which the client has come. The birth-chart has to be seen and understood as a whole. It has form in space. It establishes a definite set of planetary relationships to which the "native" is oriented in a certain way (the four angles of the chart), and these should reveal, or at least suggest, an existential process according to which this birth-potential can most adequately be actualized. A *process*. At which stage of this process of unfoldment is the native, as he comes to have his chart read? This is a most important question. It is essential for the astrologer to find the answer *as a basis for his interpretation*. What the astrologer is to tell his client concerning the birth-chart and the potentialities it reveals should depend on the stage of life-unfoldment of the native.

In broader terms, knowledge should be given to the knower in terms of his capacity to use it constructively. Knowledge has value only in relation to the knower. You cannot throw knowledge at a person's mind regardless of where this person

The Moment of Interpretation

stands in his development, and expect valid results. Knowledge can destroy as well as heal or illumine the personality — or a whole society. The *timing* of the giving of knowledge is all-important.

This is undoubtedly an area of thought in which discrimination can be crucial. It is indeed a dangerous area socially speaking; but to ignore the problem can have much worse results than to give it a not completely wholesome or risky solution. One of the basic causes of our present world-chaos is Western man's refusal to meet such a problem in the area of science and technology. Any psychiatrist faces such an issue in dealing with his confused or disturbed patients; and so does the astrologer who is at all aware of his psychological or moral responsibility. Whoever gives knowledge is to some extent responsible for the use to which it is put, especially if the use is most readily predictable in view of the character of the person (or the collectivity) to which it is given and of the circumstances in which the disclosure is made.

The psychiatrist aware of the state of mind and feelings of his patient can, to some extent at least, foresee what will be the reaction of the patient to the interpretation of an important dream or of some characteristic form of behavior. The astrologer, who should be also a good psychologist, has moreover other means for evaluating the probable response of his client to his interpretation of the birth-chart. These means come under two headings, progressions and transits; and transits can be studied not only in relation to the client's birth-chart, but also in a special way related to "horary" astrology, that is, to the time of the consultation.

In other words, when a client enters an astrologer's office, or writes him for a written horoscope, this astrologer should always ask himself: Why did this person come to me at this particular stage in his life — what prompted him to want to have his chart interpreted — and how does he fit the particular character of *this moment;* i.e., what is the relationship between the enquirer and the moment of enquiry.*

I feel that such questions are not only valid but that they *must* be answered in the mind of the astrologer, if not as a result of astrological calculations and through the erection of special charts, at least intuitively and in full realizaton of their importance. The astrologer does not deal only with the archetypal set of potentialities symbolized by the client's birth-chart, but as well with a feeling, thinking and perhaps anxious and disturbed person, possibly at a moment of crisis. He does not deal with a chart on paper, a mandala or formula; in front of him is a living person who needs an answer to his problem, even if the problem is only that of realizing why he is here — here on earth and here in the astrologer's office. This fact can never be too strongly emphasized to anyone ready to study and to practice astrol-

---

* Another question would also be worth answering: "How are we related in terms of contacts between our birth-charts and am I fit at this moment to take on the responsibility of interpreting my client's chart?"

ogy; and studying one's own birth-chart is to practice astrology upon oneself — and thus indirectly to affect all those to whom one is closely related.

What then is the astrologer to do? As soon as he has calculated the client's birth-chart, he should quickly establish — *before* saying anything to the client — at least the solar and lunar progressions, and become aware of any arc separating planets, the value of which would measure up to the number of years of the client at the time. (I use the one degree per year symbolical measure.) He should place the main transiting planets outside of the chart, and see if the client is affected by particularly significant transits. All this should enable him to speak to the person consulting him *as this person is on that day.*

This is required for any truly humanistic and existential approach to the interpretation. The interpretation must be focused first of all on the "here and now" of the existential and strictly personal situation of the client. The astrologer is meeting the client at this particular moment; and the character of this moment is all-important. This is why some astrologers, following Evangeline Adams' example, cast an exact chart for the time and place of the consultation; and insert in this chart the natal planets of the client. The House positions of these planets in such a horary type of chart can be especially revealing. They may show how the basic individuality of the client (i.e., his natal planetary *gestalt*) fits into the cosmic situation of the moment, thus why the client — unconsciously to be sure — chose this moment to come to the interview. Perhaps the choice was made by the secretary of the astrologer or in terms of apparently fortuitous circumstances; yet *nothing* is fortuitous to the astrologer. It is the *evolving relationship* between the client and his universe which established, in some irrational yet, just the same, very significant way, the "moment of interpretation," that is, a confrontation between the growing, enquiring, curious or anxious individual and his fundamental "truth of being" (dharma) — his birth-chart.

This confrontation — except in the case of a student of astrology erecting his own birth-chart — is *mediated by* the astrologer. He (or she) is the intermediary between the universe and the man or woman whose birth focalized what the universe needed at that birth moment. Now, at the "moment of interpretation," the client is facing again the universe which speaks through the astrologer. The *"birth-moment" occurred in unconsciousness; the "moment of interpretation" occurs in consciousness.* Astrology is indeed "the conscious way" to the realization of the basic "truth" of one's being as a particular person — or, at least, this is what astrology should be. And it is indeed very distressing to see how deeply it has become estranged from its original and archetypal significance.

Of course, originally astrology did not deal with "individuals," for there were no really individualized persons in archaic tribes; but astrology dealt with the Earth, or let us say the environment-as-a-whole. The Earth and not an individual person was the microcosm. The Earth, or Nature as a whole, was fashioned by celestial Hierarchies and planetary gods; and this fashioning process was unceasing. The concept of a birth-chart must have come only at a somewhat later stage, when religious and state organizations had acquired a formal and stable power, and great events related to such organizations were singled out as memorable and endowed with an "individualized" significance.

Today astrology, in current practice, deals essentially with individualized organisms: individual persons or social "persons" (nations, business firms, etc); and its main purpose is to discover the fundamental character and destiny of these persons. Humanistic astrology, however, is basically concerned with individual human beings and their personal unfoldment and fulfillment; and in a very real sense it implies the relationship between three factors: the client, the astrologer and the patterns made by celestial bodies (i.e., the state of the universe). Astrological interpretation involves these three factors; for even if a person is asking his own chart for an answer to his questions, a certain part of his total being (his objective ego-consciousness) then acts as "the astrologer."

The branch of astrology called "horary astrology" deals most specifically with the attempt to find a specific answer to a strictly defined and particular question — paralleling the type of practice consisting in throwing the *Y Ching* sticks. But whenever a person asks from an astrologer help in making a decision, or in elucidating the meaning and trend of a particular situation, the same basic process takes place. At a certain moment of time a relationship is established between the client, the astrologer and the universe.

This moment is the "moment of interpretation"; and its character differs from that of the "moment of birth." The birth-moment focused the universe into the structural pattern of the *being* of a human organism. The moment of interpretation focuses the relationship of the universe to the individual person in terms of the *conscious meaning of his existence.*

The distinction between these two moments may not be evident to many people, and they may dismiss it by saying that, of course the birth-chart is different from the progressions and transits. But the difference goes much deeper than technical means. The birth-chart is archetypal, the moment of interpretation deals with existential issues. Whoever interprets a birth-chart translates an archetypal Form into the concrete actuality of an existential situation, and the moment at which this "translation" (one could use the word, incarnation) occurs has a unique character. It is this unique character that the astrologer should intuitively sense.

If an astrologer should interpret the birth-chart of a person in exactly the same way when the person comes to see him at age 20 and at age 50, then he fails in his function. He has not understood that the moment of interpretation relates him as he is now, to the client as he is now; and that the interpretation will be deeply of value only in terms of this moment in which he and his client come together.

This situation, of course, exists even more in the field of psychiatry, or of "counselling" in general. It exists in the relationship between guru and chela. All knowledge has value only in terms of the moment it is imparted by a particular person to another particular person. This is why I speak of a "person-centered" astrology. Everything in life should be person-centered, if one understands the real meaning of "the person" and not a superficially interpreted etymological meaning. Spirit deals only with persons, with unique cases and particular "nows." God incarnates only in individuals, for God is the One; and there can only be interaction between this One and a one — as the need of the moment requires.

THE PLANETARY AND LUNAR NODES

18

Orbital Astrology and the Nodes

Astrology is essentially a study of the ever-changing relationship between man and his cosmic environment — a study which seeks not only to discover facts concerning this environment (this is the task of the astronomer), but to uncover *the meaning* these facts have in terms of his individual or collective life, his basic character and the unfoldment of his innate potential of being.

The nearest factor in this cosmic environment are the planets — including in the term, planets, for present-day astrological purposes, the Moon and the Sun. These planets move each at a different speed, and their motions are periodical. Astrology today is basically the study of these cyclic motions. And in order to pursue such a study, the motions of the planets are plotted on a background considered to be fixed. There are two backgrounds, or "frames of reference," in generalized use today: the zodiac, and the circle of the Houses based on the horizontal and vertical axes at the point of astrological enquiry.

A good deal of the ambiguity found in astrological concepts and practices is due to the fact that the astrologer today is thinking in both heliocentric and geocentric terms. He knows that our Earth is only one among several planets which revolve around the Sun, yet he also logically considers the whole solar system and the stars beyond as the environment of the Earth on the surface of which man lives, feels and thinks; thus in studying his relationship to this environment he has obviously to take a geocentric — and in natal astrology, a "person-centered" — point of view. He studies *his own* cosmic environment, as he relates to it directly.

Nevertheless man cannot ignore the fact that the solar system is a cosmic whole, that is, a more or less autonomous field of energies streaming from the central Sun. This field is only one among billions of other stellar fields which are parts of the vast galaxy, our Milky Way; and therefore the solar system as a whole obviously is affected by "galactic forces" and by the result of the interactions of a myriad of stars and solar systems. However, we know very little indeed that is specific concerning the galaxy and its stars, and at least at his present stage of evolution, the active and relevant part of man's cosmic environment is the solar system. Man looks at this solar system from his earthly point of view, yet he now knows that it is a specific field of energies; and in order to try to understand the basic character of these energies and their essential meaning, he has to think of the system-as-a-whole — this means heliocentrically, for any organized system of interrelated parts can only be understood in relation to its center or radiating core.

The structure of the solar system results from the interrelationships between not merely the places occupied by planets at any time, but more basically from the interrelationships between the orbit of the planets. Seen from the Sun, all planets describe elliptical orbits. These orbits are well spaced around the Sun. They constitute a series of more or less concentric rings, no planet ever moving as close to the Sun as the one preceding it in the series, except Pluto which about every 240 years comes closer to the Sun than Neptune, because of its exceptionally elongated orbit. However, the *planes* of these orbits do not coincide. All planets do not revolve around the Sun in the same plane. All these orbital planes intersect. The line formed by these intersections is called the line of the nodes, or nodal axis.

From the heliocentric astrological point of view each planet should be given a meaning in terms of its distance from the Sun. Indeed if we try to get at the *fundamental* meanings of the planets we can readily see that these meanings refer to their serial rank in the solar system. The series of planets represent a series of phases in a definite process which deals with the progressive differentiation of the solar force. Mercury represents bi-polar electric energy; Venus adds to this electric force magnetism and refers thus to electromagnetic fields. The Earth gives substantiality and biological properties to these fields. Mars refers to the release of energy from all organic systems, etc. (For such a study of the solar system, I must refer the reader to my book THE PRACTICE OF ASTROLOGY, Penguin Books, page 56, etc.)

In other words, each planet represents, as it were, a cosmic "quality"; but obviously it is this quality as we, human beings on this Earth, are able to see it and understand its nature; for it may indeed be that there are in the solar system planets composed of a type of substance-energy which we cannot perceive and which even our radio telescopes cannot detect. We can only measure and interpret what is within the scope of our senses and intellect. Thus when we study the basic structure of the solar system, i.e., the orbits of the planets, it is logical to refer the orbital planes to our basic life-plane, which is our own orbit around the Sun, thus, in astronomical terms, the ecliptic. Astrologically speaking, this is the tropical zodiac, or zodiac of signs (NOT of constellations) which begins at the spring equinox, or point of celestial longitude 0°.

Celestial *longitude,* from 0° to 360°, is measured along the ecliptic, which astrologers divide into twelve signs, Aries, Taurus, Gemini, etc., each sign occupying 30 degrees of longitude. But there is also a factor called celestial *latitude;* and it is this factor which is basic when one deals with the relationships between the orbital planes of the planet and our own orbital plane, the ecliptic. Each planet's orbital plane and the ecliptic intersect: and the lines of nodes represent this intersection. There is a north node and a south node. A planet is at its north node when it is at latitude 0° and moving north of the ecliptic; at its south node when it crosses the ecliptic in latitude and going southward. There are two moments in *the cycle in celestial latitude* of a planet when it reaches its extreme positions north or south. For most planets these extremes of latitude are very close to the ecliptic, thus not more than 8 degrees; but Pluto can reach latitudes of nearly 18 degrees.

The orbits of the planets are not absolutely stable; their structural characteristics vary, but extremely slowly. Astronomers speak here of "secular variations." Changes in the obliquity and eccentricity of the planets' orbits are measured by tens of thousands of years. The longitude of the planetary nodes likewise varies, but less slowly. According to modern textbooks, they gain longitude at the rates mentioned below.

Longitudes		*Annual Progress*
Mercury — Taurus	17° 42' 11''	42.6 seconds
Mars — Taurus	19° 8' 56''	27.7 seconds
Uranus — Gemini	13° 43' 30''	18.0 seconds
Venus — Gemini	16° 12' 9''	32.4 seconds
Jupiter — Cancer	9° 54' 47''	36.4 seconds
Pluto — Cancer	19° 35' 35''	48.8 seconds
Saturn — Cancer	23° 11' 38''	31.4 seconds
Neptune — Leo	11° 11' 43''	39.5 seconds

Whether this rate of progress is constant may not be certain, as some old Hindu books give very different figures. At any rate, here are the positions of the north nodes of the planets as they were listed in the American Astrological Ephemeris for 1947. The positions of the south node is always the opposite point of the zodiac; thus Mercury's South Node was at Scorpio 17°42'11" and is now about to reach Scorpio 18°.

It should be clear, however, that these are *heliocentric* positions. They refer to the intersection of the orbital planes of a planet and of our Earth. This intersection and the nodes it produces symbolize the fundamental relationship between a planet and the Earth considered as two components in the solar system. The relationship has significance in terms of this solar system as a vast cosmic field of dynamic existence. When, therefore, we apply it to the chart of an individual human being it should be evident that what this relationship — and therefore the planetary north and south nodes — mean in that chart should be referred to the most basic factors in that individual person, i.e., factors that are inherent in the essential destiny of the individual. They are factors which reach deeper than the natural bio-psychic functions which planets normally represent in a birth-chart — just because the planet as a moving small disc of light in the sky is something that the personal consciousness can normally perceive while the *entire orbit* of that planet is a cosmic fact which transcends sense-perception.

Astrology is a language which uses astronomical facts and celestial events as symbols of all-human and personal characteristics and bio-psychic developments. The more unusual or remote such astronomical events or the more cosmic or abstract the relationship between celestial bodies, the deeper or more transcendent the characteristics which they represent in the personality and the life-experiences of human beings. For instance, the Sun and the Moon's apparent revolutions through our sky are always with us, regularly perceptible and closely relatable to what is most evident in us, that is, our very existence as a living organism and our capacity to adapt to our immediate surroundings. But eclipses of the Sun or the Moon which are visible at the place where we live are relatively infrequent and quite startling phenomena; thus they refer also to unusual changes in our lives or very special traits of character, if such eclipses not only occurred at the time of our birth but were facts of human experience at this birth locality.

We shall see later on how this applies to the study of the planetary nodes in a person's birth-chart, but one more basic point should be stressed. The nodes constitute an axis; that is to say, the north or south node of planets — and likewise of the Moon — are never to be considered alone. The habit so many astrologers have of marking and considering only the Moon's north node in a chart does not make any sense. Both nodes form an unbreakable pair, *just as do Ascendant and Descendant or Zenith and Nadir*. Any characterization of the Ascendant which does not include an indissolubly related characterization of the Descendant is incomplete; yet this is what is most of the time done in actual practice and even in textbooks.

One should no more think of an Ascendant without a Descendant than of an electrical current without a positive and a negative pole. In a somewhat different yet related sense, there is no wind without a region of higher pressure and one of lower pressure. This same fact of polarity has to be considered also when we deal with astrological "Parts." The Part of Fortune relates the Moon and the Sun to the Ascendant; but it has also a polar opposite point which relates the Moon and the Sun to the Descendant — a point which I called in my book THE LUNATION CYCLE, the Point of Illumination. In our individualistic society what refers to the self is emphasized — and of course it is basic; but a person's *capacity for relationship* (the Descendant) is implied in his *attitude toward himself* (Ascendant). As a man sees himself, so does he relate to others; and the way he relates to others conditions the development of his experience of self. The same situation exists if we consider the two "ends" of any axis. The two nodes are *not* separate points each with its individual meaning; they are *the two polar aspects of one single process*. What should be studied and understood is, first of all, the process.

In the case of planetary nodes, I repeat, what is at stake is the fundamental relationship of a planet and of our Earth as two *related members of the solar system.* More specifically, in terms of individual birth-charts, it is the manner in which the *essential quality* of a planet affects the very structure and the roots of our individuality as a member of the human species.

In the case of the Moon's nodes one is dealing with a rather different situation, because the Moon actually is not a planet, but instead the Earth's satellite. The axis of the Moon's nodes also represents the intersection between the planes of the Moon's orbit and the plane of the Earth's orbit (the ecliptic); but the Moon's orbit is directly related *only* to the Earth, and therefore the lunar nodes are "geocentric" factors, while the planetary nodes are "heliocentric" factors. To try to consider these planetary nodes from the geocentric point of view not only involves very complex calculations, but by so doing one loses the true character of the nodes, which is to indicate the basic relationship of the Earth to every other member of the solar system with reference to this system as a Sun-centered cosmic organism. The geocentric positions of the planetary nodes are never exactly opposite to each other; thus they lack the very fundamental characteristic of nodes.

The nodes belong to what I called "orbital astrology"; and this is a type of astrology which deals with the absolutely basic characteristics of the planets as members of the solar system, and with very large cycles dealing with the "secular variations" of the orbits: the orbits rather than the planets as material bodies. Indeed in philosophical traditions concerning the meaning of astrology it was stated that the fundamental reality of what we call a planet is *not* its material mass, but rather the *space which its movements define*.

In ancient geocentric astrology, the universe was pictured as a series of concentric spheres each having specific characteristics related to a planet. The moving planet was considered as a lens bringing to an ever changing focus the emanative energies diffuse through the sphere which it "ruled." Today instead of planetary "spheres" we have to think of planetary "orbits." These orbits are ellipses with two foci and the Sun is the common focus of all these orbits. We consider now the entire solar system to be an integrated field of forces. It is a cosmic organism; and the planets' orbits define several *functional regions* within this organism.

According to such a concept a moving planet represents an agency dynamizing or focusing by its motion the energies of a particular region of the solar field. Thus, Mercury is the space which surrounds the Sun up to the abstract dividing line marked by Mercury's orbit. Venus is the space that extends beyond Mercury's orbit and up to the boundaries indicated by Venus's orbit, etc. The planet's position at every moment of time indicates a *point of focused release of energy*. Every point of space is filled *with potential energy;* but this energy becomes actualized in the solar system through the planet's motion. The constantly changing relationship between these planets' motion produces, as it were, a dynamic picture formed by activity-centers. Where the planet is, a "lighted point" appears; and these lighted points form indeed a pattern, a form of light.

We have a similar situation in a T.V. screen which is composed of a multitude of points potentially susceptible of becoming lighted by the electric current. It is the lighted points which in their togetherness produce the picture seen on the screen. This T.V. picture changes at every moment, and so does in a much simpler way, the overall *pattern of activity* of the solar system. Each planet acting as a focusing channel for the release of a specific type of energies, or a *quality of being* which is related to the space of its entire orbit.

Of course, this space constantly changes, for the whole solar system is moving at high speed around the core of the galaxy; therefore, the planetary orbits actually extend into spiral-forms, but their relationship to and distance from the Sun does not vary and this is what matters. Each organic system in the universe follows very complex motions because it is a part of a series of greater systems, each of which also presumably revolves around some center; yet the various components of even the smallest system retain a basic structure of interrelationship. It is such basic structures that astrology seeks to understand; and it tries to understand not only *how* the structure works, but the *meaning* of this structure and of all that it relates together and organically integrates.

Before I conclude these general but basic observations, it seems important to return to the positions of the planetary nodes already listed in order to consider more attentively the fact that the nodes of all the eight planets are bunched around the summer and winter solstices. Mercury's north node is located today at close to 18° Taurus and that of Neptune at about Leo 11°23' — thus all north nodes are found within less than a square (90°), and so, of course, are the south nodes. The mid-point of the north nodes group is the last degree of Gemini, which interestingly enough is the location of the great star Betelgeuze in Orion; and I have often stated my belief that this star has a special relationship to the "Aquarian Age" which will start, according to my calculations, at about the time Betelgeuze will reach longitude 90°, that is, the summer solstice point in the tropical zodiac (cf. my book BIRTH PATTERNS FOR A NEW HUMANITY: A Study of Astrological Cycles Structuring the Present World Crisis — 1968).

It is difficult to be sure what such a bunching of planetary nodes means, but it must be significant because it is not a constant factor. Mercury's nodes move a little faster than Neptune's, and in about four centuries the nodes of Mercury and Mars will be conjunct in mid-Gemini, and also in conjunction with Uranus' nodes. Then the group will extend between the nodes of Uranus and Neptune. In about eight or nine centuries Neptune's north node will reach Libra 0°, the fall equinox point — and therefore its south node will be at the spring equinox point.

Orbital Astrology and the Nodes

But let us consider what the situation is now. The summer solstice is a symbol of consciously individualized and stabilized power; Cancer refers to personal integration within a limited field of operation — a personality, a home. However, we must not forget that, at the summer solstice, while the Sun is entering the section of the Earth's orbit which we call Cancer, the planet Earth itself is at the opposite point, entering the sign Capricorn. These solstitial points of the Earth's orbit are particularly interesting for the reason which we shall now explain.

An ellipse has two foci; whereas a circle has only one center. All planetary orbits have one common focus, where the Sun is located; this is the great symbol of the life-force and of light. But the planetary orbits have also what I have called their "individualizing focus." This is the symbol of the *particular* function and individual "quality of being," which the whole planetary orbit symbolizes. A planet is closest to its individualizing focus when it is farthest from the Sun, thus at its "aphelion." For the Earth this point is close to the summer solstice point, when the Sun enters the zodiacal sign, Cancer and the Earth is entering the sign Capricorn.

In other words, our planet, in its orbital revolution, is closest to its individual focus when it is in the section of its orbit (the tropical zodiac) in which the south nodes of the planets are now gathered. As we shall presently see, the south node can be likened to the negative pole of an electrical system. It is a point of release, but what is released can be waste-materials, or at least the results of a highly particularized and individualized activity. At its south node the characteristic quality of a planet is almost forcibly thrown upon the Earth, while at its north node there is a much more positive and anabolic cooperation between the planet and the Earth.

The result of the present nodal gathering may therefore be related to the intense process of individualization which has gone on within mankind, and to man's specialization and stressful interest in "multiplicity" rather than in "unity" — in the *many* planets and their separate function rather than in *the one* Sun, source of light and undifferentiated power. The polarization should be particularly strong each year near the summer solstice when the Sun passes over the planetary north nodes, and the Earth over the planetary south nodes — at the very time our planet is close to the individualizing focus of its orbit. The presence of Betelgeuze then in conjunction with the Sun may tip the scales in favor of the Sun-force, and mankind may indeed move into an age illumined by a "unitive" type of consciousness.

19

The Latitude Cycle

This cylce of planetary or lunar motion in latitude is similar to the yearly cycle of apparent motion of the Sun in "declination" (i.e., north and south of the plane of the Earth's *equator*). For six months (winter and spring) the Sun "moves northward," and sunrises and sunsets take place increasingly to the north of their position at Christmas time. The Sun's northward crossing of the equatorial plane (i.e., Spring equinox) corresponds to the north nodes of the planets and of the Moon. At the summer solstice (Cancer 0°) the Sun has is maximum north declination, and this is the point of maximum solar power and consciousness — corresponding to the planets' points of maximum north latitude. After that, the Sun begins to move southward in declination and the points of sunsets also gradually move to the south in the western horizon; until the Sun reaches declination 0° and crosses the equatorial plane in a southward direction. This is the Fall equinox, seed-time — which corresponds to the south node of the planets.

The analogy between the yearly cycle in declination of the Sun and the nodal cycles in latitude of the planets is, however, not to be taken too literally, in terms of the meanings of the cycles, because different factors are involved; yet it is quite revealing in that, in both cases, we deal with two hemicycles of motion, one northward and the other southward. In the case of the solar cycle, moving northward means reaching toward the pole of the *earth-globe*; while where the nodal cycles of planets are considered the north pole is the pole of the *ecliptic*. These two poles are separated by an arc of over twenty-three degrees and have distinct characteristics in astrological symbolism, yet both have the basic meaning of the symbol of "North." And North refers to spiritual power while South represents intensity of biological experiences and emotional behavior. At least, this is what these directons have meant for millennia in the northern hemisphere of the globe; and the reasons for such meanings are varied.

The question is, of course, whether, if very original and autonomous civilizations should develop in the southern hemisphere, the symbolism will not be reversed, just as the seasons of the year are reversed. Such a reversal would seem logical, but it is also possible to believe that the poles are periodically reversed — perhaps at the close of some large cycle — and that great cultures are always born in the northern hemisphere. If Brazil were to be the seat of a new civilization it might be only after such a reversal of the poles, or at least a complete change in the electro-magnetic polarities of the Earth-field. There may once have been a great continent where the Southern Pacific ocean is now found, and Australia and Indonesia may be remnants of it; but it was perhaps directly under what then was the north pole.

The north pole, wherever located, would thus always be the *place of intake* of spiritual-cosmic power; the south pole, a place of *release*. But release of what? It can be of two basically different types of substances. The cycle of yearly plants will provide us with at least a symbolical analogy; for while in springtime we witness a mysterious surge of life under the warming rays of the sun — as if the Earth had been absorbing and assimilating new energy — when the Fall equinox arrives, we are facing the disintegration of the vegetation and the fall of the leaves to the soil dampened by autumnal rains (at least in our mostly temperate climates). But it is not *only* disintegration! The leaves fall, but so do the seed; and the seed does not decay. It carries within it tough outside covering the promise of renascent life.

As already stated, the nodes in the cycle of latitude — whether of the planets or of the Moon — correspond to the equinoxes in the solar cycle of declination. Astrologers today begin the "natural year" at the spring equinox, and what occurs then is said to affect the succeeding twelve months period. The same type of reasoning provides the north node of a planet with part of its basic meaning, in that what happens when the planet is at its north node tends to characterize the entire period of the latitude cycle of the planet. But the basic difference is that in the solar year cycle we deal with the relationship between the Sun and *the globe* of the Earth, while in a nodal cycle we deal with the relationship between a planet — always including the Moon — and *the orbit* of the Earth; and the orbit itself is an expression of the relationship between the Earth-globe and the Sun.

One of the most significant ways of thinking of the nodes is to consider them as two "gates." When a planet is at its north node, its essential function and quality in the solar system is focused upon our Earth-space which is then most able to absorb and assimilate it. When the planet is at its south node what is released as "substantial" factors are the results of the relationship between the characteristic nature of the planet and whatever in the Earth-space has absorbed its power. If the relationship has been positive, then what has been absorbed has also been "assimilated" and integrated to the Earth-consciousness and has produced a new "seed," i.e., new experiences and values. If the relationship has proven negative, what is being released or exteriorized are disintegrating materials, or negative existential results.

As to the moments when the planet reaches the points of maximum latitude, these represent turning points or moments of inner decision.

As an illustration of this cyclic process, the

latitude cycle of Uranus, which is particularly significant for the United States, should prove quite revealing.

In July, 1861, Uranus was crossing the ecliptic northward, thus at its north node and with latitude 0°. This was early in the Civil War and probably very near the time of the Union's defeat at Bull Run. Uranus reached its point of maximum latitude north in March, 1883 (latitude north 0°49), and crossed the ecliptic southward in February, 1901. The point of maximum latitude south was touched during September, 1922; and the cycle ended on July 20, 1945, a few days after the atomic bomb explosion in New Mexico. The four "critical" years (or phases) of the cycle were thus: 1861, 1883, 1900-01, 1923 — and again 1945.

The sixties of last century, if the pattern is significant, should have been a period of "intake" of Uranian energies — and so should have been, an entire cycle before, the years following 1777; and at this present time, the years following 1945. The historical record is fairly clear on these points; except of course, that some people might wish, on purely historical grounds, to choose other dates as the most significant in this connection! Nevertheless, Uranus is the symbol of the *transforming function* in man and in society. Wherever some basic metamorphosis takes place, there we must consider Uranus essentially at work — even though a complete process of metamorphosis (social or personal) requires also the activity of the functions represented by Neptune and Pluto.

Surely basic world-transformations occurred during the periods 1776 to 1789 (American and French Revolutions, U.S. Constitution, the discovery of Uranus, etc.) and 1860 to 1870 (Civil War, Abolition of Slavery, Franco-German War and the world-ascendancy of U.S.A., imperial Germany and Japan, the Proclamation of Baha-'u'llah beginning the first religious movement for a federal World-Order, etc.) Lastly, since the revelation of the possibility of use of atomic power for either destruction or complete economic world-transformation, we find humanity facing an even more momentous opportunity for Uranian metamorphosis.

As in the case of the solar year, the increase of the power of the solar rays is being felt some weeks before the spring equinox, so, in the case of all nodal or latitude cycles, an increase in the radiation of the planet's characteristic attributes is felt gradually as this planet approaches latitude 0° and its "northward crossing" of the ecliptic. Uranus had maximum south latitude in 1839-49, and from then on the planet's revolutionary power transformed utterly our Western Society and all that this Society touched. The momentum of the Industrial Revolution was most definite around 1840; but it reached only its most concrete effects in the sixties. The post-Civil-War era, with its transcontinental routes firmly established and the spread of large business corporations, marked the definite building-up of the United States as a great power. Likewise, in the religious field, the Bahai Movement began in 1844 with the Revelation of the first Persian Prophet, the Bab; but it took form as a potential worldwide structure only after Baha'u'llah's Declaration in 1863, and when this latter Prophet established the fundamental principles of a truly World-Order on a religious basis. In the field of political communism, Marx's Manifesto appeared in 1848; but the "Bible" of modern communism which made world-history in half of the inhabited globe was published in 1867, and the first Communist Revolution occurred in France in 1871, the "Commune." In the field of science, German materialism and statism developed in the forties, but Darwinism gained power in the sixties, and together with it, the whole approach to biology and medicine symbolized by Pasteur.

Of course, the influence of Neptune has to be added to that of Uranus in analyzing the Victorian Era. Neptune was at its south node in 1839, and reached its north node in June-July 1920, at the time of the formation of the League of Nations — its maximum latitude south (1°51') having been reached presumably in the fall of 1877 (Neptune in Taurus). It must have had maximum latitude north at the very close of the 18th century (beginning of the Napoleonic Era). Romanticism and the spread of German music, the socialism and humanitarianism of the eighteen-forties, American Spiritualism, the use of anaesthetics and, in industry, of oil, also large-scale nationalism and imperialism — these and other factors typical of the Victorian Era can be related to the Neptunian function releasing both its *spiritual seeds* and its negative glamor around its southward crossing the ecliptic. Finally, the more positive in-taking of Neptunian power began during the last decades of the 19th century and the new approach toward world-federalism and a global society grew in significance, culminating in the Wilsonian ideal of 1919-1920, and the victory of sea-controlling and oil-rich nations, with Neptune at its north node.

While the Victorian Era can thus be said to be characterized — in a very broad sense and according to our present point of view — by a combination of Neptune-south-node and Uranus-north-node "influences," the first half of the 20th century can be seen highlighted by a combination of Neptune-north-node and Pluto-north-node energies, developing during the passage of Uranus through its south latitude hemicycle (1901-1945) — i.e., the period between the announcement of the Quantum Theory (and, soon after, of Einstein's formula) and the final concrete demonstration of atomic power. The second half of our century, on the other hand, begins with and will be overshadowed by the north node position of Uranus (July 1945). Pluto was at its north node in September 1930, beginning its cycle just after its discovery by human eyes and minds. Its preceding cycle had begun around the winter 1682, with the south-node-crossing in 1770 and the point of maximum south latitude (17°28') in the fall 1840.

We took the relatively large periods of these three planets to illustrate the general pattern of

The Latitude Cycle

the latitude cycle but the rhythm of intake and release of the more rapidly moving planets is just as significant, provided one is able to isolate clearly the basic life-function to which each planet refers, and provided one does not mix planes of significance in the interpretation. The cyclic pattern gives also valid indication in the field of lunar activity, and provides means of dividing the lunar "month" from north node to north node. This *nodal month* is slightly shorter than the sidereal month (successive conjunctions with a fixed star), for during the latter period of 27,322 days the nodes have regressed nearly 1½ degrees. It would seem logical to consider this period from north node to north node as that to which the "lunar mansions" should be referred, as Charles Jayne also once suggested; for this nodal month refers to the motion of the Moon on her own orbital plane, and thus should be said to represent the field of purely lunar activity — the field of the Moon-function.

The Moon's maximum of latitude north or south are 5°17', and they are reached when the Moon's positions in the zodiac are at 90° angle to the nodal axis. At these points the lunar function operates with a *minimum* degree of focalization in earth-nature and in all bio-psychic organisms. The Moon is as far withdrawn from the Earth as she can be; yet, at the same time, she is most active *in her own sphere*. What happens in that sphere during these moments of maximum latitude becomes focused and exteriorized during the days when the Moon, every month, is conjunct her nodes. These are therefore days during which all that the Moon represents in the fields of man's organic psychological and social activity is brought to focus in man's consciousness.

Because the Moon's orbit surrounds closely the Earth-globe it has been said to be like a womb enfolding the life-sphere of our planet. It is therefore the symbol of the Mother principle — first at the biological level, but also at the psychological and social levels — because it is the mother who surrounds the helpless infant with care, and sees to it that he is able to meet successfully the varied and ever-recurrent needs or problems of everyday life. In time, however, the child should develop his own faculty of adaptation to his total environment, and therefore the Moon in astrology stands for whatever refers to such a faculty in its many aspects — biological, emotional and mental.

Generally speaking, any person with a natal Moon near her nodes is likely to be strongly influenced by his or her mother, or by a substitute "Mother Image." A state of dependence upon the "Mother" (in whatever form or condition) tends to be established when the Moon is near the north node; also a tendency to *repudiate* the mother and her influence should be strong with the natal Moon at the south node. But a south node Moon may refer even more to a transformation of the actual mother-relationship into a transcendent psychic Image (which may lead to religious or inspirational experiences), or to a powerful yearning for being an actual mother and for exercising maternal authority over physical or intellectual children.

The results of both these nodal positions of the Moon can be either constructive (toward sanity) or destructive (toward insanity). A strong reliance upon the mother may be transformed, as the personality matures, into a valuable emphasis upon the ability to adjust to circumstances by means of a strongly developed capacity to "feel one's way" through life. This can mean sheer opportunism and behavior dictated by pure convenience, but also diplomacy and tact, the power of sympathy for and of understanding of other people and as a result the ability to give psychological help as well as to move adroitly through a disordered society. But if the personality cannot overcome the most obvious and instinctual or psychic types of attachment to the actual mother (largely, in most cases, because of this mother's attitude), then a condition of personal maturity may never be reached. On the other hand, a natal Moon conjunct the south node can mean a negative kind of "mother complex" based on a mixture of inner bondage and strong resentment, or a deep, innate and instinctive ability to act positively as a "mother" in various kinds of relationships — to adjust situations and problems for others.

When, in a chart, the Moon is in square to her nodal axis (maximum of latitude north or south) the tendency is for the mother-function, or the capacity to adjust to everyday life, to operate in a somewhat remote and subjective, rather than efficacious and objective, manner. Finally, the distinction between a natal Moon with north latitude (i.e., between the north node and the south node, in the normal order of zodiacal signs) and one with south latitude, can be of very real meaning astro-psychological analysis — just as it is important to know whether a person is born during the spring-summer, or during the fall-winter periods of the year.

When the Moon has north latitude one should be able to discover an underlying tendency toward paying great attention to a successful adjustment to the environment; and this can mean at the social level ambition, the strong desire to control the environment, and perhaps a yearning for personal fame or at least prestige. The individual makes an issue of his personal position.

On the other hand, when the Moon has south latitude one's attitude toward the environment, especially at the psychological and social levels, is not as much a personal issue. It is taken for granted in terms of some already established collective experience. There is a deep reliance upon a power within or without, which has, in a sense, already decided the issue.

These are subtle matters, but they may become clearer by the fact that President Johnson had the Moon in north latitude, while General Charles de Gaulle had it in south latitude, the former has shown an intensely personal and ambitious approach to his society, the latter always felt himself only the agent for a national superpersonal purpose, i.e., as acting in terms of ancestral Images. Lenin and Bismarck were also Moon in south latitude types, while Stalin, Khrushshev and Hitler were Moon in north latitude types. The great yogis and carriers of the ancient traditions of India, Ramakrishna, Vivekananda and Aurobindo had their natal Moon's in south latitude.

The distincton between the two types of lunar positions at birth should not be unduly stressed, and many other factors may radically affect the situation, but I believe that this latitude factor is worth taking in consideration. It is especially significant when the Moon's nodal axis, and the nodal axis of the larger planets are identical with the natal horizon or meridian — as we shall presently see.

20

The Moon's Nodes in a Birth-Chart

The nodal axis relating the plane of the Moon's orbit to that of the Earth has been symbolized as a Dragon. The north node was called Dragon's head; the south node, Dragon's tail. The reason for such a symbolism had presumably to do with the fact that eclipses occur when New Moons and Full Moons occur near the lunar nodes. The celestial Dragon was thought to swallow the eclipsed body. There are, however deeper meanings to the allegory, meanings referring to the undulating motion of life-energies, particularly the of late much publicized Kundalini power, but also to the relative function of the two nodes. The north node, I repeat, is the point of *intake;* the south node, the point of *release or evacuation.* In animal organisms the biological functions can be shown to operate alongside of an alimentary tube; food is absorbed at one end, waste products excreted at the other end — "north" and "south."

This is the process called "metabolism." If food is not properly metabolized — and symbolically this would refer to the passage of the Moon in north latitude, from north to south node — then there may be problems of evacuation. As a result, traditional astrology has thought of the north node as a positive factor implying personal effort (the act of chewing food) but also Providential help; the south node as a symbol of behavior leading to automatism and/or "self-undoing."

What apparently has not been realized is that the region including the south end of this process in animal organisms is also that in which the *release of seed* takes place. Such a release is also, in a sense, spontaneously instinctive and nearly automatic: the sperm and ovum are periodically ejected from the male and female organisms and often this release of seed cause many problems and is related to a great deal of self-undoing; but not necessarily so. The release of seed-material may never produce procreative results; unfecundated ova are periodically rejected by the female organism, and the menstruation process may cause discomfort or even severe cramps. One could even say that the sexual orgasm is a release of accumulated and unusable nervous energy; but according to all occult and esoteric traditions, this energy can be "sublimated" and used to build a "spiritual body" — or it may be re-channeled into mental and creative (instead of procreative) developments.

The French composer, Saint-Saens, was fond of saying: "I compose just like an apple tree produces apples." The true creative artist releases almost automatically art products which his psycho-mental organism produces spontaneously and of which, in a sense, he has to get rid. He acts in relation to his culture, or to a special group of individuals constituting his potential public, as a male fecundating a female. And in peaceful times in an open society this creative fecundation should be harmonious and fulfilling, without frustration or undue excitement. It should be performed as a ritual.

From the preceding it should be clear that the nodes' meaning can be applied at *all* levels of a human life. The *north* node refers to whatever builds the personality, bringing to it new material. This material should not only be absorbed, but metabolized — and this refers to reading books and absorbing new ideas as well as to the intake of anything which can become assimilated by the consciousness of the individual person. The *south* node refers to any material whatsoever (physical, emotional-psychic, mental) which the organism no longer needs, whether it be that the substance cannot be used and is in a decaying or poisonous condition, or that it is the positive and creative expression of the natural function of the body-mind organism.

The absolutely basic fact which no astrologer should ever forget is that the nodes are the two ends of an axis; one end cannot be understood without the other. Marc Jones has spoken of the nodal line as the "axis of fate." It refers to two basic approaches to existence, both of which should be included in the harmonious life of man. Yet the position of the north node in a natal house and zodiacal sign essentially indicates where the *positive focus of conscious existence* should be established, i.e., where the "will" should find its field of most constructive action. Normally it is the field in which, through intense exertion, maximum spiritual returns to the person as an individual self can be expected.

However, because the south node should not be thought of always or entirely as a negative factor, the house and sign in which it is located are not at all necessarily fields of "self-undoing"; or else one has to realize that what is meant most significantly by "sacrifice" represent, in a sense an "undoing" of the individual person. At the south node one does not *build* personality; one may *expand* it, releasing its contents in full dedication to a community and an ideal. There are many ways of speaking of sacrifice, some quite meaningless, even actually egocentric or masochistic. But the true meaning of sacrifice is "making sacred"; and this implies a complete dedication of one's thoughts and actions to what one may call either God or mankind — or to a specific group, culture or ideal. This means a surrender of the ego-will.

In the deepest sense of the term, "destiny" may be accomplished symbolically where the south node is placed in one's birth-chart. Something greater than oneself may be fulfilled there — one's basic function in society or in the universe. And such a fulfillment may indeed mean relatively at least, paying little attention to the building and harmonious development of one's individual personality. "Individuality" and "destiny" can indeed be considered, at least in many instances, as polar opposites, if by destiny is meant one's essential relationship to what is greater than your personal self.

The position of the north node in a particular zodiacal sign will show which basic type or mode of life-energy can be most fruitfully used in building one's personality — what kind of "food" at any level is most conducive to personal growth *provided* this food is chewed well and absorbed with a conscious effort at utilizing only what is needed and can be wholesomely assimilated.

The position of the south node in a zodiacal sign above all warns you of the danger inherent in using indiscriminately and automatically (or under the pressure of an unconscious complex) *the negative implication of the sign.*

For instance, in the preceding essay we find that both Nietzsche and Sri Aurobindo have their lunar north node in Gemini, and therefore the south node in Sagittarius. In order to fulfill their personal work they had to absorb a great deal of Gemini-type of mental substance — in German and in English schools. But their destinies were to pour upon mankind ideas and visions filled with a metaphysical and prophetic Sagittarian spirit. In many ways both went to extremes in presenting their views, and their works radiated a power which drew many people into definite groups of followers. Unfortunately for Nietzsche the closeness of his natal Moon to its south node produced in him a definite anima-complex (to use Carl Jung's term), and other factors, like the squaring of the nodes and the Moon by Venus, and his several oppositions, presented problems of integration which finally tore him apart.

In President Franklin D. Roosevelt's chart the nodal situation is reversed, with the north node in Sagittarius and presumably close to the natal meridian. President Kennedy had a Capricorn north node, but also not far from the meridian and in his third House. Their south nodes near the Mid Heaven may be seen as an indication of "sacrifice" to a public destiny. In both cases the Moon had also south latitude.

It seems to me, however, that the position of the lunar nodes — and especially of the planetary nodes — in the Houses is usually more significant than their positions in the zodiacal signs. It may be because the Houses are to be considered definitely in terms of *axes* (i.e., Ascendant-Descendant, Zenith-Nadir) even more so than the signs. It may be mainly because the Houses represent basic *fields of experiences,* and that it is in terms of concrete life-experiences that the operation of the north-south nodes polarity is most recognizable.

The House in which the Moon's *north* node is located at birth usually represents the type of experiences involving the greatest amount of personal exertion, but also normally producing the most valuable results in terms of the person's capacity to adjust to his environment and the challenges it poses.

The House in which the *south* node is placed refers to a type of experience which one can easily take for granted; that is, one tends to allow the experiences to control the consciousness, instead of the conscious mind controlling the experiences. One is naturally good at meeting such experiences and therefore they represent the line of least resistance and thus of least exertion. Because of this, one tends to repeat and indulge in them. Yet in some instances these experiences may refer to a gift or faculty acquired in "past lives" (or genetically inherited from one's parents), and this may be the field in which one can express some sort of "genius." It may be also the place in which one will be called upon to "sacrifice" one's deeply cherished ego and emerge as a "representative man," a symbol of some notable achievement to one's community or to mankind as a whole.

The following is an attempt to indicate briefly the general trend associated in most instances with the position of the nodal axis in the natal Houses. It should be clear that these are only general indications and that the factors in a personal life which the Moon's node may reveal are most of the time not obvious — for the same reason that a man displaying blatant aggressiveness may do so in order to compensate for a deep-seated sense of inferiority, the typical case being that of Benito Mussolini.

Moon's north node in the First House:
The important thing for the individual is to learn from experiences in which he takes a personal stand. This may lead in some cases to a tendency to showmanship, but also to originality. As the result of such an approach to circumstances,

some valuable results may be gained in terms of partnership, marriage or any intimate association (south node in the seventh House). The danger is to indulge in all kinds of relationships and become so involved that the self becomes the slave of a yearning for losing oneself in others. A good example is the chart of Franz Liszt, the prototype of the great virtuoso who, though wasting far too much energy in the by-products of fame and adulation, nevertheless, through the sheer power of his personality, transformed the social position of the artist in nineteenth century Europe.

Moon's north node in the Second House:

The Second House is not only the realm of "money and possessions" but it refers to inherited tendencies, physical abilities and mental faculties — the first possessions of the incarnating self. The basic issue for the individual is how to manage what he owns, i.e., the proper use of his powers. If he does so successfully he will receive good rewards from partnerships (south node in eighth House). Yet he may bank too much on interpersonal or group relationships, and find these deceiving. He should stress his own tradition and background, rather than trust others too implicitly. Example: General, and especially President, Dwight D. Eisenhower. Also apparently Mary Baker Eddy, founder of Christian Science (eighth House south node?).

Moon's north node in the Third House:

The strength of the personal life and the development of a solid foundation in the world will depend mainly on a keen ability to think concretely and evaluate whole situations — and also on the capacity to formulate clearly principles of action and methods of establishing relationships between facts. The line of least resistance, however, may be a tendency to escape into vast ninth House concepts and theories, or to follow metaphysical, religious or social ideologies. The lure of the mystical or exotic should be balanced by a keen intellectual grasp of what is actually involved in the great flights of the imagination. Yet such a person may find it his destiny to be a leader in such ninth-House fields, from philosophy and religion to social-political concerns. The Presidents Franklin D. Roosevelt and Kennedy had third House north nodes; also, the great philosopher-occultist-educator-artist Rudolph Steiner.

Moon's north node in the Fourth House:

The building of a deep foundation for the personal life is the essential task, unless a strong drive for a public and professional life results from a compulsion of destiny. We see such a drive operating in the case of Richard Wagner, whose personality was neither too pleasant or harmonious, yet whose great creative gifts used as a foundation the ancestral images and myths of his culture. He drew everything and everyone to him as "food," which he then released as great music and dramatic concepts. The Hindu mystic, Ramakrishna, had this same north node position, with an also extremely full first House.

Moon's north node in the Fifth House:

The need for self-expression and creative emotional intensity — or for a progeny to project oneself into — is basic as a means to develop one's personality. If constructively satisfied it should lead to a social-cultural fruition, to friends and an easy participation in group-activity. But the south node in the eleventh House may indicate a trend toward mere dreams or escapism in utopian ideals. The dream should be integrated with an effectual work in terms of education, creative art-works or various forms of leadership. Personal frustration in emotional self-expression could produce unwholesome reactions in the eleventh House field, particularly with regards to friendships and social interplay. As example, I might give the intensely creative French poet, Victor Hugo, who also espoused a social-political Cause in his opposition to the Third Empire. He also lived an intensely emotional life.

Moon's north node in the Sixth House:

Hard work, the mastery of technique, the experiences related to personal crises or illness, and perhaps devotion to an embodied spiritual Teacher should bring great rewards, if the will and endurance are adequate. Compulsive introspection and too much passivity to the influence of social-religious institutions or collective moods may be a line of least resistance (twelfth House south node). Yet the pull toward an inner life of meditation, or a fateful involvement in social Causes may produce great results if the "Soul" is ready for these things, or if a heavy Karma has to be fulfilled. The great Persian prophets, founders of the Bahai Movement, the Bab and Baha'u'llah, had their north nodes at the end of the sixth House. Their followers consider them Divine Manifestations; one may think of them as "sacrifices" to mankind. The martyred Bab had a conjunction of Saturn and Pluto in the sixth House in square to a conjunction of Uranus and Neptune (October 20, 1819).

Moon's north node in the Seventh House:

This House refers to those experiences which a person obtains through close relationships with other persons — relationships which, theoretically at least, carry the seed-potentiality of participation in a community, or in some kind of larger whole to which the related individuals feel they belong. The House does not merely deal with close contacts between two isolated individuals, even if the relationship were to be permanent What makes the relationship a seventh House matter is the fact that it occurs within, and in function of a particular society and culture to which the relationship will bring a certain kind of fruition. This is what marriage or business partnership means. In the seventh House the individual realizes, *through* his relationship with another person, his most basic possibility of fulfilling a definite place and function within his society — or, in a still broader sense, within the whole planet, Earth, and the universe. The challenge which such a realization implies can be difficult; it may lead to the "death" of the individual ego, in the eighth House. The north node in the seventh House reveals the basic importance of interpersonal relationships to the individual person. He may have to work hard at *assimilating* in his consciousness the lessons of relationship. He may escape into a negative kind of first House south node experience; or he may become a personalized manifestation of love. A typical example is the chart of the Romantic French poet, Alfred de Musset, whose loves were tumultuous and led him to heavy drinking. As a contemporary case we may mention James Roosevelt, eldest son of F.D.R.

Moon's north node in the Eighth House:

In this House, the partners discover what is available to them in giving concrete substance to the partnership and how they have to manage their affairs and individual possessions. This is the House of business, as all business is based on transactions; but it refers also to personal experiences which result from the interactions between the partners — and this may mean the experience of surrendering one's dear ego to the larger unit. It is also the House of occultism and ceremonial magic, in the sense that these areas of experience deal with the results of group activity and of relationship to invisible entities. A second House south node may lead to financial difficulties or scandals, but also theoretically to great wealth in the case of individuals able to use relatively hidden forces. The well-known occultist, Cheiro, who became famous by his studies of the hands of kings and aristocrats, and by his various predictions, had the north node in his natal eighth House. Albert Einstein's north node was also there in early Aquarius. His formulas certainly dealt with hidden forces.

Moon's north node in the Ninth House:

Men with the north node in this House should be driven to expand, whether physical through travel or foreign adventures, or mentally and spiritually. They may tend to absorb and assimilate what is beyond man's normal reach. This can mean imperialism — and as examples, we have Hitler and the international banker J.P. Morgan, the elder. The leader of the Chinese revolution, Sun Yat Sen, Mahatma Gandhi, who did so much to liberate India through a spiritually-oriented crusade, and General Marshall (of the Marshall Plan after World War II) are other examples. The south node in the third House may refer to the negative effect of the great adventures to the close environment, but also to a remarkable capacity for planning strategy.

Moon's north node in the Tenth House:

This position may be found in the charts of powerful or ambitious men who gained and sustained social and political power through great exertion. We can give as examples Marshall Tito of Yugoslavia, and in the cultural world, Arnold Schoenberg who gained fame after many years of struggle. The balance between a public and a private life is all-important; the more successful the former, the more empty or disturbing the latter may be in some instances. Much depends on the situation affecting the first and seventh Houses, for what takes place at the Mid Heaven is basically the result of the possibilities revealed by the Ascendant. These possibilities come positively or negatively to a head in the tenth House.

Moon's north node in the Eleventh House:

Astrological tradition speaks of this House as that of hopes and wishes, and of friends; but it deals more basically with the result of the public life and professional experiences. If the latter are normally successful they may lead to satisfying friendships and the fulfillments of hopes; but they may also drive a man to want to change or at least improve "the system." It may mean hard north-node work, but also Providential help if the time for change has come. This nodal position is characteristically found in Pope John XXIII's chart, with the Sun at the cusp of the House; also in Swami Vivekananda's chart — two powerful and significant charts. In some cases the fifth House south node may produce involvement in personal emotional desires and even in gambling.

Moon's north node in the Twelfth House:

While the sixth House refers especially to personal crises of readjustment or reorientation, the twelfth House indicates a type of experience which are related either to social and institutional issues in time of transition or crises, or else to the pressure exerted upon the individual by past Karma and a desire for transcendence and rebirth. This may lead to introversion and the sixth House south node to illness or over-concern with health. The millionaire Howard Huges is an instance of the recluse spirit, but also of the ability to make huge profits from social crises. The mystic composer, Skryabin, had also such a nodal position, dying young of cancer.

A special importance should be attributed to situations in which the nodal axis is identical in longitude with either the natal horizon or the meridian, and especially the former. Then the basic structure of the individual selfhood is affected by the nodes. The situation is different from the one is which the Moon would be found just rising or culminating at the Mid Heaven. The lunar influence in the first case is more profound and more instinctive, because what is symbolically acting upon the person is the *lunar orbit* instead of the Moon *as a planetary body*.

When we consider the Moon, or in general any planet, as a celestial body in constant motion, we are dealing with a particular type of functional activity in only one of its many modes of expression; but the orbit of the Moon refers to the whole gamut of lunar characteristics, to the essential "lunarity" of the Moon factor. When we consider the relationship between the lunar orbit and the Earth orbit, we are dealing with the very structure of the Earth-Moon system; and this structure passes through a complete series of modifications in 18 years and seven months (the Moon's nodes cycle). The moments, every day, when the nodal axis is identical to the horizon and the meridian of a locality on the Earth have a special importance, because they focus the structural character of the Moon-Earth relationship, respectively, on the consciousness and identity (Ascendant factor) and the capacity for personal and public integration (meridian factor) of a human being born at that time. The effect may not be *superficially expressed* and as evident to the consciousness; but it is more profound, or one might say more "fateful" than what can be deduced from a rising or culminating Moon.

The same situation exists with reference to the nodes of the planets. If, for instance, the nodal axis of Uranus coincides with the natal horizon of a person, this person's life will be more deeply affected by the characteristic quality of Uranus than if the planet, Uranus, was rising. An individual with his natal horizon coinciding with the line of Uranus' nodes will in most cases be almost irresistibly impregnated with the cosmic, essential character of Uranian activity. He is, in a very real sense, fated to act as an agent of this impersonal Uranus power. He tends to be overshadowed by it. His very presence induces changes in those who relate to him. His destiny is to act as a tranforming, perhaps revolutionary, force in his environment; even though he may not want to do so, or is not really aware of the profound challenge he brings to others.

When astrologers claim that the *planet* Uranus should logically be rising in the U.S. national chart (Gemini 8° Ascendant), they forget, among many other things, that the chart with Sagittarius 13° has the Uranus line of nodes practically identical with its horizon. Uranus' south node is at the Ascendant and it is the *compulsion* to act in the world as a transforming agent (and what is more, a self-righteously Sagittarian agent) which characterizes the deepest aspect of the "American" prototype. In that chart the *planet* Uranus is where it should most logically be, i.e., in the sixth House — the House of labor and of health, and also of personal crises; for indeed America has utterly transformed the condition of work (assembly line and mass production) and of the workers. It has seen a mushrooming of new medical techniques, and a constant occupation with health, self-improvement and with psychological problems unknown in other countries. It has given to the national Services a rather different character, and produced such weapons as the atom bomb.

What has just been said of the Uranus nodes applies to the nodal axes of other planets; but it is more relevant in the cases of the more remote planets, Jupiter, Saturn, Uranus, Neptune and Pluto; for the planets close to the Earth show a great difference between the geocentric and the heliocentric positions of their nodes — and here I have only considered the heliocentric nodes. The closest planets deal with the more personal aspects of the human being, and their essential nature — i.e., the places they occupy in the solar system — is affected by the geocentric point of view just as a person's natural character is most of the time distorted by the pressures of their family and socio-cultural environment.

These "distortions" are very real, of course, from the existential point of view; they occupy the attention, and fill the bank accounts of psychiatrists, educators, and medical men. They refer to the "outer man" living in society under great pressures of which he may not even be aware and to the "ego" which controls normally the relationship of the individual to his society. But a time should come in man's evolution when he is able to identify himself not merely with conditions at one particular locality on the surface of the Earth-*globe,* but with the essential character and destiny of Man — a character and destiny symbolized by the entire *orbit* of the Earth.

This is what is really or "hiddenly" implied in statements to the effect that man is "the whole zodiac" because the zodiac IS the orbit of the Earth — and thus the sum-total of the possible modes of relationship of his organism to the source of all life, the Sun. Man as the zodiac relates himself to the planets of the solar system in a new way — an "orbital" way, a structural, cosmic way. Then the planetary nodes assume their full meaning; and so also the Moon's nodes, for the Moon, as it revolves around the Earth, plays a most significant role in relating what is *outside* the Earth's orbit to what is inside of it.

21

The Moon's Nodes Cycle

The axis of the Moon's nodes has a retrograde motion in the zodiac; and retrograde motion, in geocentric astrology, means motion in a direction opposite to that which the Sun and the Moon always follow. As these two "Lights" symbolize essentially, in terms of any earthly organism, the bi-polar life-force, a retrograde motion is one that takes place in counterpoint to the life-force. In times when the worship of this life-force (cults of fertility, sex-oriented rituals, etc.) was the basic factor in tribal religions and agricultural societies, retrograde motion was usually given a more or less negative meaning. Today the situation is quite different. Any type of retrograde motion is seen rather to indicate an *inward directed* process. It is linked therefore to introversion. Such processes run against direct and spontaneous self-exteriorization in outward directed activity, but this certainly does not mean that they should be given a negative value in terms of the over-all development of an individual person.

These remarks apply especially to the retrograde phase of the planets' cycle.* — a phase resulting from the combination of the motions of the planets and the Earth as celestial bodies. Thus the time when Mercury is retrograde may not be the best time to start some definitely outward directed project; but it is during such a period that the mind of the individual may be able to separate itself from its natural or original bio-psychic subjection to the demands of life's survival and expansion, and thus to gain greater objectivity and independence from instinctual drives and gland-controlled emotions. The retrograde period of Venus may also be an excellent time to regrasp and revalue the meaning of past emotional experiences or cultural achievements; and that of Mars, a time to reexamine and reassess one's characteristic type of behavior and motives for action.

In the case of the Moon's nodes, however, we do not deal with the combined motions of celestial bodies but with the relationship between two orbits. What happens is that the plane of the Moon's orbit has a sliding ''backward'' motion with reference to the plane of the Earth's orbit, the zodiac. This motion is continuous; the Moon's nodes never go ''forward'' in longitude. This fact can be related to the symbolical character of the Moon, for actually the Moon function of adaptation to everyday life is one that is based on

---

* What is called "converse progressions" in astrology — i.e., going backward in the ephemeris from the date of birth, one day per year of the life — also refers to the fateful results of the past of the Soul, i.e., to basic "Karmic" occurrences.

past experiences, whether it be the past of the individual person or that of the human race. The Mother function itself is deeply rooted in the racial past and the unconsciousness of instincts. The contemporary trend, especially in America, to replace maternal instinctual behavior by a conscious type of book-knowledge — even if called "scientific" — is one of the tragic features of our actually disintegrating Western civilization.

The retrograde motion of the Moon's nodes, being an expression of the manner in which the essential character of the Moon affects the Earth-being, deals therefore fundamentally with the past — which does not mean that it has to be given a negative or pejorative meaning! In a collective sense, it can be said to deal with what, in occultism and among esoteric Brotherhoods, is meant by "the Tradition." All religions and esoteric movements are founded upon some kind of "original Revelation," upon the appearance among men of great Beings who incarnated as well as distributed spiritual-cosmic knowledge and taught basically sound disciplines or techniques of living. Progress for the confused and untrained person may thus mean, in a sense, a "return to Source." We still see this operating in the "Great Books" concept and the so-called "Humanities," which imply learning from the past of the race and the great moments of history and culture.

If this process today arouses very little enthusiasm, to say the least, among many youths, it is because they deeply feel that our entire Western civilization has brought mankind to an impending catastrophe and that therefore its past is of little or no value; they long for either a totally new creative divine outpouring, or for a still more remote past whose Great Tradition by far antedates the beginnings of Western civilization in Greece and the Near East some 2500 years ago.

Be that as it may, the symbolism of the retrograde motion of the Moon's nodes refers to a process by means of which an individual can not only recapitulate his past in search of the deepest meaning of its outer experiences, but perhaps also reach deeper sources of knowledge in terms of his relationship to the events and the basic needs of the time in which he lives. This process has a definite rhythm which stresses the numbers 19 and 9. The north node regresses by some 3 minutes in the zodiac every day; it returns to its natal place in 18.6 years, and the nodal axis is reversed — i.e., the north node reaches the place of the natal south node — in a little over 9 years.

This Moon nodes cycle is important in astronomy because it has a direct connection with the cyclic recurrence of solar and lunar eclipses. These eclipses occur when a New Moon or a Full Moon takes place in the vicinity of the zodiacal degrees occupied by the north and south nodes. These occurrences were carefully computed in Chaldea and two significant cycles were known. The *Metonic* cycle refers to the return of the New Moon to approximately the same zodiacal degree; some of these New Moons are solar eclipses, but not all. The *Saros* cycle lasts 18 years and 11 ⅓ days, and refers to the recurrence of an eclipse in relation to its actual visibility on the Earth's surface. This period contains 223 lunar months and includes 70 eclipses; 41 are solar, and 29 lunar. Every 18 years and 11 ⅓ days an eclipse belonging to a particular Saros series occurs, and it occurs (because of the ⅓ of a day, i.e., of the daily rotation of the Earth) 120 degrees of geographical longitude more to the West. Thus in three Saros cycles totalling 54 years one month and one day an eclipse occurs about the same *terrestrial* longitude, but *not zodiacal* longitude. However, if it is a solar eclipse, its track will be found several hundred miles farther north or south in terrestrial latitude.

From the archaic, strictly geocentric and vitalistic point of view, eclipses were obviously startling phenomena; and they still are spectacular when full, but they are important, astrologically speaking, mostly in terms of the lunation cycle. From the point of view of orbital astrology, they relate most significantly the Moon-factor not only to the Earth, but to the Sun, the main focus of the elliptical orbit of the Earth. If the Moon represents the "past," the Sun stands for the "present" — simply because it provides the power to exist as a living organism here and now. In a solar eclipse the past tends to obscure the present; in a lunar eclipse the present tends to obliterate the past. This need not be considered catastrophic, and most of what archaic or classical astrology states about eclipses should be dismissed, if only for psychological reasons, as the fear of an eclipse over one's natal Sun or important planets may be highly detrimental. Great success has come to men when a solar eclipse fell on their birthday; but this success sometimes is not permanent. Strongly karmic factors may be involved and a sudden eruption of what Carl Jung called "contents of the Collective Unconscious."

From the point of view of the Moon's nodes cycles, what is basic is the periodic motion of the nodal axis around the chart. This retrograde motion usually reveals moments of great individual significance when the nodes touch the two Lights or some planetary groupings, and come to coincide with the natal horizon and meridian. The 19 year period is indeed well worth studying and I can vouch for its importance in my own life as I approach the age of 76 (four times 19) while writing these pages. I suggest that everyone should study how it, and the 9 year cycle (often used by numerologists, particularly by the great pioneer Azo Neith Cochran), relates to important turning points or achievements in his or her life. In some cases the exact nodal returns, in others the more abstract and numerological 19-year cycle, turns out to be the most revealing.

As the nodal cycle has a *mean* 18.6 years value it refers to both the numbers 18 and 19; and interestingly enough in the Tarot symbolism, 18 is symbolized by a "weeping Moon" and 19 by a radiant Sun. The "New Age" calendar inaugurated by the Persian Avatar, the Bab, contains 19 months of 19 days each plus four or five intercalary and festival days just preceding the spring equinox.* The Bab had 18 disciples, himself representing the number 19; and it is interesting to compare this with the Christ-situation with Jesus and his twelve disciples. The zodiacal number 12 is a solar number; 19 refers to the soli-lunar cycle.

To give examples of how the Moon's nodes cycles refers to important turning points in an individual life is rather futile, as what is involved is often very personal and does not refer to outer events, though sometimes it clearly does *and we can see emerging* a definite rhythm or destiny. I shall only mention the case of President Truman who assumed his office under particularly critical circumstances after the death of Franklin D. Roosevelt.

Harry Truman was born on May 8, 1884 with the 17th degree of Libra rising, and the North Node at 21°48' of Libra. In this case the Nodal axis and the birth-horizon nearly coincide, which tends to show a life controlled by Fate or Destiny; that is, a life in which the *present* is directly a consequence of the *past* or against the *present* a life controlled by Karma — and let us not forget that there is a racial-national Karma as well as a personal one.

After Truman's birth, the North Node moved "backward" along the upper half of his natal chart — a half in which we find all planets except the Moon. This Moon, however, rules the whole

---

* The 19th month is a period of fasting. Each month carries such a name as Splendor, Glory, Beauty, Grandeur, Light, Mercy, etc. ending with Dominion and Loftiness. The days in this calendar, officially adopted by the present Bahai Faith, begin at sunset. There are cycles of 19 years, and a period of 361 years.

chart as it is in the first House, and it rules the 10th House, while Venus (ruler of Libra rising) is in the lunar sign, Cancer. This made of Truman an opportunist with a remarkable capacity for adaptation to public situations — and most likely with a strong mother complex of one kind or another (and there are many kinds).

At the end of August 1893, Harry Truman was in his tenth year and the Nodes had reversed their positions, the North Node being now where the South Node was at birth. Late in December 1902 and again in late in July 1921, the North Node returned to its natal place. We shall consider only the last mentioned return, for it is then, at the age of 37 that Truman's political life really began. He became a county judge in 1922 with the help of Tom Pendergast's political machine which ran Kansas City and the county; and in 1926 he was elected "presiding judge."

In the 1932 Elections (when F.D. Roosevelt rose to national power) Truman tried in vain to become governor of Missouri. The transiting North Node was now in the natal South Node hemisphere, the South Node passing through the natal North Node hemisphere and over Uranus (late April 1932). In 1934 at the request of Pendergast Truman ran for the U.S. Senate and was elected as the transiting South Node moved through his natal tenth House and was about to reach his natal Jupiter. He was "releasing" in his new public function the capacities he had built through the years of his judicial career, close to a political machine. He worked hard, followed consistently the New Deal line, and stood firm when the Pendergast machine was investigated and broken up. He was reelected in 1940; he was in his fifty-seventh year. The North Node had returned to its natal place *in mid-March 1940.* This new nodal cycle was to be the crucial one.

Then came the organization of a Senate special committee for the investigation of the national defense program. As its chairman, Harry Truman obtained national fame and prestige, and in the summer 1944 he was picked by the Democratic Party as its candidate for Vice-President. In view of Roosevelt's health condition this fourth term of his presented the probability of Truman becoming President of the United States. This happened all too soon (April 12, 1945), only less than three months after the new Administration was sworn in. The North Node was on that day at 13°23 Cancer, very close to Truman's Mid Heaven (Cancer 18°45') and to the mid-point of the arc between his natal Venus and Jupiter (Cancer 16°3').

He was reelected in 1948 in spite of many predictions he would not be. Interestingly enough the South Node was then on Truman's dominant natal Moon, and there had been a solar eclipse exactly on his natal Sun of the preceding May 9th, and another, near his natal Moon, came on November 1st — which shows that solar eclipses *can* mean an intensification of the natal planet they touch — for Truman's Moon rules his tenth House and his public status. The contact between the transiting South Node and this Moon released what had been built up while the North Node was moving through the North Node hemisphere of the chart, dynamizing most of the chart's planets — the last contacts being with the natal Neptune and Sun (January-February 1948). Interestingly enough the North Node had moved over Truman's natal Moon in July-August 1939 — at the time of the Russo-German Treaty which set the stage for Hitler's invasion of Poland, the beginning of World War II. Actually, even if indirectly, it was World War II which brought Truman to the Presidency, and gave him the awesome responsibility of ordering the use of the atom bomb over Japan.

22

The Planets and the Nodes

In concluding this condensed study of the nodes I should say a few words concerning the significance of finding a planet close to one of the Moon's nodes; but I should mention the fact that the position of these nodes given in ephemerides is a "mean" position — just as the position of the Sun actually is. The reason why these mean positions seem valid is that astrology deals basically with *cycles of motion* rather than with *celestial bodies* as material masses. In this sense astrology is definitely a study of abstract factors, and this is why in my book ASTROLOGY OF PERSONALITY (1936) I spoke of it as "the algebra of life." Of course, it could be, and it has been considered differently and we have seen that claims have been made to its being, and having been since its assumed beginning(?) in Egypt and/or Chaldea, an "empirical science" concerned with exact events and precise celestial positions. If this claim is accepted, then many things in current astrological use have certainly to be given up, and one of these is all "mean positions" and much that relates to the Houses of a chart. Also the positions in latitude of the planets should be considered, especially in relation to the natal horizon, for a planet below the horizon in terms of its zodiacal longitude may already have risen above this horizon because of its latitude.*

Nevertheless what is probably the most important thing in astrology is the way one approaches it and how the use of its language of symbols may broaden the mind and establish a new consciousness of one's individual relationship to the universe. As one seeks to relate the basic functions represented by the planets to factors which divide the birth-chart and thus the whole universe in two-dimensional projection — such as horizon, meridian, nodal axes, and even the axes constituted by the equinoxes and the solstices — one may learn, in the attempt, to interpret everything in terms of polarity and complementary factors.

Thus one can give a broad meaning to the fact that all, or all but one, planets are above or below the horizon, or east or west of the charts' meridian line — or also on one or the other side of the Moon's nodes. The nodal axis of the Moon establishes two half-circles, one which in some

---

* A now departed French astrologer, Neroman, who founded the College Astrologique de France, devised a very beautiful gadget "le Cosmographe" thanks to which one can see at once where a planet stands in latitude when close to the horizon. Unfortunately his remarkable work seems not to have been kept alive.

way has a north-node character, because it begins with this node; the other, a south node ambiance. The point is, however, what portion of the chart is it that "follows" the north node?

In the past I have accepted the statement that the north node hemisphere was constituted by the 180 degrees of the zodiac after the north node, following the natural order of the zodiac. If the north node is at say, Scorpio 6°, then the north node section of the zodiac would be between Scorpio 6° and Taurus 6° where the south node would be found. However, it has occurred to me recently that this was not logical, for the *nodes' motion is retrograde!* Everything in which the Moon's nodes are an active and basic factor should therefore be interpreted in the direction of the nodes' motion.

As a result the example I gave in ASTROLOGY OF PERSONALITY (page 405 and 409, hardbound edition) should be interpreted in a reverse manner. Mussolini had all his planets above the horizon and, as the north node nearly coincided with the Scorpio 11°40' Ascendant, in the north node hemisphere, counting clockwise or in retrograde fashion.

The half-circle below the horizon is said to be that to which the Ascendant gives its meaning, because after birth the Ascendant will move through this below-the-horizon half of the natal chart. In Mussolini's chart in which all planets are found above the horizon Scorpio-Taurus they are said to refer to the life of relationship, because the Descendant pervades with its meaning the 180 degrees of the zodiac from Taurus to Scorpio in the order of the signs, i.e., *counterclockwise;* the Descendant begins this zodiacal half because it is moving into it. But as the Moon's nodes axis is nearly identical with the horizon and the north node is just above the Ascendant, this North node after Mussolini's birth moved *clockwise* away from Scorpio into Libra, then Virgo, etc. All the planets are therefore in the north node's, and *not* in the south node's hemicycle, as I had stated.*

I also said in ASTROLOGY OF PERSONALITY that the north node's hemisphere "refers to the power of developing new spiriual faculties" while the south node's hemisphere "refers to the working of past tendencies," but the term "spiritual faculty" is rather confusing, even if it befits the type of approach characterizing Jung's psychology and his "individuation process." In this early book of mine (written in 1934-35) I followed much of the so-called esoteric tradition, more do than I do now; for I feel that the present time requires a more "cosmic" and less archaic type of symbolism. This is why I am developing in this essay the concept of orbital astrology. What the Moon's nodes tell us is not so much something about the relationship of the Sun and the Moon — with special attention placed on eclipses — but how the essential nature of the Moon symbol affects Earth-beings. The basic

---
* Mussolini's chart has been reproduced in the preceding essay, FIRST STEPS IN THE STUDY OF BIRTH-CHARTS, as an example of the Cluster Pattern.

factor is the Moon itself, not as a "Light" as much as a satellite of the Earth.

The Moon's north node is the gate of "intake" of this basic lunar nature. In the north node's hemisphere the Moon's power is absorbed and (hopefully) assimilated. Planets placed in that hemisphere tend to be used a great deal in connection with the process of development of a greater or new capacity for adjustment to existence. They may be made to serve this process. Thus in Mussolini's chart all planets are enlisted for the development of the individual capacity to deal with immediate problems, opportunities or emergencies. On the other hand, the organic functions represented by planets in the hemisphere which begins (in a retrograde sense) with the south node may be called upon to give a certain coloring to the release of whatever is automatically required for the fulfillment of a specific destiny, or the working out of karma.

However, unless all or nearly all the planets are located in one of the nodal hemispheres, it seems unnecessary to give much attention to this factor. What is usually more important are situations in which a planet, or a group of planets, is located very close to one of the Moon's nodes — and also to the nodes of the larger planets, beginning with Jupiter. Such a situation indicates that the planet affects in some manner the absorption or release of the Moon's, or of some other planet's force.

I mentioned already the cases in which the Moon

itself is located at its own nodes. This is by far the most important situation, psychologically speaking. When the Sun is close to the Moon's nodes a strong effect can be expected; and this most often means a birth near an eclipse. In the case of the Persian Prophet, Baha'u'llah, the Sun at the Ascendant is two degrees further than the Moon's south node in longitude, and also on the heliocentric position of Mars' south node which is moreover the longitude of the star North Scale. As Mars is retrograde and completely isolated and forming a T-square with Neptune and Pluto, a powerful release of power is in evidence, the key to which may be the star Regulus exactly on the Mid Heaven, H.P. Blavatsky, initiator of the Theosophical Movement, and Karl Marx, inspirer of the Communist Movement were born with the Sun near the Moon's north node, Marx (it seems) during a solar eclipse.

In Chief Justice Earl Warren, under whose chairmanship the U.S. Supreme Court made crucial decisons, Pluto was exactly on the Moon's north node in his fifth House. This perhaps indicates the depth to which he sought to meet absolutely basic social issues. General Marshall who was Army Chief of Staff in World War II had Mercury one degree away from his Moon's north node, stressing his capacity for planning and organization, and he was born the day of a partial solar eclipse. J. Pierpont Morgan had also Mercury in conjunction to his ninth House north node, with the Sun close by. The pioneering composers, Schoenberg and Charles Ives had birth-charts with Neptune (often related to music) at their north nodes.

A planet at its north node is powerful, perhaps in an insidious or compulsive manner. The function it represents is focused upon the consciousness of the individual person as sunlight through a lens. With the planet at its south node its function may become wasted or negatively applied, though in some cases an intense release of energy may be experienced at some crucial moments of the person's life.

INTERPRETING A BIRTH-CHART
AS A WHOLE

23

Preliminary Considerations

The last section of the essay entitled "First Steps in the Study of Birth-charts" dealt with what I call "The Moment of Interpretation." This is a factor to which very little attention, if any, is given by the ordinary astrologer who is simply concerned with telling to his client what he sees in his birth-chart and what is in store for him in the near future. I stressed in that chapter the essential importance of evaluating, as much as is possible under ordinary conditions, the stage of unfoldment at which the client is at the moment of interpretation, that is, at the time of his life when, through the intermediary of the astrologer, he is being confronted with his birth-chart — the archetypal pattern of his individual being and destiny, his "celestial Name." Knowledge prematurely disclosed may be deeply harmful; and as I wrote: "Knowledge should be given to the knower in terms of his capacity to use it constructively . . . timing of the giving of knowledge is all-important." I also stressed the vital significance of the relation to astrologer to client — a relation as crucial as that of psychiatrist to patient, and in terms of spiritual unfoldment, of *guru* to *chela*.

Because of this, it should be obvious that nothing may be more psychologically unsound, if not futile, than the "blind" reading of a chart; that is, interpreting the chart of what is then merely an abstract entity, perhaps of unknown sex, with which the astrologer can have no personal relation. Truly, a chart erected for a particular time and location on the Earth's surface pictures for us *the archetypal character of whatever is born then and there*. But in natal astrology, at least from the humanistic point of view, we are dealing with living, feeling, growing persons, and not merely with abstract forms. In a similar sense a Jungian analyst, face to face with a client who tells him about a revealing dream, is not dealing with the archetype of the "devouring Mother" or the "Ideal Lover," but with a person whose psyche had reached a stage of its development which had tuned in to these broadly defined great Images inherent in human nature as we know it today.

For these and other reasons it should be easy to understand my reluctance to discuss "in the abstract" a particular birth-chart without being confronted with a particular person having particular needs. If I did this, then I would be in fact telling the reader interested in humanistic astrology how he should go about studying and interpreting *any* birth-chart at *any* time. Yet, essentially, each living situation bringing together the interpreter and the chart of a real person requires its own particular approach. The tragedy of our modern civilization, lost in the sand dunes of an uncompromising intellectualism, is that it deals most of the time with abstract entities and intellectual models of situations which one has to meet according to pre-conceived "how to" programs, with a statistical allowance for minimal error. Much can be achieved by following this approach; but this type of achievement is materialistic or at least ego-centered. You achieve what your intellectually eager ego sets itself to accomplish.

When man accepts this way of doing things, he can never go beyond the boundaries of his ego and the official stereotypes of his society. He plays golf on the moon — what a characteristic achievement! Wherever he goes he finds only the image of his own ego-barrenness and of the mechanistic model he has made of his body functions. Because most people today want to know how to *do* everything, they cannot go out of the circle of their own concept of "doing." This is why we witness today a strong reaction against this setting-up of standardized situations and an eagerness to open one's consciousness wide — often too wide, by compensation! — to the irrational and the aleatory.

There is a middle path. One can tell a student what *in principle and in most cases* is worth doing — how to start in ordinary cases, and what it is better not to forget. But such directions should be learned in order soon after to be able consciously to forget them, retaining only the faculty to move at once to what is essential *in any particular situation.*

Education today rests on two very serious mistakes. The error of most professors consisting in imparting to the student a mass of more or less unrelated data and information of various kinds referring to how to act in standard situations. But all this data and these recipes tell only how mankind has reached the place where it is now in his evolution. What matters is not what has been done in past occurrences, but the development of the power to recognize, accept or create new situations and develop new and more adequate human responses to them. On the other hand, many young people and a relatively few progressive educators are tensely concerned with discarding all set patterns and discovering new situations, without realizing that they should *first* develop the faculty required constructively to meet new situations into which they most often run unprepared, and thus at great risks of self-deceit or mental confusion.

If in these series of essays, and in all my works I have constantly interjected considerations which to many people seem to be digressions from the main line of study, it is because it is not so much what one studies that matters, but *how* one studies it. Data have evidently to be remembered, at least basic ones from which, as needs arise, all the others could be derived deductively as well as intuitively; but they are only the foundations on which a meaningful and creative approach to what one deals with can rest. It is *the approach* that is important. It alone will tell what you will find.

The way one poses a question already has in germ the solution. Rigidly set scientific laboratory experiments give results which are inherent in the way the experiments were planned. Very often it is due to completely unplanned "chance" occurrences that an important discovery is made. Yet, without having previously developed the faculty of being aware of meaning, if the unexpected occurs there will be no discovery. What is involved also is the capacity to give up old and cherished concepts and expectations — a very difficult achievement for most people, trained scientist included.

All this applies to astrology and the attitude one should develop to the interpretation of the birth-charts of individual persons if one seeks to follow the humanistic approach. In this approach what is first of all required is the ability to consider the chart as a whole, and what is more, as an *organic* whole. Everything in this chart is related to everything else. No factor is independent from the others, whether or not it makes any of the conventionally classified "aspects." It is true that the chart is a formula of relationship between a variety of component parts and functions and that therefore it can be considered an abstraction. Yet, I must repeat that in actual fact, existentially, it reveals a unique being confronting you at this particular moment of interpretation. Somehow the interpreter has to *accept* this confrontation as a situation which is part of his own life — and as a challenge to the development of his own awareness of human values and human problems.

Using a now fashionable term in psychiatry, the astrologer should develop "empathy" toward what the chart represents; or if he or she cannot do so, it would be best to abstain, for not all confrontations can be productive of a significant harvest. They cannot be productive, if there is no feeling-realization that they constitute real "encounters" — meetings which may in some ways introduce a new factor in human lives.

A most needed element in such meetings is, for the astrologer, a sense of humility. Not cleverness or intellectual brilliance in the interpretation, but the humble realization that he, as an astrologer, is merely a "mediator" between a human being, who may be confused and uncertain, and the universe — or Life as a whole, or God. He should take to heart the statement of a great psychologist, Dr. Jacob Moreno, who often stated that he was not the one to heal a patient; God only did the healing. The astrologer likewise may reveal to his client most constructive and healing facts or aspects of his individuality and destiny; but the revelation is only focused *through* his mind. It is the universe, the Sky-God, the client's Higher Self — names matter little! — that spoke through him. When the practice of astrology, or the practice of medicine and psychiatry or psychoanalysis, becomes mostly if not exclusively a "business," then a vital factor is missing.

Preliminary Considerations

The situation linking astrologer and client at the moment of interpretation presents also an important difficulty, one which is also more or less found in medical or psychological consultations. The consultant has acquired knowledge in terms of some definite set of symbols — and all technical words, categories of symptoms and names of diseases are indeed symbols. These symbols have definite meaning for the consultant; they may awe or confuse the patient or client who may have either no knowledge or, what is worse, a superficial and perverted knowledge of their meaning — and especially of their meaning *in his particular, more or less unique case.* The problem of true and complete communication can thus be a hard one to solve. In the astrologer's case this problem is most of the time very serious, because the symbols used — Saturn, a square, an eclipse on the client's Sun, etc. — have a mysterious and fateful ring. On the other hand, if the astrologer does not mention to a client who is vaguely familiar with them the names and symbols used as the background for the interpretation, he risks having this client feel that he is only speaking "out of his hat," according to some psychic intuition. The effectiveness of the interpretation may thus be at least partially lost.

A middle course is also possible and advisable in all such cases. Some simple and basic statements concerning the purpose of an astrological interpretation and the meanings of the main planetary factors in a birth-chart should be made.

A clear and easily readable chart should be shown to the client who thus will be confronted with his "celestial Name," or as I previously wrote, with a fundamental "set of instructions" concerning his place in his planetary environment and the function which he would naturally and spontaneously assume if he were not also perhaps under the disturbing pressure of family, social and religious-cultural forces.

What I have said so far, and other matters mentioned elsewhere,* refer to the approach a humanistic astrologer should take toward the interpretation of a client's birth-chart. What comes next depends on the situation in which the process of interpretation takes place. The most fruitful situation is, I believe, one in which the astrologer meets the client first as a human being, rather than as client waiting to be told something, and the client either presents his problems as he sees it, and gives a few basic data concerning his environment, his parents, his social condition and a few turning points in his life — or what *seems to him* to have been decisive turning points. The client should be clearly told that the purpose of the coming consultation should not be the satisfaction merely of his curiosity, and that the astrologer is not interested in "proving" the validity of astrology. In most cases such a preliminary interview is not possible, considering the usual way in which astrology is practiced; if so, it

---

* cf. the first chapters in the book THE PRACTICE OF ASTROLOGY (Penguin paperback books)

should be replaced by a letter giving the necessary information and a couple of snapshots of the would-be client. In either instance, a contact should be established at the existential level — a "meeting" of consciousness, allowing for a feeling or intuitional response.

Then the astrologer should erect the birth-chart, preferably while alone, rather than in the client's presence. One of the reasons for this is that a fairly large number of items have to be calculated and related to each other, which demands a great deal of concentration and care. If the birth-moment is not exactly known and a process of "rectification" is required, the client's presence may help; yet in most cases this presence induces over-haste and an insufficient study of past astrological aspects, progressed New Moons, transits, etc. and their correlations with the few basic events mentioned by the client. Besides, in this first stage of the study, it seems best for the astrologer to use his mental faculties at the level of archetypal values — that is, in terms of number, rhythm, form and essential meaning. When, after this is done, the client is met face to face, then the level of the interpretative operation becomes existential and personal. To the basic factor of "essential being" is added that of "existential becoming"; and the latter acting upon the former sets in motion focalizing process directly related to the living experience of the client, as this experience has made him *what he appears to be at the moment of interpretation.*

There would be little sense in explaining here

the calculations required for the erection of a birth-chart. Any number of textbooks and now of inexpensive paperbacks are available for this purpose. There is great value in at first writing down on a piece of paper all the elements of the chart; then in making a chart which is eminently readable and which gives a clear picture of what the sky at birth looked in two-dimensional projection. The problem of determination of House cusps is very important and every student, and especially every practicing astrologer, must solve it to his satisfaction. As I stated many times, astrology is a system of symbolism, a "celestial language"; and various types of language are possible and can be effective, *provided* the kind one selects is consistently and intelligently used, and one does not jump from one system to another. Every system that is truly consistent and based on astronomical facts — and not mere psychic intuitions or supposedly clairvoyant or clairaudient "communications" — is in principle valid *at some level of understanding.*

Likewise a dream can be interpreted according to Freud, Adler, Jung, etc.; and the various interpretations can be valid in terms of the different approaches implied in the system of these psychologists — approaches conditioned by their temperaments and life-purposes, as their birth-charts easily reveal. For the same reasons, patients can be cured by allopathic, homeopathic, naturopathic, osteopathic, etc., systems of medicine — each patient, being attracted, according to his particular need and temperament, to one or the other system — at least if all schools were allowed to freely operate.

However, at least for people born in temperate regions, I strongly recommend the use of a House-system and of a chart-disposition in which the natal horizon and meridian are represented by the horizontal and vertical lines of the chart. The European way of making charts, giving to each degree of the zodiac an equal space on the outer circumference of the chart, does not logically fit in a person-centered type of astrology. In such charts the Houses are given different sizes and usually the meridian line is not perpendicular to the horizon. Yet a chart should show the sky exactly as it is experienced at a particular time and place on the surface of the Earth. Every other type of chart is *not* person-centered.*

In a birth-chart, each House represents (in two-dimensional projecton) thirty degrees of *the actual space* surrounding the newborn; but, because of the distortion introduced by the terrestrial latitude of the birth-place, thirty degrees of actual space contains either more or less than 30 degrees *of the zodiac*. As I see it, the 12 Houses symbolically constitute a spatial frame of reference for all individual experiences. Every celestial body, and as well the degrees of the zodiac, are *contents* within this twelve-compartmented *structure*.

However, in order to make the matter clear at first sight as one looks at the chart, it is good to mark across the circumference of the chart

───────────────
*A detailed study of the Houses will soon be published in book form.

where every zodiacal sign begins within the Houses. This makes it unnecessary to add the zodiacal sign after each of the planetary symbols. Also, to add to clarity and to the holistic and immediate visual perception of the chart and its contents, it is important to link with colored lines the planets forming aspects. I use blue pencil for "soft" aspects (trine, sextile) and red lines for "hard" aspects (oppositions, squares, semi-squares). Other colors can be used for quintiles and septiles, or these aspects can be marked separately on the side of the chart, together with other relevant matters.

I cannot discuss here the problem of "rectification," for it is a complex and difficult issue. It is almost impossible to be sure of the exact moment of the first breath, when there is no record of it within at most a half an hour, unless perhaps the matter of life-events is unusually sharply defined and the rising sign seems fairly evident — and this, in most instances, applies only to persons at least past thirty-five or forty. The time of the first parent's death is usually a strong and reliable indicator. The transit of slow planets over the four angles of the chart are valid indications up to a point; yet as most often these transits are repeated three times within one or two years it is difficult to see which one of the three crossings gives the correct degree for the angle. If the indications given by the transits of two or three slow planets point to the same birth-moment, then of course the latter may well seem fully reliable.

The progression of the Moon over the angles, and especially the Ascendant, can also be used as broad means of rectification; but what is indicated is a period of days or months, and there may be factors delaying the type of change normally related to such lunar progressions over an angle. The older a person becomes, the greater may be the lag.

In general, one should avoid expecting that an astrological event will inevitably correlate with an existential life event or crisis of growth. A birth-chart does not tell what will happen; it reveals only a *set of potentialities.* It tells what Nature — or the universe, or God — "intended" in producing such a birth. But the pressure of family, school, and society expectations — plus the interplay of interpersonal relationships of all types — introduce a multitude of factors affecting the actual life-events. The basic structure of destiny symbolized by the chart remains what it is — the acorn *will not* turn into an apple tree — but the actual life-contents of the structure are essentially unforeseeable. The growing oak may be stunted or partially destroyed by a variety of occurrences from which the tree cannot protect itself; neither can a human child.

Prevision is possible within limits because the structural factor in a human life is still very strong in spite of the person's possibility of giving to what happens an individual meaning, and therefore of making "free choices." The individual's free choice resides essentially in his ability to select *the meaning* he gives to the many crises of growth marking the beginning and mid-points of the smaller sub cycles dividing his over-all life-span.

The study of a birth-chart can proceed in a variety of ways. Each astrologer may discover a procedure — i.e., a particular sequence of investigations — which he feels produces better results. Yet I must repeat that from the holistic and humanistic standpoint it is essential to consider first of all the overall structure of the chart — and this means the overall disposition of the planets in relation to the two basic axes, horizon and meridian. I have discussed this *gestalt* approach in the fourth essay of this series. The chart is thus seen to belong to a particular type; it is given a particular "form" — a significant form.

The next step is evidently the study of the contents of this form. The form represents the structure of an organism; and within this organism a number of basic functions operate. They are represented by the planets — including the Sun and the Moon. The two "Lights" symbolize the most essential functions in any living organism. Thus they should be considered first — separately, then in relation to the four angles of the chart — thus their "House positions."*

---

* The House in which the Sun is located tells at once the time of the day the person is born. As the astrologer often has to use ephemerides some of which give noon positions, others midnight positions, it is rather easy to make an error in making the initial calculations from the given birth-data. The simplest check on the accuracy of the calculation is the position of the Sun in a House. If the birth date says 1 a.m. and the Sun is placed above the horizon, it is clear at once that the calculations were wrong. Such checks are valuable, especially if calculations for

Preliminary Considerations 317

First, then, the chart is seen structurally to belong to several kinds of categories or basic types; the overall *gestalt* type (Cluster, Hemispheric, Tripod, etc.), the solar-zodiacal type (Aries, Taurus, etc.) and the soli-lunar types (New Moon, First Quarter, Full Moon, etc.) defined in my book THE LUNATION CYCLE. Other general classifications are provided by the well-known categories of Fire, Earth, Air, Water signs, and of Cardinal, Fixed and Mutable signs. Some signs may contain several planets, others none. The absence or the concentration of planets in one of the "quadruplicities" (the four Elements) or of the "triplicities" is a significant factor; and here we deal with what Marc Jones called "focal determinator."

It is very important to try to find in a birth-chart a factor (or perhaps several factors) which somehow stand out, thus polarizing one's attention. Here we are dealing actually with an esthetical" process. Confronted with a great painting, an onlooker finds his eyes drawn to some color, or form, or implied movement relating several forms, around which perhaps the whole picture may seem to revolve. Every person one meets and comes to know tends to be characterized by certain traits or combinations of traits. The caricaturist seeks to discover some dominant feature

---

several charts have to be made quickly in the presence of the client. The procedure of erecting a chart is simple enough, yet it allows for the possibility of a great many errors. This is why perhaps computers are welcome, and the day will come when every astrologer can call up by phone a computer service and have all the data available in a very few minutes. But, of course, computers can be incorrectly programmed!

in the face or the bearing of an individual, then exaggerates it. The astrologer has to avoid this process of exaggeration, yet he has to recognize emphasis, accentuation, repetitive pattern, etc. When such attention-focalizing factors exist; and they nearly always exist in one way or another, even if the accentuation is only slight. If there is *no* emphasis at all, this too is obviously an emphasis, a negative one.

The focalization of attention has a two-fold significance. It concentrates the mind of the astrologer upon some relatively outstanding feature of the chart, but it does more if the mind is open and able to "resonate" to the universe. It polarizes a response from the sky; for the chart *is* an image-symbol of the universe. It is one single moment of the universe within which the client is born — born to fulfill a function, as every cell of a living organism does fulfill a function. The universe in its organic wholeness speaks with its myriad of stars, suns and planets. In some way the astrologer has to become attuned to that cosmic Voice. To do this he may find it easier to seek that factor or feature in the chart which, because it stands out, is like the keynote of the cosmic chord which indeed this chart is. It can truly become a key that unlocks the door to the revelation of *either* the basic meaning of the whole life, or the need which led to the person seeking advice or greater understanding at the particular time of the consultation.

When only one relatively brief consultation is possible, the most important, or at least urgent, aspect of the astrologer-client encounter is most often the solution of a particular problem of the moment. For this reason, the use of a "horary" type of technique can be very significant *in connection with* the basic theme of the chart (i.e., the planetary *gestalt*). A specific horary chart can be made or, as already stated, the natal planets in the client's birth-chart can be introduced in a horary frame of reference — i.e. in a House-circle calculated for the time of the beginning of the consultation.

This recourse to a horary procedure is not necessary, and it requires a special skill of interpretation. Whenever it is used, its purpose is to focus the attention of the interpreter upon some factor or factors in the birth-chart which can polarize an intuitive inner response, a deep resonance to the need of the seeker for understanding.

The solution of any of our problems is always around us, because this is a holistic universe. An individual person, just because he has become "individualized," has become relatively separated from the universal whole; or rather he *thinks* of himself as being isolated and insulated. And because he is seemingly isolated, he longs for contacts with other individuals. This is the cause of his problems. But the solution is surrounding him; and this solution is essentially to reunite himself in thought with the whole around him — that is, to stop insisting he is separate — which means, to surrender the ego in him that isolates him.

This is the reason why horary astrology, in particular, can work. It can work because at all times the universe surrounds an individual person with the solution of his problems, as the glove surrounds the cold hand. *The shape of the problem is as well the shape of the solution.* Problem and solution are two aspects of the same fact: an individual has separated himself from the universe around him, but the universe still remains around him, as the sea remains around the fish which is only a bubble of seawater separated from the ocean by a skin. But the fish does not know the ocean, and individualized man in most cases does not know that he is a bubble of "spirit" gesticulating in an ocean of spirit.

Essentially, interpreting a birth-chart to a client should mean establishing a conscious connection between the ego-centered and ego-bound individual and the universe. He is a tiny portion of that universe surrounded by a "skin" of mental consciousness. Within that skin all kinds of troubles develop. Astrology, like Jungian psychotherapy, or Assagioli's "psychosynthesis," or true yoga — should be a process of *whole-making* that is, a way of becoming *and remaining* in a state of resonance with the universe by fulfilling the function (*dharma*) for which one was born within the universe.

The "mystery" is that you are born "out" of the universe, yet remain "within" the universe; only, you *forget* this "within" state, because you are intensely ego-proud to be what you are: "I myself." The function of astrology could be — but most rarely is, indeed — to dis-ego-ize the consciousness, by allowing the universe to enter into it and to reflect itself upon the inside walls of the mind; these mind-walls acting as a movie-screen on which the great movements and patterns of the universe cannot only be watched, but allowed to tune-up and harmonize the consciousness. If the individual "lets go" (the great secret taught by Zen and all truly valid techniques of meditation), what Jung called "the cramp in the conscious" can be relaxed, and peace may be a constant presence within the assuaged heart.

"Philosophy, metaphysics!" the reader may say. But this is just what true astrology is. It was so to the ancient Chinese, to Pythagoras, to all the men who sought to help human beings to live in harmony with the universe, as functional parts of the universal whole. And in case one should believe that this is an "easy" life, a passive life of subservience to an external "Fate," I must add that a total acceptance of one's function and "dharma" *whatever the consequences might be,* and (as the Bhagavad Gita enjoins us to do) the wholehearted surrenduring of "the fruits of action" on the altar where dwells the divine Presence of the wholeness of the universal Whole — these are certainly not easy and passive modes of activity.

The study of astrology has for essential purpose a discipline of the mind. But I am not one of those who speak glamorously of "the religion of the stars." It might be called a yoga with the universe; and I have spoken of it in preceding essays as a "karma yoga." But a yoga is not a religion; it simply provides us with a technique for reaching — through understanding or through total surrender in action and love — a state of unity with the universal Whole. Likewise the study and application to one's life and consciousness of the many variables in astrology can become a technique of understanding of all essential life-processes, and through such an understanding, of identification with the great symbol of the universe, the Sky.

Because all life-processes are founded upon polarization, what is to be sought in a chart is the way in which polar opposites interact *in any situation*. To rise "above" the opposites by fulfilling them is the eternal task of human consciousness. Any astrological chart one interprets involves such a task; for nothing in the chart stands alone. The Ascendant implies the Descendant; the north node, a south node; Jupiter is nothing without Saturn; Venus without Mars, or Mars without Venus.

Any chart can be an endless subject for meditation. Each one is the whole universe perceived and understood from one particular center of consciousness. One can write endlessly *about* it; but it is rather to be experienced, to be lived. Unfortunately this is not what astrology means today to 99 percent of its devotees. And interpretative situations are almost never right or ripe for the release of true understanding, for such true understanding implies the overcoming of ego-fears and ego-passions. Alas, our present-day society is a society of egos, by egos and for the ego's greatest glory. This is the great human tragedy.

24

President Franklin D. Roosevelt's Birth-Chart

In order to bring to a more concrete focus what has just been stated, I shall present an interpretation of two birth-charts: that of a very well-known personage, President Franklin D. Roosevelt, and that of a young man born on September 25, 1949 in Southern California. My purpose in studying in print these charts is not to give the kind of interpretation which would be based on a direct personal contact between a person seeking advice and a greater understanding of himself at a particular time of his life, but rather to show how a set of interpretative procedures outlined in the preceding chapter can be applied in two very different cases. We know what F.D.R.'s life has been; the young man's destiny is still largely a pattern of potentialities.

In the first instance we can have in retrospect an example of how to seek a more profound and objective understanding of the manner in which a powerful individual person was able to attune his personality to the need of the critical time in which he lived and thereby gave a personal direction to certain historical trends. In the young Californian's case it is what is ahead of us, wrapped in futurity, which is important. This time of history is certainly as critical as that in which F.D.R. rose to fame and power; but the young man is meeting the challenge of history with an obviously most different kind of personality and potential destiny. The astrologer's task in this case is to evaluate the potentiality and to help its actualization. To focus such an evaluation, a horary chart will also be presented; it was made for the time I decided to use the chart after asking my young friend for the permission to do so. It was also an important time in his life, for it was just past his 21st birthday and he was beginning a new and potentially very fruitful association.

THE BASIC CHARACTER OF PRESIDENT ROOSEVELT'S CHART

According to F.D.R.'s mother he was born around 8:30 p.m. with the possibility that birth might have happened as late as 8:45 p.m. (according to what seems to have been the father's testimony). This was "local time" as New York State adopted standard time only in 1883.

The chart I used in my book THE LUNATION CYCLE is the one that has most often been accepted as valid, perhaps because Saturn was just at F.D.R.'s Ascendant when he was struck with polio on August 10, 1921 (Virgo 23°3'). However I have never felt quite satisfied with the angles of this chart. F.D.R.'s father died when he was 18 years and about 10 months; and it seemed to me that the arc between the Mid-Heaven and the most characteristic Mars retrograde at 27°01' Gemini should refer to this death. Yet, according to the system of rectification which seems to be reliable in many instances in which the moment of the first breath is accurately known, this would give Gemini 8°09' at the Mid Heaven — and an apparently too early birth-time.

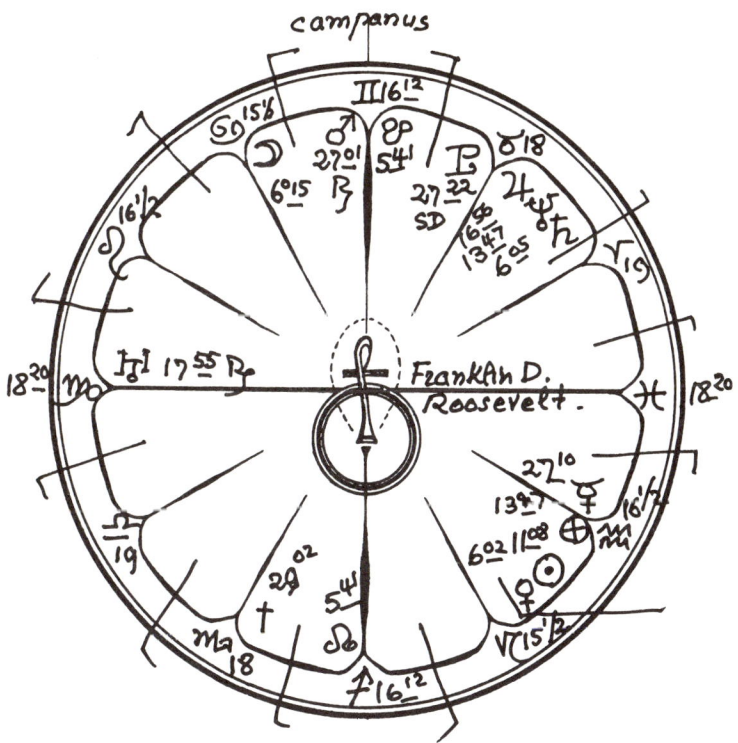

However, in re-considering F.D.R.'s chart for this present essay, I was struck with the idea that the death-event may be represented instead by the arc between Pluto at Leo 27°22' (nearly "stationary direct") and the Mid Heaven. This gives Gemini 16°12' for the Mid Heaven and a Virgo 18°20' Ascendant with Uranus just at the Ascendant. The angular degrees of the chart carry significant symbols and I feel that this is probably the most accurate chart. The fact that Saturn crossed the Ascendant on September 26, 1920 (and was "stationary direct" within two or three minutes of the natal Uranus on May 21, 1921) very likely refers to what may have been the basic cause of the polio attack. Just getting cold after a swim in the ocean (on August 10, 1921) seems hardly of itself to justify such an attack. There must have been antecedent causes, at least a predisposing weakness or inherited condition; various factors during F.D.R.'s official trips to Europe (1918-1919) may indeed have provided the background for the "polio attack." Strange things happened at the time in Paris and Versailles!

At any rate, I shall assume for the purpose of this study that the chart printed here is correct, and proceed with the outline of the steps I would normally take in studying such a chart.

The Planetary Pattern:

This is quite obviously a "Tripod Pattern." Uranus at the Ascendant is isolated and occupies the most important position. Another group of planets in Aquarius includes the Sun and the Two inner planets, Venus and Mercury; and the Part of Fortune is also in Aquarius, adding to the emphasis. The third group of planets is located within the sextile of Saturn to the Moon (the parental planets).

In this chart no "grand trine" can be found, but a powerful trine aspect links the rising Uranus and Jupiter (near the cusp of the ninth House), with Neptune just behind this Jupiter in Taurus. One can also mention a rather weak, because separating, trine between Mercury and the Moon. The Tripod Pattern in any case suggests that the life should witness a great deal of growth in consciousness, if no too strong obstacle blocks the innate capacity of the individual to participate in a larger social frame of reference along lines of reform and as well self-transformation. The rising Uranus, in trine-relationship to the four planets in Taurus, is the "Signature" justifying such a statement. The planets in Aquarius, and particularly the conjunction of Venus and the Sun in the fifth House (self-expression, creativity, etc.) add to the power of Uranus. A powerful self-generated "drive" for self-transformation is evident. How it is likely to be used cannot be seen from the birth-chart; and there were no doubt other persons born on that day with Uranus rising who responded in different ways to the *potential situation and the "set of instructions"* revealed by his birth-chart; this because of their heredity and their personal environment, and other spiritual factors which transcend the possibility of astrological interpretation. Nevertheless, within their individual field of operation, they presumably experienced in some manner the same inner subjective urge to expansion, reform and participation in some sort of social or religious field of activity which allowed them to express themselves quite powerfully *in relation to what was possible to them according to their birth-environment.*

It should become evident at once to the student of such a chart that something quite powerful would nevertheless act as an obstacle, or as crisis-producing factor. I am referring mainly to the broad square of Mars to Uranus and the exact square of Pluto to Mercury. The fact that the Mid Heaven is situated within the semi-sextile of Pluto to Mars, and especially that the tenth-House Mars (the most elevated planet) is retrograde, gives a great deal of power to these squares. Moreover we can see, at a glance, that the three planets in Aquarius are squaring the four planets in Taurus. The former are celestial factors *within* the Earth's orbit; the latter are four of the most distant outer planets. One may well think therefore of a tension between the more intimate personal factors, and the broader social and possibly spiritual and transcendent factors.

The disposition of the four Taurus planets is very interesting: Saturn and Jupiter are a natural pair of complementary factors at the social, political, or religious level; and so are Neptune and Pluto at a more transcendent or universalistic level which normally is that where the power of mutation and self-repolarization operates. These two pairs of planets are intertwined. However, the *center of gravity* (i.e. the mid-point) of the fourfold grouping is at Taurus 16°43½ within a few minutes of arc of Jupiter. This stresses the significance of Jupiter, and of its trine to Uranus. Besides, the fourth House has a Sagittarian cusp and is therefore "Jupiterian" by nature.

The fourth House refers to the mother — or at any rate, *always* to the parent who has the more meaning or importance in the development of the feeling-nature of the person — and F.D.R.'s mother was a quite strong and remarkable individual.

One of the factors difficult to interpret is the elevated Mars retrograde which traditionally "rules" Aries and thus the eighth House of the chart. It makes a close trine to Mercury in the sixth House, and — as I already said — a very distant square to Uranus. A more ominous septile of Mars to Saturn should be noticed; and, most important, we find in the chart also a septile of the Moon to the center of the Jupiter-Neptune conjunction, and a bi-septile of Venus to Jupiter.

If we add to these aspects the strong quintile of the Moon to Uranus, and a near novile of this Moon to Pluto, and also an exact novile of Mars to Jupiter, plus a sesquiquadrate aspect of the Sun to Mars, we realize that we are looking at a chart unusually rich in the type of aspects which are most often called "minor," yet which in some cases, like this, can assume a far more than normal importance — at least *if* the individual whose chart it is is developed or sensitive enough to respond to them. President Roosevelt's life — we now can see — evidently did respond, especially to the quite "fateful," because transcendent, septiles, and the Moon-Uranus quintile (to which we might add a near-quintile of Mercury to Saturn).

But to return to Mars: it affects the two planets which can be considered "ruling planets" of the chart, Mercury and Uranus, and it obviously occupies a very significant place in terms of the professional and public life, which is also "ruled" by Mecury, Gemini being at the Mid Heaven. The important point, according to the basic concept of Humanistic astrology, is not what kind of events are to be expected in terms of this Mars position, but rather how the person should meet professional challenges and opportunities. This is what I would have had to consider if young Franklin had come to me for a consultation, say after his father's death.

The answer would have had to take in consideration a multiplicity of factors which we have not yet touched upon, in particular the Sun and the Moon; but from the point of view of the overall distribution and placing of the planets in the chart, the attention would have been drawn first of all to the Tripod character of the chart, and to four outstanding factors: Uranus just rising, the Aquarius group in which the Sun is surrounded by Venus and Mercury (and the Part of Fortune) the very broad and "separating" conjunction of Mars and the Moon in the tenth House, and the four planets in Taurus.

What this all totals to — when seen from a broad perspective — is transforming activity powered by deep emotions, a will to self-expression, self-overcoming and expansion, and a restless mind pulled by contrasting forces and possibly requiring sharp confrontations for its full development.

Mars retrograde is usually a puzzling factor for it can operate in many different ways. As Mars represents *all outgoing activity,* and this outgoing is always dependent upon some kind of muscular process — unnoticeable as it may be, except by very sensitive instruments — the fact that Mars is retrograde may affect the muscular system, though it certainly need not do so in any observable way. What it basically means is that, as a person is urged spontaneously to reach out toward, or to fly from an object which has aroused a "feeling judgment" (the Venus function) of being valuable or dangerous, something happens in that person which tends to stop him and forces him to reconsider more cautiously or attentively whether to object is *really* worthwhile, or to be avoided. The action which is thus delayed will probably be performed, but the performance will tend to be less spontaneous; it may be strongly colored by a psychological complex — or, as in F.D.R.'s case, it may have to be forced against natural difficulties requiring deliberateness and the exercise of conscious will-power.

This mechanism related to the retrograde phase of the Mars cycle (the briefest of all planetary retrograde phases) may not be at all obvious, even to the individual person himself, if what is involved is a psychological complex blocking the spontaneous outflow of the psychic energy or libido; yet I believe that it can always be discovered at work, however subtly. And of course, as we previously saw, Freud is the most characteristic case of such a Mars retrograde position, with a completely isolated Mars. In Roosevelt's life, the situation took on a most acute physical form, but I doubt that a study of the birth-chart alone would have led to the prognostication of his illness. The most dangerous factors, in this connection, were the septile of Saturn in the eighth House to Mars which almost suggests some "occult" force at work; and the square of Pluto to Mercury (possibly referring to a trip abroad.)

In any case, what could be deduced from the over-all pattern is that we are dealing here with a complex situation in which the outer manifestation of a strong power of creative and transforming self-expression will meet definite opposition or "tests," inner as well as outer. On the other hand, the strong Moon in Cancer and the four Taurus planets suggest a rather conservative or at least traditional background; on the other hand, the rest of the chart reveals just the opposite trend in terms of the truly individual character of the person.

It is interesting to note that the upper group of planets in spring and early summer signs of the zodiac is contained within an exact sextile of the Moon and Saturn. In F.D.R.'s case we see there the constructive power of a strong family background and heredity; yet the Mars retrograde in the House of the Father could suggest that the paternal inheritance presented some problems

— whether at the intellectual level or in relation to the nervous system.

One should note also that Mercury and Uranus are in "mutual reception" (Mercury ruling Virgo, and Uranus said to rule Aquarius), and Mercury is powerfully aspected, but in the sixth House which at least partially refers to health. It refers more generally to the realization that the type of self-expression related to the fifth House usually leads to, or requires for the best results, re-training and a close attention to the results of a too emotional or too egocentric release of energy. With the conjunction of Venus and the Sun in this fifth House, such results could be expected to need being reconsidered and revaluated — especially as the fifth House is ruled by Saturn (Capricorn at its cusp) and Saturn makes the ominous septile to Mars already mentioned. And here again Saturn refers to the father, or at least the Father-Image and the ancestral tradition.

The Lights:

I believe that it is better to study the over-all pattern of the chart and the distribution of the planets in the House *before* one focuses one's attention upon the Sun and the Moon; but this is evidently not essential, and where the planetary pattern is not sharply defined and suggestive, one may find it easier to pay attention first to the positions and the aspects formed by the two Lights. The Sun and the Moon symbolize respectively the nature of the life-energy (i.e., its most characteristic mode or rhythm of operation) and the way it is distributed to the whole field of the personality to meet everyday demands for adaptation to ever changing inner states or outer situations. The angular relationship between the Lights describes the phase of the soli-lunar cycle at which one is born — or what I have called one's "lunation birthday" and one's soli-lunar type (cf. my book THE LUNATION CYCLE for information concerning the 8 types).

In F.D.R.'s chart the Moon is in its "gibbous" phase, about 35 degrees short of "full," or more accurately about three days before Full Moon. This means that he was born within a lunation cycle that had begun on January 19, 1882 with a New Moon on the last degree of Capricorn — a degree which Marc Jones has spoken of as "the White Lodge degree"; or, less occultly, a degree of executive deliberation and control. The first New Moon after F.D.R.'s birth occurred on February 18th at 29°24' Aquarius; and it corresponds by secondary progression to the winter 1900 — age 18 — less than a year before his father's death. This was undoubtedly the start of his more individual life.

The next New Moon (at Pisces 28°47') corresponded to the summer 1929, not long before he was reelected Governor of New York, thus insuring a solid base of operation for his 1932 campaign for the Presidency. The progressed Full Moon of that 30-year long progressed lunation cycle referred to the summer 1944. Victory was at hand and the physical process of disintegration brought about by enormous pressures and responsibilities could no longer be arrested. The two main opponents in the global confrontation, Roosevelt and Hitler, who had risen to power in their respective nations at about the same time and both on the basis of economic collapse, died in the same month of April 1945.

The lunation cycle and the natal Sun-Moon relationship can be used as a frame of reference within which various astrological factors can be given special meaning. The position of the Part of Fortune very close to the Sun should be considered (cf. again THE LUNATION CYCLE) and the position of the planets within the angle formed by the Sun-Moon relationship. As the Moon progressed after F.D.R.'s birth the first planet it touched was Uranus; which can be considered as an indication that what F.D.R. had to stress in this life is the power of transformation (or reform) of Uranus. Before reaching the next New Moon, the Moon crossed also over Venus and Mercury. This suggests that at the end of the life-experience, the inner factors of being were to enter into play — a personal culmination of effort beyond the realm of outer events.

Obviously much can be made of the fact that F.D.R. was an "Aquarian" — too much probably if one looks at what such zodiacal type characterization has brought to popular astrology. The interesting fact is nevertheless that this Aquarian Sun stood in psychological contrast to the Cancerian Moon in the tenth House — a very strong position for the Moon. What this means can be interpreted in various ways: a strong mother whose ambition for her son may have been a dominant factor, especially during his illness — also an equally strong wife. A good approach to one's public and warm response from women in public matters may also be indicated. At any rate, the individual with such a natal Moon should pay much attention to women and/or public moods in all professional matters.

Beside its already mentioned and concretely effective sextile to Saturn, the Moon forms a quintile to Uranus, and a septile to the Jupiter-Neptune, pair. A numerologist would be very interested by these angular factors 5, 6 and 7. One might add also a novile (38°53') to Pluto. This variety of aspects could be interpreted as referring to a keen ability to adapt to public situations in terms of creative, practical and super-personal or planetary values.

On the other hand, the Sun (backed as it were by Venus nearby) makes only tense aspects: a massive square to Saturn, Neptune and Jupiter, and a sesquiquadrate aspect to Mars. These aspects confirm, as it were, the meaning of the Mars-Saturn septile already mentioned. This Sun-Venus pair can also be said to form a broad Y aspect to the quintile of the Moon to Uranus. It is not the typical kind of Y-aspect which theoretically involves a sextile and two fairly exact 150° aspects, yet Venus is in exact 150° aspect to the Moon, and the Sun forms the same aspect to Uranus — though Uranus actually forms a bi-quintile (144°) to the Sun.

These solar aspects imply definite challenges to the vitality; but the Sun also refers to the inner Will of the individual (i.e. the sense of purpose or "destiny") — provided this Will can be mobilized; and this depends mainly on the stage of spiritual evolution of the person. In the Sabian series of symbols, the twelfth degree of Aquarius is represented by the Stairway of Life's evolution — which suggests the capacity to move upward to a new level of experience. Such a moving upward implies quite inevitably harsh challenges and the need to overcome them. It may evoke the possibility of an "Initiation" — a much abused term, alas! — or at a more mundane level, a forceful ambition. The elevated Mars in the tenth House can evidently be said to reveal a strong drive toward achievement, and the sesquiquadrate of Sun to Mars suggests that this drive is probably the result of an ancient Soul-past — or even of a family tradition. The symbol for the Ascendant degree fits well in such a picture, for it reveals "A swimming race"; it even fits in with F.D.R.'s illness, its at least apparent cause (a swim in the ocean) and his constant efforts at helping his muscular disability through swimming.

The symbol for the Part of Fortune (in Aquarius and in the fifth House, at 13°27) is also revealing: "A train entering a tunnel." It suggests a strong will to pierce through obstacles, even if it be in defiance of nature. The square between the planets in the fifth and eighth Houses fits in well with such a symbol, for these seven planets in fixed signs tend to indicate not only a capacity for a "regeneration" of personal egocentric urges, but great perserverance and a fixity of purpose.

Progressions:

It is not my purpose here to attempt a study of secondary progressions. As I have stated in THE LUNATION CYCLE and THE PRACTICE OF ASTROLOGY, the "progressed lunation cycle" and its 30-year cycle provides the most general and best frame of reference for all progressions. In F.D.R.'s case the progressed New Moons divide his life as follow: from birth to 1900 — from 1900 to 1929 — and up to his death in 1945. At 18 the young Roosevelt presumably was entering college; in 1929 (age 47½) he had sufficiently overcome the effect of illness to have been elected Governor of New York state in 1928 — his new political life had begun, after an impressive comeback. Mars, which became direct (by progression) in 1885, had moved over the natal Moon in 1927-28, thus correlating accurately with the new ambitions and successful effort. The effort took place during the "seed period" (the last three years) of the progressed lunation cycle which had begun in 1900.

The progressions of the Moon over the four angles of the chart, especially the Ascendant, are often very significant. We find the progressed Moon crossing F.D.R.'s Ascendant in the spring-summer 1915 (he had already been given the position of Assistant Secretary of the Navy in 1913) and in the fall of 1942, less than a year after Pearl Harbor, and at a time when the progressed Sun and the progressed Mars were moving in close square formation — a difficult time for the United States. What is even more significant, from the Humanistic astrology standpoint is that the passage of the progressed Moon through each House normally emphasizes the realm of individual experience upon which it is *advisable* for the person to focus his attention. However, one has to interpret the meaning of the Houses in a consistent and logical manner, realizing that the Houses constitute *twelve successive phases of a cyclic process* — this process referring to man's inherent capacity to consciously experience life and its constant modifications, within himself and in relation to the outer world. Each House represents a specific *field of experience.* Passing successively through these fields and responding to what they bring to the consciousness an individual person gradually becomes aware of himself and his world, and learns to adjust himself to, or control (which may mean to upset!) the sources of these experiences, i.e. his inner and outer environment.

When F.D.R. became the President of a nation in economic chaos and confronted by the possibility of a revolution, his progressed Moon was passing through Taurus. During his summer 1932 campaign it was moving over his three Taurus planets, especially Jupiter and Neptune, and through his natal eighth House. When he assumed power and he wielded it at once in an imaginative and striking manner his progressed Moon had entered the ninth House. He surrounded himself with far-seeing minds using new principles of social and economic value.

He prepared for his second term while the progressed Moon was in the tenth House and returning to its natal place. The progressed Moon was in his twelfth House when Japan struck at Pearl Harbor; the President had to face the "karmic" result of a long cycle of diplomatic fumbling which had begun with the Presidency of another Roosevelt, T.D.R., the man with the "big stick" policy who completely ignored the portents of Japan's victory and angered the rising nation which never forgave that President's intervention at the Peace Treaty. And evidently F.D.R. was also then reaping his own Karma — the challenging results of his own ambition and his feeling of destiny.

In any complete chart-interpretation one has, of course, to study the cycle of the other progressed planets; but the Moon is the only planet whose progressions can complete a cycle during a natural human life. It is for this reason, if for no other, that its progressed cycle is so basic, especially in terms of the progressed lunation cycle, because the Moon should never be fully separated from the Sun as they constitute a fundamental polarity — the symbolic basis of all life on this Earth. The movements of progressed Mercury can, however, be very significant, for this planet often changes direction twice during a lifetime. In F.D.R.'s case, progressed Mercury turned retrograde in 1895-96 (adolescence time), and became *direct* again in 1918 when he went to Europe after World War I. In 1924 progressed Mercury reached once more its natal place, as progressed Venus was entering Aries. This very likely refers to the time when it became evident that the future President had mentally conquered his illness and was gathering his forces for a new life.

Transits:

I believe that it is rather senseless to interpret progressions and transits as if they referred to the same level of significance. It is true that once a birth-moment is given, the positions of all the planets during the entire life of the person are also given, and thus the relationship of these positions to the natal positions on any day is also *implied* in the birth-chart. Nevertheless the transiting positions of the planets (including Sun and Moon) are theoretically the results of the observations of the celestial environment by the mature person; they are *outer events;* thus they logically should be correlated also to "events" in the person's life. They represent the relationship between an individual and his planetary and social as well as cosmic environment; which in most cases means first of all the pressure or impact of this total environment upon the person — even though the person's responses do affect, in ever so slight a measure, his planetary environment, and, in some cases, quite strongly indeed, his social environment. This effect of the individual upon society in terms of transits should never be forgotten. For instance, a President may have transiting Saturn over his natal Sun when he takes office, and this refers to the man experiencing a massive increase in his responsibilities, in working hours, in the protocol and public aspects of his daily existence. But it means *as well* that the man's Sun is relating itself to the world's Saturn; that is, his purpose of destiny is impressing itself upon all that Saturn represents to his nation and to mankind.

Secondary progressions have a very different character. They refer to the completion of the process of gestation *at the psycho-mental level* during the three months following the nine months of intra-uterine development of the body (*bio-physiological level).* A whole solar cycle has to be completed since the moment of conception; thus a twelve-month period. The *body* has normally to be developed during the first nine months within the dark, protective and *closed* environment of the mother's womb; but the *mind* (or what I have called specifically "intelligence," i.e., the power of consciously adjusting to the environment through processes of interchange) requires that the organism operate in at least relative independence in an *open* environment, giving to it as well as receiving from it (if only through breathing, vocal sounds and simple gestures).

What the secondary progressions thus represent (on the basis of one year per day of actual living after birth) is the process of unfoldment of potentialities latent in the human organism, but needing the relationship with an open environment for their development or actualization. In a more general sense these progressions refer to the process of germination of the seed of a plant. The seed (the birth-chart) contains in potentiality what the full-grown plant will, or rather *may,* become. The process is essentially an *interior* one in that it demands, in a sense at least, nothing from the exterior. By contrast the transits refer to the interaction between the basically permanent (or archetypal) structure of being (the birth-chart) and the cyclic patterns made by the rhythm of the ever-moving and dynamic components of the solar system which our senses perceive, the planets. There may be as yet unperceived components, but they are not parts of the language of astrology, just as the word, neutron, did not exist as a word until atomic physicists needed it to characterize some until then unperceived element.

The concept of "transit" in astrology should not be entirely limited to what happens when some moving celestial body passes over the degree of the zodiac on which a natal planet or an angle was located. Such an event only serves *to bring to a focus a cyclic process.* Such processes can be defined in two ways. There are simple cycles, which I have called "cycles of positions"; and complex ones, called "cycles of relationship." The time it takes for a planet to return to its natal position defines its cycle of position. The cycle produced by the successive conjunctions of two planets moving at different speeds — for instance, the cycle defined by the succession of New Moons, or of conjunctions of Jupiter and Saturn — is a cycle of relationship. Both types are transit cycles, and important for the interpretation of a chart. What is to be considered in connection with cycles of relationships is the place at which the successive conjunctions occur.

In the case of the lunations, nothing too significant may be indicated; yet, if a New Moon falls exactly on a natal planet or angle, this planet or angle is usually dynamized — and the indication may be more important if the New Moon is a solar eclipse. What the planet or angle signifies should be intensified. The opportunity, or need, is indicated; but the individual is not obliged to meet it. Indeed most human beings are always eager to avoid confrontations, if these will tend to upset the *status quo.*

Solar eclipses are not necessarily fateful omens if they occur on one's birthday, or on some natal planet. They simply stress the fact that Sun, Moon and Earth are in exact alignment, and that the Sun's energy is therefore, as it were, channelled through the Moon. In ancient occultism it was stated that the most mysterious "seventh Ray" of the Sun — the *Sushumna* Ray — goes to the Moon. It produces, one may assume, "occult" transformations — perhaps "redemption from the past," a karmic process. It may vitalize the form of the past, only to eventually shatter it. At least the first effect can be a kind of ego-glorification.

In September 1931 there was an annular solar eclipse on F.D.R.'s Ascendant. He was undoubtedly preparing himself from Albany for the Presidency. Another — a partial one — came very close in September 1942 when he was preparing the country for a war he most likely felt inevitable if not necessary. He died just after a New Moon in his eighth House; Venus and Mercury, both retrograde, were contained within the five-degree arc separating the Moon from the Sun. The Ascendant was at Virgo 10°, according to some data, with Jupiter retrograde rising close to F.D.R.'s natal Uranus. Neptune, also retrograde was squaring, from the first House, Saturn about to pass over his natal Moon. Mars was about to leave his sixth House forming, from the seventh House of the death-chart, a T-cross with the tenth House Uranus and the first House Jupiter.

One of the important transit cycles is that which is defined by the successive conjunctions of Jupiter and Saturn. The House (and sign and degree) in which these conjunctions occur at 20-year intervals can give very interesting indications. F.D.R. was born not long after such a conjunction (April 1881) which fell in his eighth natal House. The following one occurred in November 1901 in Capricorn at the end of his fourth House, a year after his father's death and while he was in college. Another took place on September 10, 1921 *just after* his polio attack at Virgo 26°39', thus in his first House. The last one was three times repeated in 1940-41 when Hitler was overcoming all European armies; and that one touched his Saturn, Neptune and Jupiter once more in the eighth House (about every 60 years Jupiter and Saturn return to their natal places). Thus the eighth, fourth and first Houses were emphasized in F.D.R.'s life, insofar as social-political factors within his personality were concerned.

In the case of President Kennedy the Jupiter-Saturn conjunctions of his life fell (according to Campanus Houses) in his twelfth (1921), his seventh (1940-41) and just past his fourth House cusp (1961-Capricorn) — an interesting problem of interpretation.

Once we have noted these turning points in the development of the complementary functions represented by Jupiter and Saturn we can then consider the transits which these planets make as they cross the other planets and the angles. The Jupiter cycle of positions lasts less than 12 years; the Saturn cycle, about 29½ years. The former has been associated with financial matters, but also with the growth of the "social sense." The Saturn cycle is very interesting inasmuch as it lasts close to the period of a progressed lunation cycle.

In analyzing the simplest division of these two cycles of positions one naturally thinks of the passage of these planets through the four quarters of the birth-chart. These quarters — at least in such a connection, but also with reference to the cyclic motion of the progressed Moon — can be given the following meanings:

First Quarter: "Growth in essential being" (in three phases: first, second and third Houses)
Second Quarter: Growth in faculties
Third Quarter: Growth in power and opportunities, essentially through relationships
Fourth Quarter: Growth in influence

I have stressed here the positive factor of "growth"; but any phase of a cycle can turn negative. If the transits through the third quarter have been connected with a negative approach to, and/or a failure in relationship, the fourth quarter can represent a decrease in influence, perhaps an empty feeling of frustration and ineffectual protest or rebellion.

When Roosevelt was stricken by illness Saturn had entered the first quarter of his chart (first, second and third Houses). What the illnesses brought him was indeed "growth in essential being." Saturn had previously entered his fourth quarter (1913) when President Wilson appointed him Assistant Secretary of the Navy; this was the climax of his first ascent along the path of political power. Very likely his personal development at that stage would not have been adequate for greater responsibilities. Thus when Saturn crossed his Ascendant the stage was being set for a new cycle of growth. The stage-setting may somehow have begun on October 1920 when Saturn crossed the Ascendant of the chart I am presenting here. On May 21, 1921 Saturn was "stationary direct" at Virgo 17°58', and in August the crisis reached the plane of physical shock.

During 1928 Saturn entered by transit the second quarter of F.D.R.'s chart; and he was elected Governor of New York. His Administration began on March 4, 1933, immediately after Saturn crossed his natal Sun. It reached the Mid Heaven in June 1943 — a year of conferences between the chiefs of State. The concept of the United Nations had already been formulated. As already stated, at his death Saturn was about to cross his natal Moon.

The transits cycles of the faster planets, Mercury, Venus and Mars can also be significant, even though they recur frequently. Some astrologers make a great deal out of Mars' transits; every one, it seems, has some favorite! For others, Saturn, Jupiter, or Uranus are the most important factors. It is far moe valuable to think of each transit cycle as significant only in terms of the functon which the transiting planet symbolizes. When Uranus reached F.D.R.'s Venus he became Assistant Secretary of the Navy. It moved over his Sun in January 1915, while Saturn crossed his natal Mars, and Jupiter his natal Mercury; Venus being also at the Nadir of the chart. This should have been a very basic turning point, but I know of no special event mentioned in his biography. He was then 33. This may have referred to a very personal, perhaps an emotional, matter — perhaps even something that could have led to his illness later on. The transit of Uranus over the natal Sun is nearly always an indication of some inner crisis of transformation, or of an external turning point in the personal and/or public life; yet there may not be any definite *outer event* connected with the transit. Uranus began to cross F.D.R.'s Taurus planets in May 1936, as the campaign for his second term of office began; it ended in March 1942 with Uranus's final transit over natal Pluto — the dark days of

Japanese conquests. F.D.R. died before Uranus reached his Mid Heaven.

Neptune crossed his Ascendant and his natal Uranus during late 1936 and 1937. These were crucial days when Hitler had risen to power and was testing the will-to-fight of France and England, when Mussolini had revived a pseudo "Roman Empire," when the Civil War in Spain was challenging the "Free World" and Japan was conquering China. This was, in a sense, the start of World War II; just as World War I had actually begun with the Balkan Wars of 1912.

Opinions vary concerning the value of the transits of the Moon's Nodes; but there is no reason why they should not be considered. They correlate with "eclipse seasons" which may affect planetary groupings in the birth-chart. When the transiting nodes correspond with the natal horizon and the meridian, basic changes in consciousness and in the public life often indeed are experienced. The North Node was conjunct F.D.R.'s Ascendant in April 1923, which I presume marked his recovery, for he was able a year later to present the name of Alfred E. Smith to the Democratic Convention in New York. It had come to the cusp of the fourth House as World War I ended (October, November 1918). It reached F.D.R.'s Descendant in August 1932 during his campaign for the Presidency. It was once more at the Ascendant and conjunct Uranus — significantly indeed — just as the Pearl Harbor tragedy occurred (December 1941).

One can even find value in progressing the

Part of Fortune*; but, as I have used such progressions, I calculate the progressed Part of Fortune with reference to the *natal* Ascendant (i.e. by referring the progressed Moon and the progressed Sun to this natal horizon). One can also calculate it by considering what is called the "progressed horoscope" which was popularized by Alen Leo. Personally, I prefer to retain the angular structure of the natal chart as a permanent lifelong frame of reference. The motion of the horizon and meridian are no doubt also significant, and these are various ways of calculating their positions year in, year out. One can also use "primary directions" beside the "secondary progressions." There are indeed so many techniques that can be used! And now the "cosmobiological" system of Ebertin — and before him of the Uranian School of Germany — is being widely spread.

All these systems, if logically and consistently developed and carried out, can find their place in a very detailed study of charts; but their mastery demands a very long period of study and the variety of often contradictory information they provide can be, and indeed usually is, very confusing — just as the mind of a person can be confused by his ability to express his thoughts in several languages. What is essential is to know what one is looking for; i.e. what astrology is to be used for — and to focus one's attention upon that. If one wants to deal with precise outer events, this is one approach. It is *not* the approach of Humanistic astrology. This approach is purposive

---

* For a study of the Part of Fortune, I refer the reader to my book THE LUNATION CYCLE.

rather than analytical. It does not seek to know what *will* happen, but to understand the meaning of what *has happened* and to know how best one can meet present situations and the turning points or crisis of growth which one can see taking shape in the future as the result of the rhythmic development of the potentialities inherent in the individual person.

25

A Young Man's Chart

This is the chart of a young man, J.A., who was born in Southern California on September 25, 1949. The exact birth-moment was said to be 7:55 a.m. but because of the crucial early death of his father at the exact age of 7 (arc of Mars to Mid Heaven and also of Saturn forming by direction a semi-square to Mid Heaven 7 years after birth), it seems necessary to rectify the birth-time to 8:02 a.m. His appearance is more typical of Libra than of Scorpio; but with the Sun in Libra and a rising Venus, it is expectable that the Libra character would have marked rather deeply his features and to some extent at least his character.

I have known him for several years, at first through his family, and for at least three years as an individual with a rather outstanding intelligence and sensitivity. His development became particularly accelerated and significant when Uranus, then Jupiter passed over his natal Sun in November 1968. When, last Fall, I thought of using his birth-chart in this essay and I asked him his permission to do so, we talked a little more than before about his chart. He had

A Young Man's Chart

just reached the age of 21, the beginning of a very important 7-year cycle which assuredly will establish more definitely what can be expected of him during his mature period as an individual. I made a horary chart at the time and I am using it much as I might have used it then if he had come for a consultation. (I no longer give such consultations.) We shall presently see that this horary chart was quite significant, as he was then just entering a new phase of his emotional unfoldment. But before we come to this, let us examine the young man's natal chart.

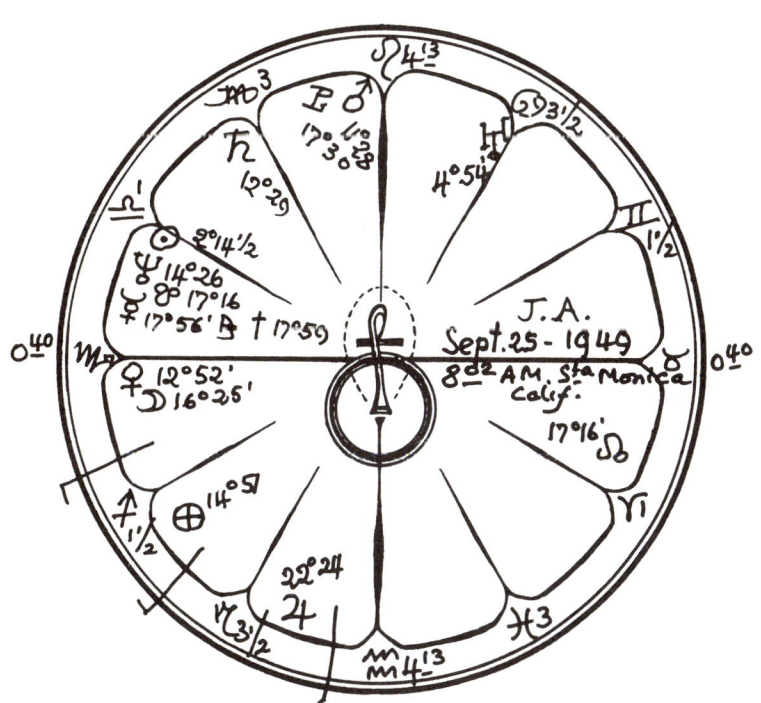

We see at once that most planets, except Uranus in the ninth House, are located in the "eastern" half of the chart. However, Jupiter is separated from the closest planet by a 66 degree angle (sextile) and by an empty second House (I do not count the Part of Fortune or the Moon's Nodes in evaluating the overall planetary pattern, or *gestalt*); moreover this Jupiter in Capricorn is in too wide a relationship to allow us to speak of an opposition; and there are no other opposition aspects in the chart. Thus while at first sight the chart gives the impression of belonging to the Hemispheric Type defined in a previous essay FIRST STEPS IN THE STUDY OF BIRTH-CHARTS), nevertheless it would perhaps be better to consider it as a Funnel Type. If we place the natal planets in the frame of Houses of the symbolic horary chart above-mentioned, it will be seen that Jupiter stands most definitely isolated. The planets on that September 26, 1970 showed also a Funnel Pattern with an isolated Saturn in the fourth House.

In the essay just mentioned I gave as an example of Hemispheric pattern the chart of Harold Wilson, the Ex-Premier of England, and this chart and that of J.A. have a common appearance; but Wilson has a planet in the second House and thus all Houses were occupied east of an opposition of Mars retrograde to Uranus. The difference between the two patterns is quite real, and of course the planets themselves have very different positions by House and sign. Still, there is a certain similarity due to the five empty Houses and I shall suggest, after a while, what this situation implies.

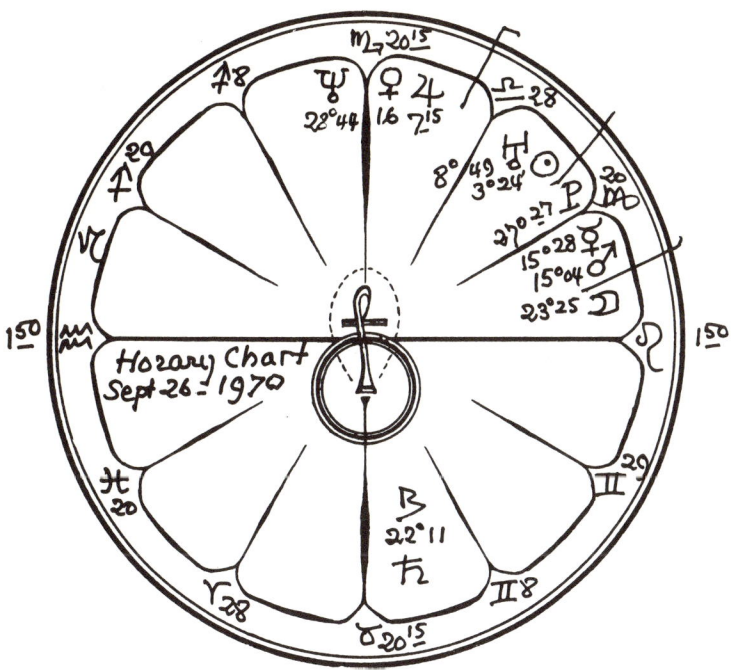

If, however, one interprets the chart as a Funnel Type then Jupiter in the third House can be considered as a point of release for the energies, and the tensions, generated in the grouping of planets between Uranus and the Moon. Jupiter in Capricorn is supposed to be "weak" as it is in a Saturnian zodiacal sign, and interestingly enough it is located on the north node of Saturn; one could also consider the two planets of the social consciousness as being in a very broad trine aspect, especially as both form sextiles to the Moon which stands very close to the mid-point of this trine.

Moreover if one calculates the "center of gravity" (or mid-point) of the planetary grouping between Uranus and the Moon — a grouping occupying about 131½ degrees, thus a sesquiquadrate aspect — this center of gravity falls at Virgo 10½° quite close to Saturn and about 132 degrees away from Jupiter — a sesquiquadrate aspect. The sesquiquadrate between Uranus and Moon divides itself into a square of Uranus to Sun, and a semi-square of Moon to the Sun. Thus in terms of the Lunation Types, J.A. belongs to the Crescent Type, the Moon to Sun angle being so close to 45 degrees. Theoretically the new release of power at the preceding New Moon, which occupied on September 22, 1949 at Virgo 29°08' had reached, at J.A.'s birth, a level of intensity at which it was ready to challenge the remaining structures of the past cycle — unless the aspect should operate in a negative aspect as a result of "a failure to repolarize one's capacity for personal or social relationship." (cf. THE LUNATION CYCLE, page 64-65, first edition, p.50-51 new edition). J.A. may have to watch lest this negative attitude develop because of strong Neptunian "influence" over the twelfth House Sun and Mercury. However, the conjunction of Mars and Pluto in the tenth House in constructive sextile aspect to Neptune and Mercury suggests that sooner or later J.A. is most likely to take a very positive approach to social situations — an approach tempered by a practical and objective Saturn, yet not without great emotional intensity (square to Venus and Moon). But planetary squares and tensions are needed to generate forcefulness, and in "fixed" zodiacal signs (Leo and Scorpio — also the signs of Mid Heaven and Ascendant), they show a fixed determination to overcome obstacles, including those provided by one's subconscious "ghosts."

The chart offers a tight interweaving of squares and sextiles, the latter producing rather broad trines. All categories of Houses (angular, succedent and cadent) are represented, but cadent Houses are emphasized (ninth, twelfth, and third); and zodiacal signs of the four "elements" are accentuated by planets, but cardinal signs (Cancer, Libra and Capricorn) are stressed — then come fixed signs. One should consider Venus and Mars as ruling planets; but they are in square aspects, and the planets close to them, respectively Pluto and Moon, are also in square aspect. The first aspect which the Moon made after birth was indeed is square to Pluto — then a sextile to Jupiter. However, these tense aspects are balanced by sextiles. The "forming" square of the Sun to Uranus is perhaps the symbol of the greatest tensions in the chart — together with the square of the Moon to Pluto in angular Houses.

As the Sun is on its way to meet Neptune, we see that the two Lights are in quite intensified relationship to the most distant planets, which represent the action of transcendent forces — or of catharsis-producing factors in the depths of the psyche. As Uranus dominates the ninth House, the influence of philosophical and/or "exotic" ideas is stressed. This may lead to long journeys and contacts with "foreigners," and these Uranian factors may produce basic challenges to the psychic depths — to the "Unconscious."

The retrograde Mercury, rising after the Sun (as Venus also does) can be considered a symbol of an "inward turned" mind, seeking guidance and/or confirmaton from a source within — or in terms of some kind of broad social-cultural Movement. Historical objectivity should be favored. Mercury's closeness to the Moon's South Node could be interpreted in several ways, especially as the Moon is quite close to Mercury's South Node (17° 42 Scorpio) — an interesting interchange which may suggest a "past" of intellectual achievements or a strong reliance on intellectual concepts, as a means to insure emotional security.

There might be also a tendency to develop some subtle kind of psychic dependence on a Mother-Image; but here one has to consider the rising conjunction of Venus and the Moon in Scorpio — a somewhat ambiguous aspect, in terms of whatever Scorpio may represent in J.A.'s temperament, inasmuch as the two celestial bodies square the "elevated" conjunction of Mars and Pluto.

This could refer to difficulties with the mother. A strong relationship with a sibling may also be implied. Some kind of psychological or even psychic involvement in which the Woman Image plays a role is possible. But the intuition, or psychic sense should be very strong, if it can be held within a clear mental structure.

The symbol for the Moon's degree (Scorpio 17°) suggests a capacity for receiving spiritual energies of a fecundant nature; and the Venus degree symbol pictures a capacity for carrying a creative work to its completion. The symbol for the Sun is "Dawn"; and birth occurred in the morning. The possibility for expansion of consciousness and vivid realizations of a larger order of realities (cf. Ascendant degree-symbol) is certainly evident. But there will be obstacles (social as well as personal), inner tensions to overcome, and perhaps confrontations with "the Establishment" at whatever level it might be.

With most planets located on the Eastern side of the chart, problems dealing with the self and the place one occupies in society are almost inevitably to be experienced. But, from the Humanistic astrology point of view, the challenges are there to be met "squarely" — not to be avoided. In other words, the natural pull of the personality is toward a strong concentration upon what is required for self-unfoldment and there would be no sense in resisting it; *but* this leaves the field of interpersonal relationship and partnerships all open as a kind of void; or, let us say, as an unconscious demand for fulfillment through relationship in order to balance the urge toward self-development. As, moreover, the sign Libra in the 12th House and Venus rising are emphasized (and Venus rules the House of relationship), this gives added power to this demand for fulfillment through relationship — and even more perhaps for seeking to touch the deepest psychic depth of "man's common humanity" through whatever Scorpio represents in this individual instance; which may mean far more than sexual experiences. This may lead to some kind of mysticism or capacity for "transpersonal" contacts or communicaions. Neptune being a strong presence in the unconscious — or, we might also say, in terms of a subconscious "memory" of past lives.

The horary chart I erected provides a strong confirmation of what has just been stated, even though it be a purely symbolical one. The emphasis in the chart is reversed — and, if one inscribes the natal planets in the horary framework of the Houses, the same result is found; that is, a concentration of planets in the West-South sector of the chart. It is indeed very interesting to compare this chart with the natal one, and to see what happens to the natal planetary pattern when placed in the new framework of Houses with the first degree of Aquarius rising. This places the natal Jupiter in the twelfth House and the over-all planetary picture definitely reveals a Funnel pattern.

As already mentioned, J.A. was at the time entering a new phase of unfoldment which has been generating profound development of his feeling-nature. In the horary chart, the Sun and Uranus are in "forming" conjunction in the House of "regeneration," with Mars behind them; and indeed the transit conjunction of Uranus to

J.A.'s Sun in the fall 1968 did mean a deep arousal of new values and the development of an unusually mature and intuitive mind.

The difficulty an astrologer would have met if he had been definitely asked in the summer 1968 what kind of opportunities such a Uranus transit could bring, and how best to meet them, refers to the rather ambiguous character of any twelfth House. This House symbolizes the last phase of a cycle of individual and conscious experiences; but it represents also the preparation (the "seed sowing") preceding a new one. One speaks of it usually as the House of the subconscious, of Karma, of social bondage, etc.; but I have often stressed the fact that it could also be the field of experience in which one reaps the social rewards of a "successful" cycle of activity in one's community. One may "retire" with honors and wealth, or end the cycle in jail or a hospital; and there is no reason why the twelfth House should mean the latter alternative rather than the former. In most cases, of course, the situation falls in between the two extremes.

Another difficulty is also that if one would use, say, the Placidus House system, J.A.'s natal Sun would fall in the eleventh instead of the twelfth House; but, as I stated in a previous essay, the astrologer should abide by what he considers the most valid and sound system, and no amount of "research," statistical or otherwise, can "prove" that one system is better than another — except perhaps in rare cases. The individual himself, if thoroughly familiar with the language of astrology, may feel definitely inclined to use one system rather than another; and this ambiguity is in itself an indication that every man or woman has the privilege of giving his or her own meaning to the "words" astrology spells in his or her birth-chart. Astrology is certainly *not* an exact science; but even in supposedly exact sciences like physics the results of an experiment can often be interpreted in several ways, and other results might be obtained if the technique used would have been different.

This is why a chart should always be interpreted in terms of the present situation and the vital need of the client — and of one's own need if one studies one's own chart. And in 1968 as Uranus was about to cross his natal Sun, J.A.'s need was presumably to arise and transform within his subconscious nature the end-results of what in the broadest sense I would call his "past."

One may look at the matter by considering the chart of the New Moon which began the lunation cycle in which he was born some three days later. This New Moon occurred, as we already saw, at Virgo 29°08'; and the Sabian symbol for this 30th degree of Virgo is rather intriguing. Marc Jones has interpreted in a curious way what he originally recorded; and it is this interpretation which I followed in 1935 when writing THE ASTROLOGY OF PERSONALITY as I had just begun to study the set of symbols. However, the original record (cf. Marc Jones SABIAN SYMBOLS) was different and what the symbol seems to refer to is a final test *before* the process of self-transformation — or one might say "initiation." The individual ready for the great step has succeeded in developing such a one-pointed attention to what is, potentially. at least, ahead of him that he has become impervious to illusory demands made upon him. He simply does not hear or acknowledge them. Nevertheless this is still only a preparatory state of consciousness, and the momentum of that state must complete its appointed course. The course, in the situation now being discussed, is the full lunation cycle which, having begun on September 22, 1949, ends in the next New Moon on October 21, at Libra 28°48'. The symbol for this twenty-ninth degree refers to man's essential drive toward knowledge — at last, knowledge at the particular level which can be attained by a collective, cultural effort.

In terms of the progressed lunation cycle J.A. will reach this progressed New Moon in December 1975 — thus at the age of 26. The progressed Full Moon of the cycle which began before his birth occurred in 1961 — age 12. The progressed last quarter occurred in 1969 and may correspond to a more definite break away from his family and cultural traditions. It may be worth noting that his father (who died accidentally on September 22, 1956) had his natal Uranus at Leo 5°52' very close to J.A.'s Mid Heaven. The Mid Heaven represents the father, or at least the Father Image in a psychological sense, and in a more spiritual sense, the "Father within" — the divine Presence within the total person, but also the "star" that is not in the zodiacal field but at the true zenith of the birth location.

In 1962 the progressed Sun crossed natal Neptune while Neptune moved by transit over the natal Moon; this was a time of inner confusion. But the sextile of the progressed Sun to Pluto in 1965, and the conjunction of this progressed Sun to Mercury in 1966 began to dispel the psychic fog. The square of the progressed Sun to Jupiter in the winter-spring 1970 — prolonged through the first part of 1971 (progressed Sun squaring *progressed* Jupiter) — very likely gave an added incentive to the development of the mind, and also led J.A. to a new environment.

The most interesting period ahead is that which will correspond to the crossing of his natal Ascendant by the progressed Sun. This may help to clarify further the matter of the most correct ascendant. It should happen in mid 1978, if the Ascendant I suggest is verified. But before this occurs the first progressed New Moon after J.A.'s birth will have occurred at the very close of 1975. The 1978 date is interesting because he will then be in his twenty-ninth year, having reached the age of 28 on September 25, 1977; and this twenty-eighth birthday begins not only a 7-year period, but the second of the great 28-year periods which — at least today — divide a human life into three basic cycles, in a kind of "dialectical" sequence of thesis, antithesis and synthesis.

These dates should mark the successive phases of an *interior* process of "self-actualization"; but giving power and momentum to this process, we can see the transits of Uranus and of Pluto over the very sensitive areas of the twelfth and the first Houses. We saw that Uranus (backed by Jupiter) crossed J.A.'s Sun during November 1968 and lastly in August 1969. As I am writing these pages Uranus is retrogressing over his natal Neptune; it will cross Mercury in 1972 and 1973. Then the most important transit over the Ascendant will occur at the end of November 1974 and again in September 1975; thus *nearly at the same time as the progressed New Moon;* quite an extraordinary coincidence and J.A. will then begin his twenty-seventh year. That fall period will also be the opening of the last quarter of the century, exactly one hundred years after the beginning of the Theosophical Society in New York — very likely a crucial 25-year period for mankind.

Then there are the less easy to interpret (or to understand) transits of Pluto. About the time this brief analysis is made public, Pluto will come close to crossing J.A.'s natal Sun, repeating thus the series of transits made by Uranus (The exact transit will occur a year later). The two planets, Uranus and Pluto, were conjunct in 1966 just on J.A.'s "Part of Spirit" (which I have discussed in my book THE LUNATION CYCLE); and it could be that this marked the reestablishment of an ancient spiritual pattern, or the breaking up of it in connection with a friend, or some inner influence. In any case this conjunction of Uranus and Pluto has certainly been the "Signature" of the present phase of revolutionary upheaval which has spread from California — and more precisely Berkeley — to the whole youth of the world. In J.A.'s case that time presumably started him off and out of a confused period — and I already mentioned the progressions of the Sun to Pluto and Mercury during 1965 and 1966 (age 16-17).

Pluto, then, is slowly, and I believe far more definitively and irrevocably, deepening up the pathway which Uranus opened in 1968. Whether or not the transit will correlate with important external events is, in a sense, quite unimportant. The traditional effort which countless generations of astrologers have made to show the correlation between astrological motions and physical plane events is, to a Humanistic astrologer, beside the point. There may be events, and there may not be. What counts is only whether or not one *understands* whatever is happening, and one *uses* the situation being formed in order to make more conscious, more complete, more radiant and/or creative the process of self-actualization.

Pluto will pass over J.A.'s Mercury in 1979; and it will cross his Ascendant in 1983-84. But it is hardly worthwhile to speculate on what these fairly distant transits may indicate. What is more relevant is the coming transits of Uranus over J.A.'s Mercury in October 1972. This could mark a highly stimulating period at the intellectual level. There are obviously many lesser transits which should be studied in a detailed analysis, but this present study aims merely at indicating *main lines of enquiry.*

I have not spoken yet of the Moon's Nodes, but these constitute a factor which can be very significant. In this case, if we consider the chart as being divided into two zones, one containing all the planets, and the other empty, we see that the South Node is placed close to the center of gravity of the planetary mass which is located in mid-Libra very near Neptune in the twelfth House. This could be interpreted as signifying a strong tendency toward introversion, conceivably based on practices or at least attitudes subconsciously "remembered" from some ancient past — thus as a somewhat "automatic" type of response to life-situations; and this could mean in certain circumstances, a withdrawal into Neptunian abstractions or psychic glamor. On the other hand, it could mean, according to the positive sense of the South Node, a kind of "genius" at developing transcendant (psychic or spiritual) faculties. In either case, it suggests that J.A.'s conscious attention is drawn toward such twelfth House matters, and this according to the Libra temperament.

Interestingly enough Uranus has been criss-crossing this "center of gravity" of the occupied half of the chart throughout 1971; and this could indicate a transformation of this center of attraction within the inner or psychic life — one might say a drying up of Neptunian waters (fantasies of the unconscious perhaps, or utopian dreams.) By "drying up" I do not mean that the Neptunian waters should be considered as a negative factor; even though they can be negative in many instances, if the mystical or abstract urge is not balanced by other influences. The balancing factor and the point of self-exertion — and as a result of "Providential" assistance — are represented by the North Node in the House of work, retraining and in some cases discipleship.

While speaking of "balance" I cannot help restating what I have repeated many times, i.e. that Libra and its symbol "the Scales" do *not* refer to what is so commonly and superficially called "balance" by astrologers. It is true that scales balance one thing against another, but the important factor is the *purpose and meaning* of the operation. When an object is weighed, it is weighed against a collectively agreed upon standard of measurement and value. What an individual brings to society (for instance, to the market place) is being *evaluated according to a social standard.* The important factor in the weighing is not that the two sides of the scales are "balanced," but that, for instance, the product of an individual's work (such as vegetables he has grown, or piece of gold he has discovered) is given a *collective* value. Libra therefore refers to all processes which lead to ascertaining the value to society of an individual and his work — and thus to the first active integration of an individual person in the collective patterns of the group, culture and nation to which he belongs, or which he wishes to join.

This, to me at least, should be obvious; but astrologers are so traditionalistic in their response to symbols, and particularly to the superficial

A Young Man's Chart

aspect of what a symbolic situation depicts, that the idea that people born with the Sun in Libra are "balanced" people — when there is no real evidence for this at all — will undoubtedly persist. People born with the Sun in Libra are rather persons whose vital energies, and often life-purpose, are deeply conditioned by a basic urge to *assess their value* in terms of social or group responses. In the case of J.A., the group could be a transcendent more than a social collectivity, and his interest in occultism, astrology and the development of psychic or intuitive faculties is evidence of this *possibility*. The presence of the Moon's South Node in the midst of his Libra planets and between Neptune and Mercury could well indicate that he had brought such a interest from the past.

One of the problems he may face is what to do with the rising Venus-Moon conjunction in Scorpio. This problem may have to be faced when Uranus will transit these two planets during 1978. He will then be 29; and such a period has already come up in this study, for it is then that J.A.'s progressed Sun will reach his natal Ascendant. This could be a time of decision, with life-long consequences.

A factor which I discussed long ago in an article and more recently in a lecture for an astrological organization in Chicago might be validly considered in J.A.'s chart. It is what I have called "the Point of Redemption." This Point is very logical as it is the extension of the technique which gave to astrology the Part of Fortune and the

Part of Spirit. It is found by adding the longitudes of the Moon and the Sun, and by subtracting from the sum the longitude of the Ascendant.

In order to evaluate significantly the meaning of such a point we have to realize that, if we consider the relationship of the Sun, the Moon and the Ascendant in terms of *time*, the Sun stands for the present, the Moon for the past, and the Ascendant for the future. The Sun is the "present moment," for it is solar energy that makes us alive *now*. The Moon represents the "past," because the patterns of distribution of solar energy and the capacity we have to adapt to everyday situations is conditioned by our culture, our ancestry and in most cases by our relationship to our mother, for the mother (the past of the race and the womb from which we emerged) gave us our first example of how to adjust to cold, heat, hunger and in general any biological, and perhaps later on psychological needs. The Ascendant represents the "future" because it refers to the set of individual potentialities which it is our task to actualize as we live and grow.

Now, when we calculate the Part of Fortune, we actually add the arc between the forward moving Moon and the Sun to the Ascendant; and this is a way of showing what the phase of the solilunar relationship is in terms of the framework of the Houses (especially the Ascendant). As the relationship of the Moon to the Sun deals with the nature of the vital energies and with the way they are being distributed, this relationship *applied to the Ascendant* reveals the best way we can use these energies in order to actualize what we potentially are.

If now we consider the relationship of the Moon to the Ascendant we see that it can be interpreted as the relationship of the past to our individual future, i.e. to the person we are meant actually to become. This relationship plays at all times upon our "present," i.e. it affects the solar and vital forces which we constantly use. We obtain the Point of Redemption by applying the distance between the Ascendant and the Moon to the Sun. The Moon, however, does not merely represent the past; it indicates as well the *potentiality* of overcoming, or of coming to terms with this past — because indeed every factor in a birth-chart indicates *how best* to approach the function to which this factor refers. The same thing applies to what is so often misunderstood as "karma." Any so-called karmic event or contact gives us the opportunity to harmonize a past failure — a fault of omission as well as of commission.

The Moon therefore shows us *by implication* how we can best handle our past karma; but this handling of the past inevitably affects what we think of as our "dharma" — i.e. as the process of fulfilling our individual purpose (Ascendant). The relationship between these perhaps conflicting directions affect our solar-vitality; it makes demands upon it, and these may be crucial. It is to this whole situation that the Point of Redemption refers. In a very broad sense, it should reveal to us the nature of our basic opportunity to "redeem" the past, i.e. to neutralize our karma — or at least the general approach which we should best take in order to understand and meet this karma. At Moon-rise the Point of Redemption is conjunct the Sun; thus when the karmic factor arises in the consciousness, the position of the Sun (basic life-purpose or spiritual Will) represents the way of overcoming.

In J.A.'s chart the Point of Redemption falls at Libra 17°59' exactly conjunct to Mercury retrograde. Considering the quite emotional squares between Leo and the Scorpio planets, one may see in this position a suggestion that mental objectivity and a deep inner search for values and motives are the best ways to handle karmic problems. But as the Point of Redemption is located in the twelfth House it suggests that it is in the very subjective depths of the being that the confrontation with the "ghosts" of the past is likely to be met. This implies the need to develop a strong capacity to deal with factors referring to the inner life and the subconscious mind — and referring also to the collective mentality of the age and of mankind in general. However, I have found that in a number of cases, the position of the Point of Redemption is more significant in a *solar* House (i.e. in its aspect to the natal Sun) as in a *natal* House. In J.A.'s case this would place this Point in the first solar House.

In the chart of the Russian Czar Nicholas II whose execution by the Bolsheviks had a social-political character rather than a personal one, the Point of Redemption falls at the cusp of the eighth *solar* House (i.e. 210 degrees ahead of the natal Sun.) He had become a political symbol and in his death he, as it were, assumed a national karma — which, from the individual point of view, is a great spiritual achievement! The Point fell in his fourth *natal* House, again suggesting identification with the land, in which he was rooted. Interestingly, Lenin's natal Saturn was within one degree of the czar's Point of Redemption.

Space forbids to go into more detail concerning J.A.'s chart, though it is quite evident that many factors have been left untouched. The position of the Part of Fortune could have been discussed, and far more attention should have been given to the symbols of the degrees on which planets and angles are located. Also, charts should have been made for the New Moon before birth, and the one following birth. This last one is important in that J.A. is still living within the lunation cycle it opened up. A close study of the progressed New Moon which he will experience at the close of 1975 may reveal more information concerning the essential character of the 30-year period — and especially the period until the next progressed Full Moon — which will follow.

The progressions of every planet should be studied; but one should remember that only the progressed Moon makes a complete cycle around the birth-chart, and astrology deals essentially with factors capable of making complete circuits in the sky (i.e. wholes in time and space). For this reason I feel that the progressions of the planets should be studied within the frame of reference provided by complete progressed lunation cycles. Each progressed lunation cycle in the lifetime of an individual is given meaning, not only by the position of the progressed New Moon (and secondarily by the chart erected for the exact moment of this progressed New Moon at the place where the infant experienced it — i.e. most likely at his birthplace), but also by the aspects between progressed planets (Both progressed-to-natal and progressed-to-progressed aspects can be used).

I personally do not use the "progressed horoscope" popularized by Alen Leo; but it may prove valid. I prefer to keep the framework of the natal horizon and meridian as a permanent frame of reference; partly at least because the daily motion of the horizon and the progressed movements of the planets belong to two different frames of reference. For a similar reason I do not feel that the transits of *actually moving* planets over the positions of *symbolically moving* progressed planets should be considered. At best the transit of a planet over a degree occupied by a progressed planet might be said to emphasize the symbolic character of this *degree;* it has nothing to do with the planets so related.

It may nevertheless be significant to indicate in some way the place occupied each year by the "progressed" Mid Heaven and Ascendant. But I prefer to use what I called in THE ASTROLOGY OF PERSONALITY, the 28-year cycle of the Point of Self, or AUM Point. In J.A.'s case this Point is now passing through his tenth House because he is 22 years old. It is conjunct Pluto, as Pluto is nearing a conjunction with his natal Sun (October 1972). It was still close to Uranus when Uranus was transiting this same natal Sun (1968). The progressed Moon was also conjunct Pluto during this last winter 1971. The Sabian symbol for Pluto's natal degree is "A teacher of chemistry." This could mean a deeper awareness of the powers and opportunities locked in matter; and to a person whose attention is strongly drawn to subjective factors and abstract concepts related to the self, this awareness would indeed be most valuable.

With this I must close this study hoping that it will indicate a general line of approach to the birth-charts of individuals. The more intimate and definite possibilities of strictly individual meaning can only take verbal form in the presence of the person himself and in terms of his ability to accept and to constructively assimilate what might be said — thus of his response to more general and formal statements such as this study contains. Because of this inevitable fact the study should not be taken as revealing the essential value which a truly "humanistic" or person-centered interpretation can release. What I have talked about are natural tendencies. These should be clearly seen by the client, but this is only the foundation of a process — a vital and psychological process. It is what you do with these "natural tendencies" which is important — or, I might say again, how one comes to understand, then apply the "instructions" contained in the coded message of one's birth-sky.

EPILOGUE

Seven and a half years have passed since the first chapter of this book, *Astrology for New Minds*, was published as the first of a series of six booklets dealing with what I then for the first time called 'humanistic astrology.' This humanistic approach, however, was already evident in my first volume on astrology, *The Astrology of Personality* (1936) and I had used the terms 'harmonic astrology' and 'harmonic psychology' since 1932.

As a result of the widespread youth movement which developed during the fateful and revolutionary Sixties—the Hippies, the protests against the Vietnam quagmire, the many-sided struggle against 'the Establishment' and our materialistic and computerized society—groups of various types mushroomed all through the U.S. striving to help spiritually and culturally uprooted individuals reorient their approach to life, their consciousness, and their interpersonal relationships. At one time the term 'counterculture' was emotionally bandied about as a rallying standard, together

PERSON-CENTERED ASTROLOGY

with long hair, convention-defying clothing and community-living in often substandard conditions. The exciting days of that period are now largely memories, and the drug-taking revolutionary youths are in their late twenties or thirties; the colleges are peaceful, and now the main focus of attention is the 'personal growth movement'! Hundreds of groups provide the young and not-so-young with seminars, conferences, conventions, directed trips to special places of inspiration in which they are given supposedly new techniques and often magical passwords assuring growth in consciousness, more integrated or successful lives—even business lives—thus, more self-assured, emotionally freer, more mentally aware and objective, better adjusted and happier personalities.

Many years ago Carl Jung built his psychological practice on the concept of the integration of personality through a process he called "individuation." Also during the first half of our century the American New Thought Movement featured a cult of personality, success and happiness with a more or less religious background, particularly emphasized in Unity. Today these movements are given a more sophisticated and focused form through long and often exhausting sessions of concentrated personal and group training; and we see in this the widespread influence of a great variety of Near-Eastern, Hindu and Tibetan teachers-gurus who, especially since the arrival on the Euro-American stage of the notorious Gurdjieff, have made people work hard to gain the promised ability to solve all their mental, emotional and physical problems.

The not too obvious fact—not obvious at least to the individuals caught up in the excitement of working with the new techniques—is that the end-result of this self-conscious attempt at developing well-adjusted and successful personalities, seemingly free from the cruder forms of subservience to our Western Puritan morality

Epilogue

and our Scholastic rationalism and materialism, actually is a subtler, but very pervasive and dominant, ego. This is true even where much stress is in theory placed upon ego-surrender. And the reason for this is quite evident. If the ego is to be surrendered, *what* does the surrendering, and *to whom* is the surrender made?

We reach here a very subtle metaphysical as well as psychological issue, which cannot be understood and met in purely psychological terms; yet it is the central issue. It has to be met either in religious terms—the ego and personality being surrendered to Christ, or to God under whatever name He is called—or in so-called esoteric or occult terms. These imply the belief in the existence of superphysical realms of existence and consciousness, and of more-than-human (or 'divine') beings of great power, love and knowledge to whom a merely human person can be intimately related. The relation may be thought of and perhaps experienced in various ways. For the Christian and Hebrew mystic it may take the form of a 'dialogue' between the "I" and the supreme and absolute "Thou," God; for the Theosophist the relationship may be experienced in physical or transphysical meeting with the "Master" once the individual has resolutely entered upon the occult Path leading to Great Initiations, foreshadowed by the many types of lesser initiations dispensed by a variety of gurus.

This is not the place for discussing such transcendent matters in any detail, but they had to be succinctly mentioned because the practice of the kind of 'person-centered' astrology to which this book refers will inevitably bring them to the fore, if this practice is pursued truly in the spirit I have intended it to be pursued. Since I gave some publicity to the term, humanistic astrology, numerous astrologers have called themselves 'humanistic astrologer.' Classes are given and articles are written about 'humanistic astrology'; and the way the words are used associate their user with the above mentioned 'personal growth movement.' Planets in a chart are thought to refer to 'energies' operating within the personality and the basic problem a person faces is how to integrate or harmonize these energies so that he or she may live a fuller, better adapted and thus, more successful life.

Some astrologers are content to use astrology as a purely *descriptive* procedure. They tell their clients the way the energies most likely operate in them, what are the good and bad points in their characters, what they can expect in terms if not of actual events, then at least of important turning points and crises in their lives. Other astrologers take a more *purposive* approach, suggesting ways of improving the client's life and character, of harmonizing discordant influences, and of selecting compatible partners and a satisfying profession. This approach can lead to a kind of astro-psychotherapy and can be of great value to the usual psychotherapist, whether he be a psychiatrist or a family counselor. It can take the place of the religiously oriented approach according to which a confused, distraught or guilt-ridden person sought comfort and advice from a priest or minister acting as the mouthpiece for a hallowed and revered tradition. At a time when this tradition has lost most of its effectiveness and credibility for strongly individualized and egocentric persons, person-centered astrology can indeed fulfill an important function in many lives.

We are, however, at a time when an increasing number of individuals are deeply feeling or intellectually realizing that the achievement of personal well-being, happiness and self-fulfillment may not be the most important goal, at least as long as this goal is defined and desired in terms of the old order characterizing our Euro-American society. It has become banal to say that mankind is in a state of deep-seated crisis; and not only fans of astrology, but a vast variety of schools of

Epilogue

thought speak of an impending Aquarian New Age. Even the reverse side of the Great Seal of the United States 200 years ago dedicated our nation to a "New Order of the Ages." What all this means is that we may have to think of the fundamental keynote of our present period not as fulfillment, but as transformation. This implies a radical change of attitude and orientation in psychology and in the arts, particularly in our attitude toward ourselves and our 'self-image.'

If this change constitutes today the most basic issue we have to face, the 'personal growth movement' has evidently to be given a new meaning. It may represent a necessary step, but more as a means than as an end. In principle, a wholesome and well-balanced personality should in any case be a valuable asset; but, if it is only a means to an end, focusing one's attention and efforts almost exclusively upon the means is likely to defeat the end. If today the process of transformation of mankind is the essential evolutionary end to be reached, individual persons may contribute to this end by developing a particularly outstanding inherited capacity—genetically or in terms of past lives—at the expense of other faculties the use of which would serve no great purpose in the present human situation; and this may lead to a relatively unbalanced and one-sided personality. Students of occult philosophy have often been told that the apparent failings of a disciple may be used by the Master to produce needed results.

The basic question is whether or not a wholesome, harmonious and happy personality, operating as a physical-mental organism and socially successful according to the standards of our Western culture, is the highest 'spiritual' status a human being can attain. Such an individual may represent the most perfect *form* our culture can produce, but if the crucial need today is *trans-formation* of the basic values and standards of this culture, then perfection of a probably obsolete form (the beau-

PERSON-CENTERED ASTROLOGY

tiful people!) can be an obstacle rather than a help. A person can be a very warm, generous, talented and beautiful ego; but being so may make the surrender of that ego to the Divine very difficult—and we see this fact already stated in the Gospel parable of the wealthy man who could not give up his many possessions to follow Christ.

This has a direct application to the practice of astrology and the approach an astrologer takes to the interpretation of a client's birth-chart, its progressions, transits and related techniques. Is the astrologer to tell his client how to avoid crises which might be the necessary means for spiritual transformation? Should he (or she) send this client to a new locality where, according to astrological theory, the effect of some potentially nefarious planetary aspect could be made inoperative? Should the astrologer strongly veto the selection of a mate because a comparison of his client's and the potential marriage partner's charts show that the union might be stormy and produce conflicts? Yet conflicts may generate challenges and dynamic responses which both partners may need in order to transform agents in their society, thus serving a collective superpersonal evolutionary purpose.

Such questions may be answered in several ways, and the answer is rarely an easy one. It entails the kind of responsibility most astrologers are not prepared to assume; yet they may assume as much responsibility when routinely predicting events, for by so doing they become, consciously or not, parts of a life-process in which the prediction and the fear it causes can be important factors. Here I may refer the reader to the ninth section of this book, *Astrology as Karma Yoga*. More recently, the way I have theoretically answered the above mentioned questions is to develop what I have called a *transpersonal* astrology—an astrology of transformation. What it implies has been discussed in a small

Epilogue

book, *From Humanistic to Transpersonal Astrology* (Seed Center, Palo Alto, 1975) and a larger volume which carries my ideas much farther: *The Sun is Also a Star* (E. P. Dutton and Co., New York, 1975).

The last mentioned volume, whose subtitle is "The Galactic Dimension of Astrology," deals particularly with the Study of Uranus, Neptune and Pluto. These trans-Saturnian planets are shown to be the main agents for transformation; they are 'transpersonal' planets whose allegiance, as it were, is to our Galaxy, a vast cosmic organism of billions of stars. Our sun is only one small star within this celestial whole, so huge that it takes the Sun 200 million years to revolve around a still mysterious galactic core.

Our solar system proper—the *heliocosm* (from *helios*, sun)—ends at the Saturn orbit; and radiationally this ringed planet has always been the symbol of limitation and boundaries, but also of the concentration and solid organization required for the development of individual consciousness and self-conscious identity. The "solar wind"—direct emanations of solar particles—apparently does not reach farther than Saturn. But just as a human body, which we normally perceive as bounded by the skin, actually reaches farther in surrounding space through an electromagnetic aura, so the aura of the heliocosm reaches beyond Saturn. This aura is the realm where Uranus, Neptune and Pluto move in a remarkable threefold geometric pattern; and it is through these planets that, symbolically speaking, the power of the Galaxy mainly operates. They are galactic agents whose transcendent power beats the cosmic rhythm of cyclic transformation for the denizens of the solar system.

By studying the positions of Uranus, Neptune and Pluto in an individual birth-chart (especially in the houses and on particular zodiacal degrees), their relations (aspects) to the other planets and the chart's four angles, and also their interrelationships in the zodiac, the astrologer can visualize the basic rhythms of the process of transformation which may affect the client's life. I say "may affect," for many people are either too insensitive and unevolved, or they refuse to be transformed. Such a refusal, in a sensitive personality, usually leads nevertheless to crises and often (but not always) to upsetting events. What matters in any case is not the event, but the individual's response to it; and no one can quite foresee what this response will be, for this is the area of individual freedom—possibly the only area.

However important it is to be transformed, there can be no real transformation where there is no form to be transformed. Transpersonal astrology in no way detracts from the value of a person-centered astrology. It adds another dimension to the interpretation of individual birth-charts, and on a larger scale, to that of mundane charts erected for collective persons such as nations. What is written in this book provides a practical as well as philosophical foundation for any more transcendent approach to astrology; and at a time when astrologers are impelled by the pressures of our modern living and the urge to produce or demonstrate their skill in the use of new techniques—which often are only gimmicks or short-cuts—it seems particularly important to state and restate basic principles without which a psychologically and spiritually constructive use of astrology cannot stand.

October 1976
Palo Alto, California